L

THE BASICS

Now in its third edition, *Literary Theory: The Basics* is a clear and engaging introduction to this core area of study. Exploring a broad range of topics, from the New Criticism of the 1930s to the Ecocriticism and Posthumanism of the twenty-first century, it guides the reader through the sometimes confusing world of literary theory to answer such questions as:

- Why is theory so important?
- Can I use modern theories to analyse texts from other periods?
- What are issues like gender or race doing in literary theory?
- How do I decide which theory to use and must I pick just one?
- What comes after theory?

Now with updated case studies and suggestions for further reading, *Literary Theory: The Basics* is a must read for anyone wishing to approach the many debates and theories in this field with confidence.

Hans Bertens is Professor of Comparative Literature at Utrecht University, the Netherlands.

The Basics

LITERARY THEORY

THE BASICS

Third edition

Hans Bertens

Routledge
Taylor & Francis Group

LONDON AND NEW YORK

Third edition published 2014
by Routledge
2 Park Square, Milton Park, Abingdon, Oxon OX14 4RN

and by Routledge
711 Third Avenue, New York, NY 10017

Routledge is an imprint of the Taylor & Francis Group, an informa business

First published 2001 by Routledge
Second edition published 2008 by Routledge

British Library Cataloguing in Publication Data
A catalogue record for this book is available from the British Library

Library of Congress Cataloging in Publication Data
Bertens, Johannes Willem.
Literary theory : the basics / Hans Bertens. – Third edition.
pages cm. – (The Basics; 3)
Includes bibliographical references and index.
1. Criticism–History–20th century. 2. Literature–History and criticism–Theory, etc. I. Title.
Pn94.B47 2013
801'.950904–dc23
2013010557

ISBN: 978-0-415-53806-0 (hbk)
ISBN: 978-0-415-53807-7 (pbk)
ISBN: 978-0-203-48883-6 (ebk)

Typeset in Bembo
by Taylor & Francis Books

Printed and bound in Great Britain by
TJ International Ltd, Padstow, Cornwall

CONTENTS

INTRODUCTION

There was a time when the interpretation of literary texts and literary theory seemed two different and almost unrelated things. Interpretation was about the actual meaning of a poem, a novel, or a play, while theory seemed alien to what the study of literature was really about and even presented a threat to the reading of individual poems, novels, and other literary texts because of its reductive generalizations. In the last thirty years, however, interpretation and theory have moved closer and closer to each other. In fact, for many people involved in literary studies, interpretation and theory cannot be separated at all. They would argue that when we interpret a text we always do so from a theoretical perspective, whether we are aware of it or not, and they would also argue that theory cannot do without interpretation.

The premise of *Literary Theory: The Basics* is that literary theory and literary practice – the practice of interpretation – can indeed not be separated very well and certainly not at the more advanced level of academic literary studies. One of its aims, then, is to show how theory and practice are inevitably connected and have *always* been connected. Although the emphasis is on the 1970s and after, the first three chapters focus on the most important views of literature and of the individual literary work of the earlier part of the twentieth century. This is not a merely historical exercise. A good understanding of, for instance, the New Criticism that dominated literary criticism in the United States from the mid-1930s until 1970 is indispensable for students of literature. Knowing about the New Criticism will make it a lot easier to understand other, later, modes of reading. More importantly, the New Criticism has by no means disappeared. In many places, and especially in secondary education, it is still very much alive. Likewise, an understanding of what is called structuralism makes the complexities of so-called poststructuralist theory a good deal less daunting and has the added value of offering an instrument that is helpful in thinking about culture in general.

This book, then, is both an introduction to literary theory and an admittedly somewhat sketchy history of theory. But it is a history in which what has become historical is simultaneously still actual: in the field of literary studies a whole range of approaches and theoretical perspectives, those focused on meaning and those focused on form, those that are political and those that are (seemingly) apolitical, the old and the new, operate next to each other in relatively peaceful coexistence. In its survey of that range of positions *Literary Theory: The Basics* will try to do equal justice to a still actual tradition and to the radical character of the new departures of the last four decades. We still ask, 'What does it mean?' when we read a poem or novel or see a play. But we have additional questions. We ask, 'Has it always had this meaning?' or, 'What does it mean and to whom?' and, 'Why does it mean what it means?' Or, perhaps surprisingly, 'Who wants it to have this meaning and for what reasons?' As we will see, such questions do not diminish literature. On the contrary, they make it even more relevant.

In recent years, a number of critics have expressed a certain impatience with what is now simply called 'theory' – and which has, as we will see, ventured far beyond strictly literary territory. There is no denying that theory, in its eagerness to uncover hidden patterns and bring to light hidden assumptions, has sometimes pushed things to rather implausible extremes or that theory's desire to be radical has occasionally seemed a goal in itself. Especially after 9/11 and subsequent events theory's more extravagant claims seemed to some commentators armchair exercises that had little or no relation to what happened in the real world.

But a return to modes of critical interpretation that are not, in one way or another, informed by some form of theory is impossible. As I have already noted, most literary critics would claim that all interpretation is governed by certain assumptions and that interpretation can seem theory-free only if we are unaware of those assumptions – if we are, in effect, blind to what we are doing. If we prefer awareness, our interpretational practice will inevitably be marked by the theoretical interventions of the last forty years. We could, of course, choose to work with the assumptions of traditional interpretation, but we would (ideally) have thought long and hard about them and have realized that these assumptions, taken together, in themselves constitute theories with regard to reading and literary value. We can't go home again. Or, to be more precise, perhaps we can go home again, but not with the illusion that our home is theory-free.

Theory, then, is here to stay and the great majority of literary academics would not want it otherwise. They believe that theory has dramatically sharpened and widened our understanding of a great many fundamental issues and expect that theory, in its restless grappling with ever new issues, will continue to enhance our understanding (even if it may in the process also come up with things that severely test our intellectual patience). A case in point is the relatively new field of ecocriticism, which also illustrates theory's flexibility. More than earlier theoretical ventures, it recognizes the importance of empirical, even scientific, evidence for its political project, in this case that of raising our ecological consciousness.

This new edition of *Literary Theory: The Basics* has been revised, brought up to date, and expanded with discussions of posthumanism, animal studies, and very recent developments such as 'world literature'. And, like the earlier editions, it casts its net rather wide. Since the theories that have emerged within literary studies have been so thoroughly assimilated by various other disciplines, a book on literary theory has much to say about the wider world of the humanities and beyond.

READING FOR MEANING
PRACTICAL CRITICISM AND NEW CRITICISM

ENGLISH MEANING

If we want to understand English and American thinking about literature in the twentieth century a good starting-point is the nineteenth-century figure of Matthew Arnold (1822–88), English educator, poet (once famous for his rather depressing but much anthologized 'Dover Beach'), and professor of poetry at Oxford University. Arnold's views, which assigned a very special role to literature, and further enhanced its prestige, were not wholly new. In fact, his central idea that, apart from its aesthetic and pleasing qualities, literature also had important things to teach us was already familiar in antiquity and we see it repeated time and again over the ages. So we find Thomas Jefferson, future president of the future United States of America, observing in a 1771 letter that 'a lively and lasting sense of filial duty is more effectually impressed on the mind of a son or daughter by reading "King Lear" than by all the dry volumes of ethics and divinity that were ever written'. However, Arnold is not interested in the more practical aspects of the idea that literature is a source of instruction – moral or otherwise – but places it in a spiritual context.

Writing in the second half of the nineteenth century, Arnold saw English culture as seriously threatened by a process of secularization that had its origins in the growing persuasiveness of scientific thinking and by a 'Philistinism' that was loosened upon the world by the social rise of a self-important, money-oriented, and utterly conventional middle class, which is characterized by 'vulgarity', 'coarseness', and 'unintelligence'. With the spiritual comforts of religion increasingly questionable now that the sciences – in particular Darwin's theory of evolution – seemed set on undermining the authority of Bible and Church, Arnold foresaw a crucial, semi-religious role for poetry especially:

> More and more mankind will discover that we have to turn to poetry to interpret life for us, to console us, to sustain us. Without poetry, our science will appear incomplete; and most of what now passes with us for religion and philosophy will be replaced by poetry.
>
> (Arnold [1880] 1970: 340)

'The future of poetry', Arnold tells his readers, 'is immense, because in poetry … our race, as time goes on, will find an ever surer and surer stay.' This radical claim for poetry – made in an 1880 essay called 'The Study of Poetry' – is in fact the culmination of claims that Arnold had for decades been making on behalf of what he called 'culture' and which in a book called *Culture and Anarchy* (1869) he had defined as 'the best that has been thought and said in the world' (Arnold [1869] 1971: 6). As this makes clear, that 'best' is not necessarily confined to poems, but there is no doubt that he saw poetry as its major repository. The special importance that he accords to poetry is not as surprising as it may now seem. It accurately reflects the status of pre-eminent literary genre that poetry, especially in its lyrical form, enjoyed in Arnold's time. Moreover, in giving poetry this illustrious, almost sacred, function, Arnold builds on ideas that earlier in the nineteenth century had been formulated by Romantic poets like Percy Bysshe Shelley (1792–1822), who had attributed a special, visionary status to poetry, and on a long tradition, going back to the classics, that likewise gives literature, and especially poetry, special powers. It was only natural, then, for Arnold to put forward poetry as the major embodiment of 'culture'.

What does Arnold have in mind with 'the best that has been thought and said in the world'? Strangely enough, *Culture and Anarchy* is very outspoken, but not very clear on this point. Arnold has no trouble making clear by what forces and in which ways that 'best' is threatened: the evil is summarized by the 'anarchy' of his title, which includes the self-centred unruliness of the working class and 'the hideous and grotesque illusions of middle-class Protestantism' (63). He is, however, not very precise in his definitions of 'the best'. This is partly because he assumes that his readers already know: he does not have to tell them because they share his educational background and his beliefs. But it is also due to its elusiveness. Arnold can tell us where to find it, for instance in Hellenism – the Greek culture of antiquity, with its 'aerial ease, clearness, and radiancy' (134) – but can only describe what it expresses: an attitude towards life, a way of being in the world. Included in this attitude we find 'freedom from fanaticism', 'delicacy of perception', the 'disinterested play of consciousness', and an 'inward spiritual activity' that has 'for its characters increased sweetness, increased light, increased life, increased sympathy' (60–64). What culture would seem to amount to is a deeply sympathetic and self-effacing interest in, and contemplation of, the endless variety that the world presents. For Arnold, poetry probes life more deeply, is more sympathetic towards its immensely various manifestations, and is less self-serving than anything else, and so we must turn to poetry 'to interpret life for us'. Because poetry has the power to interpret life, we can also turn to it if we want to be consoled or to seek sustenance. With the persuasiveness of religious explanations seriously damaged, poetry has the now unique power of making sense of life, a sense from which we can draw comfort and strength. Moreover – and here we see the idea of 'instruction' – culture allows us to 'grow', to become more complete and better human beings. As Arnold puts it in *Culture and Anarchy*: 'Religion says, *The kingdom of God is within you*; and culture, in like manner, places human perfection in an *internal* condition, in the growth and predominance of our humanity proper, as distinguished from our animality' (47).

CONTINUITY OR CHANGE?

Let me for a moment turn to one of Arnold's major examples of the culture he extols: 'Hellenism', the complex of intellectual and emotional attitudes expressed in the civilization of ancient Greece.

Like all university-educated people of his time, Arnold was thoroughly familiar with classical history and literature. So familiar, in fact, that in some ways he sees Greek epics and plays that are more than 2,000 years old as contemporary texts. The classics and the ideal of culture that they embody are timeless for Arnold. This is a vitally important point: 'the best that has been thought and said in the world', whether to be found in the classics or in later writers, is the best for every age and every place.

From Arnold's perspective, this makes perfect sense. After all, culture and its major means of expression – poetry – must take the place of a religion that equally was for every age and every place. But this introduces what many literary academics now see as a serious problem. Arnold does not consider the possibility that what is 'the best' for one age may not be 'the best' for another, when circumstances have completely changed, or that what within a given period is 'the best' for one party (say, the aristocracy) is not necessarily 'the best' for another (poverty-stricken peasants, for instance). Arnold's culture and the poetry that embodies it demand an intellectual refinement and sensitivity, and a disinterested otherworldliness that under a good many historical circumstances must have been a positive handicap. Arnold would probably not deny this but he would argue that, all things being equal, there is only one cultural ideal – embodied in 'the best' – for which we should all strive.

The way I am presenting this – with peasants pitted against the aristocracy – could easily create the impression that Arnold is an elitist snob. But that is not necessarily the case. Arnold's ideal of culture is certainly exclusive, in the sense that it defines itself against money-grubbing vulgarity, narrow-minded fundamentalism, upper-class arrogance, and so on; but it does not seek to exclude anyone on principle. If we allow ourselves to come under the influence of 'culture', we can all transcend the limitations imposed on us by class, place, and character, and acquire the cultured sensitivity and respectful, even reverent, attitude towards the world that 'culture' holds up for us. In fact, this is what Arnold would like all of us to do: to escape from the place and the time we live in and transform ourselves into citizens of an ideal world in which time does, in a sense, not pass and in which we are in some ways – the ways that count – all the same. After all, in Arnold's view 'culture' is of all time: it exists in an autonomous sphere where time- and place-bound personal, political, or economic considerations have been left behind. We can fully enter the realm of culture only if we choose, at least temporarily, to disregard the here and now of personal ambition, political manoeuvring, and economic gain.

LIBERAL HUMANISM

Although that may not be immediately clear, this view of culture has important implications. Arnold is of course aware that culture will always reflect (to some extent) its time and place of origin – in the sense that, for instance, medieval and early modern literature will assume that the Sun revolves around a static Planet Earth – but with regard to what it *really* has to tell us it stands apart from time and place; that is, from history. With regard to its essence, culture *transcends* history. We must assume, then, that its creators – the poet supreme among them – also transcend time and place, at least as long as the act of creation lasts. A timeless culture must be the creation of timeless minds; that is, of minds that can at least temporarily disregard the world around them. This brings us to an important question: where does a creative mind that has temporarily soared free of its mundane environment find the insights that will allow it to contribute to 'the best that has been thought and said'? The answer must be that the source of that wisdom can only be the individual creator. Poets find what is valuable and has real meaning in *themselves*; they just *know*.

Arnold was by no means unique in his view of the creative individual. It was shared by the large majority of his contemporaries and by the countless writers and critics who in the course of the twentieth century would more or less consciously follow his lead. More importantly, it is still the prevailing view of the individual – not just the creative ones – in the Western world. This view of the individual – or *subject*, to use a term derived from philosophy – is central to what is called *liberalism* or *liberal humanism*, a philosophical/ political cluster of ideas in which the ultimate autonomy and self-sufficiency of the subject are taken for granted. Liberal humanism assumes that all of us are essentially free and that we have – at least to some extent – created ourselves on the basis of our individual experiences. It is easy to see that this view of the subject is pervasively present in our culture and in our social institutions. The legal system, for instance, starts from the assumption that we have a certain autonomy. If your lawyer succeeds in convincing the court that the murder you thought you could get away with was not a conscious act that you could have decided against, but was ordered by those voices in your head, you will be declared insane. Likewise, democracies do not set up elections with the expectation that people will wander mindlessly into a voting booth and make a completely arbitrary choice between the candidates. Our social institutions expect us to be reasonable and to be reasonably free. Because of that freedom, we ourselves are supposedly the source of the value and the meaning we attach to things. As liberal subjects we are not the sum of our experiences but can somehow stand outside experience: we are not defined by our circumstances but are what we are because our 'self' has been there all along and has, moreover, remained remarkably inviolate and stable.

Not surprisingly, in much of Western literature, and especially in lyric poetry and realistic fiction, individuals present themselves, or are portrayed, along these lines. In the realistic novels of the mid-nineteenth century, characters again and again escape being defined by their social and economic situation because they are essentially free. Since what they are – their 'self' – is largely independent from their situation, the circumstances in which they find themselves can be transcended. Realism suggests that the characters that it presents find the reasons for their actions and decisions inside themselves. Because this liberal humanist view of the individual is as pervasively present in our world as it was in the nineteenth century, it also characterizes much of our contemporary literature.

For many present-day critics and theorists this is a deeply problematic view. In the later chapters of this book we will encounter various objections to this liberal humanist perspective. Let me here just point at one possible problem. What if access to Arnold's 'the best' depends, for instance, on education? If that is the case, Arnold's campaign for a 'culture' that supposedly has universal validity begins to look like arrogance: we would have the educated telling the uneducated that they are barbarians. Arnold might object that ideally all of us should get the same – extended – education. And he might also point out that education does not benefit those who refuse to be educated – after all, *Culture and Anarchy* does not hesitate to group the English aristocracy and the Anglican establishment with the 'Barbarians'. But he would have to admit that educational opportunities are not evenly distributed over this world; there are, even within every nation, sharply different levels in education. A sceptic might easily see Arnold's campaign for his idea of culture as a move in a struggle for power and status: for the power to define culture, to decide what the 'best' is, and for membership of the cultural elite. In fact, even if we grant Arnold's claim and accept that his idea of culture does indeed represent the most humane, most tolerant, most morally sensitive perspectives that human civilization has come up with, we would still have a problem. Would we have the right to impose that culture on people who couldn't care less?

In short, there are serious problems with Arnold's humanist conception of culture and poetry. I should, in all fairness to Arnold, say that it has taken almost a hundred years for these problems really to register and that even now his views are still seductive. Isn't it true that many of us, at least at some point in our lives, want to see literature as a high-minded enterprise by and for sensitive and fine-tuned intellectuals that is somehow several steps removed from the trivial push-and-pull of ordinary life? It is an alluring prospect: to have a place to go where in a hushed silence, the sort of silence that we very appropriately find in a library, we meet with the kindred, equally sensitive people who have written the works we read. It is a place where time does not pass and where in some ways – the ways that count – we are all the same. 'The best books', the American philosopher Ralph Waldo Emerson (1803–82) tells us in his famous essay 'The American Scholar' (1837), 'impress us ever with the conviction that one nature wrote and the same reads' (Emerson [1837] 2007: 1142). We, the readers, are of course only the passive consumers of what they, the writers, have actively produced, but doesn't that difference tend to fall away? Especially so since the texts we read are, in the act of reading, lifted out of their historical context and so to a certain extent cut loose from their creators?

It is too good to be completely true, even if it is not necessarily wholly untrue. How can we, apart from everything else, possibly know whether the seemingly kindred spirits that we meet in that timeless place do indeed share our perspectives and concerns? What guarantee is there that we do not see our concerns in such sharp relief only because we ignore what we do not want to see? Perhaps

Arnold is right about Hellenism's 'aerial ease, clearness, and radiancy', but where in that phrase are the murder and mayhem of so many of the Greek classics? Can the Greeks, or can Chaucer, or Dante, or even Shakespeare, who all lived in worlds dramatically different from our own, really have been in some important way similar to ourselves? Perhaps 'delicacy of perception', the 'disinterested play of consciousness', and the other qualities that Arnold attributes to his ideal culture are indeed of all times, even if in different periods and places they will have been framed by different historical circumstances. But since we cannot travel back in time we will never know. 'The past is a foreign country: they do things differently there,' the narrator of L.P. Hartley's novel *The Go-Between* (1953: 9) tells us, and he may well be right. In the final analysis, Arnold's historical continuum between Hellenism and the high culture of his own time – the poetry that must interpret life for us – is an act of faith.

LITERATURE AS CIVILIZATION'S LAST STANCE

When Matthew Arnold died, in 1888, English literature was fairly well established as an academic subject in both England and America. Interestingly, in British India English had already, since the 1830s, served to familiarize the 'native' elite with 'Englishness' and to anglicize them to the extent that they were prepared to have themselves anglicized. However, English literature as it was studied in the late nineteenth and early twentieth centuries could not very well be regarded as a serious intellectual discipline. Academic English was largely devoted to the history of the English language and to its older forms, such as Middle and Old English (the absolutely unintelligible language of *Beowulf*). The study of literature was largely the province of well-educated men of letters who preferred high-minded evaluations and discussions of an author's sensibility to critical analysis and attention to the structure – the actual workings – of literary texts.

What really changed things and moved them in a direction we can more readily recognize is the intervention of a young American poet, T.S. Eliot (1888–1965), who had moved to England before the outbreak of the First World War, and the British government's desire to find a place for the study of English literature somewhere in its educational schemes. While Eliot, with whose views I will deal in a moment, was primarily influential in the universities, the govern-ment-controlled Board of Education gave English literature a solid place in secondary education. It is worth noting how closely the so-called 'Newbolt Report' of 1921 that the Board had commissioned follows in Arnold's footsteps: 'Great literature', it tells us, is 'a timeless thing'. It is 'an embodiment of the best thoughts of the best minds, the most direct and lasting communication of experience by man to man' (Newbolt Report 1921: 15), and it may form a new element of national unity, overcoming class differences. As the Report tells us, 'An education fundamentally English would, we believe, at any rate bridge, if not close, this chasm of separation' (22). Great literature, with its focus on a spiritual realm of unselfish harmony where all petty quarrels are forgotten or have become irrelevant, could over-come social conflict and anti-patriotic sentiment. What the Report in fact suggests, although it never says so in so many words, is that social and economic inequality pales next to the equality we can find in the study – or perhaps the mere reading – of great texts.

It is always easy to criticize the ideals of the past and we should perhaps not come down too hard on these English educators or on their American counterparts, who somewhat earlier had put for-ward the study of English and in particular American literature as an important binding principle in a nation trying to assimilate large numbers of immigrants. Apart from everything else, they may also have had the spiritual well-being of British and American students at heart. Still, the idea that literature might be instrumental in for-ging national unity has some consequences we must look at because it introduces a criterion that is absent from Arnold's view of poetry as the interpreter of life. If literature is supposed to promote national unity, it makes good sense to throw out those texts that emphasize disunity – tension between social classes, between reli-gious denominations, between regions – or that are openly unpa-triotic. For Arnold such texts, if they were sensitive and intelligent enough, were perfectly admissible. In fact, Arnold's 'disinterested play of consciousness' will inevitably – although of course not exclusively – lead to critical assessments of the outside world. But if literature is used to foster national unity – in other words, if it is used to create or keep alive a national identity – critical assessments of the nation's mercenary politics or its cultural vulgarity will no longer be very welcome.

ARNOLD'S ACADEMIC HERITAGE:
THE ENGLISH SCENE

As I have just noted, in the more academic sphere the most influential spokesman for Arnold's vision was the young expatriate American poet T.S. Eliot, who had settled in London before the First World War. In the early 1920s Eliot did what Arnold had largely avoided: he set out to define the criteria that 'the best that had been thought and said in the world' would have to meet and he undertook the mission actually to identify that 'best' in so far as it had been expressed in literary form. In other words, after drawing up the admission requirements he used them to establish which texts met those criteria and which failed to do so. The canon – the list of good and even great literary works – that he set out to construe in the 1920s would dominate virtually all English and American discussions of literature until the 1970s, and it is still a powerful influence today.

For Eliot, poetry – the genre in which he was most interested – was profoundly impersonal. This is not to say that he denied poets the right to express themselves in their poetry, although it would not be too difficult to extract that position from his writings. In 'Tradition and the Individual Talent', for instance, we find him claiming that the poet has 'not "a personality" to express, but a particular medium' (Eliot [1919] 1972: 75). Eliot's main aim, however, is to deflect his readers' attention from everything he considers of – at best – secondary importance – the poet's personal or social circumstances and so on – and to get poetry itself on centre stage. Eliot, then, objects to highly emotional outpourings and personal confidences because they tend to focus our attention on the poet rather than the poetry. What is more, from Eliot's perspective, they also make for bad and superficial poems. This does not mean that he is against the expression of deep feelings in poetry. However, expressions of profound emotion should not have an autobiographical dimension. Even if the emotion is unquestionably the poet's, it should be conveyed in such a way that the poet's private life plays no role in its presentation. What the poet needs to look for, Eliot tells us in 'Hamlet', another essay from 1919, is an 'objective correlative': 'a set of objects, a situation, a chain of events which shall be the formula of that particular emotion' (Eliot [1919] 1969: 145). Emotion must be conveyed indirectly. The poet's emotion should be invested in a carefully selected and appropriate 'objective correlative', which will then evoke the proper response in the reader. Moreover, emotion must always be kept in check by what Eliot called 'wit', a quality that he required of all poetry and by which he means an ironic perception of things, a – sometimes playful – awareness of paradoxes and incongruities that poses an intellectual challenge to the reader. It follows from this that Eliot had little use for, for instance, the low-key, soft-focus emotionality of Alfred Tennyson (1809–92):

> Tears, idle tears, I know not what they mean,
> Tears from the depth of some divine despair
> Rise in the heart, and gather to the eyes,
> In looking on the happy autumn-fields,
> And thinking of the days that are no more.

('Tears, Idle Tears', 1847)

In contrast with this sort of poetry, Eliot's own poetry presents what might – somewhat unkindly – be described as a terse, tight-lipped, ironic melancholy that signals in its striking use of images, juxtapositions, inversions, and other poetic strategies just how intellectually agile and alert it is. It is a poetry that fully demands the reader's close attention. '[P]oets in our civilization, as it exists at present, must be difficult,' as Eliot told his readers in 'The Metaphysical Poets' (Eliot [1921] 1969: 289). The corresponding complexity of its language and form forces us to take it seriously in its own right and makes it difficult to see it in, for instance, autobiographical terms.

The integration of intellect and emotion, and, less insistently, of profundity and playfulness, that Eliot sees as an absolute condition for good poetry drastically limits his list of worthwhile poets. In fact, for Eliot, writing in the 1920s, literature had taken a wrong turn more than two centuries before. In 'The Metaphysical Poets' he argues that the so-called 'Metaphysical poets' of the seventeenth century still knew how to fuse thought and feeling, and seriousness and lightness, in their poetry. After their heyday, however, a 'dissociation of sensibility' had set in in which intellect, emotion, and other formerly integrated qualities had gone their separate ways (288). For Eliot this had led to poetry that errs either on the one side – sterile rationality, for instance – or on the other – excessive emotion or a levity that turns into irresponsibility – and that is always condemned to superficiality because of such failures.

With hindsight, we can see that Eliot proclaims his own poetic practice and that of his fellow modernist poets of the early twentieth century as the general norm. With hindsight, we can also see that Eliot's nostalgia for a past when people were supposedly still whole in the sense that they knew how to combine thought and feeling – reason and emotion – harmoniously was fed by a deep dissatisfaction with the contemporary world in which harmony seemed sadly lacking.

It may at first sight not be clear what this has to do with Eliot's views of literature. However, Eliot, following Arnold, consciously places poetry – and by implication all literature that meets his criteria – in opposition to the modern world. He seeks in poetry the sort of profound experience that the modern world, in which materialistic values and a cheap moralism have come to dominate, cannot offer. For Eliot, the natural, organic unity that is missing from the world and that we ourselves have also lost with the advent of scientific rationalism and the utilitarian thinking of industrialization – the 'dissociation of sensibility' – is embodied in aesthetic form in poetry. So even if poetry has no answers to any questions we might ask, it is still of vital importance and it allows us to recapture temporarily a lost ideal of wholeness in the experience of reading. As Eliot's fellow American Robert Frost (1874–1963) phrased it from a slightly different perspective, poetry provides 'a momentary stay against confusion'. Because of its integration of thought and feeling and of opposing attitudes in a coherent aesthetic form, poetry, rather paradoxically, could even serve that function if the confusion itself was its major theme (as, for instance, in Eliot's 'The Waste Land' of 1922). Simultaneously, poetry deepens our awareness of the important things in life.

Although Eliot is obviously very much interested in poetic technique and in the *form* of specific poems – an interest that would be worked out by a group of American poets and critics, the so-called 'New Critics' – he is ultimately even more interested in a poem's *meaning*. Poetry should convey complex meanings in which attitudes that might easily be seen as contradictory are fused and which allow us to see things that we otherwise would not see. Our job, then, is to interpret poems, after which we can pass judgement on them; that is, establish how well they succeed in creating and conveying the complexity of meaning that we expect from them. 'Here lies Fred, / He is dead' does not pass muster. The idea that we read poems, and literature in general, because they contain deep *meanings* is now a commonplace. However, as will become clear in the course of this book, the meaning of a specific literary work cannot have a mono-poly on our interest. An interest in the *form* of the poem, novel, or play in question – and, by extension, in the form of literature as a whole – is equally legitimate, as is an interest in a literary work's *politics*. But those complications will have to wait.

CAMBRIDGE, ENGLAND

Eliot, although trained as a philosopher, was not affiliated with a university. But he was one of the most exciting poets of his genera-tion and also one whose philosophical interests made him think long and hard about the nature and function of literature. Inevitably, his views of literature were immediately picked up by young university teachers. Eliot's most influential following emerged at Cambridge University with the literary academic I.A. Richards (1893–1979) and the group that would somewhat later be led by the critic F.R. Leavis (1895–1979). Although each of them in his own way disagreed with some of Eliot's claims, Richards and Leavis initiated two intimately related 'schools' that would give shape to English and American thinking about literature for almost fifty years.

In Richards's hands Eliot's emphasis on the poem itself became what we call *practical criticism*. In a still fascinating experiment Richards withheld all extra-textual information – author's name, period, explanatory commentary – and asked undergraduate stu-dents (and tutors) to interpret poems that were thus completely stripped of context. It would be difficult to think up a more text-oriented approach. We are now so familiar with this that it is difficult to imagine how revolutionary Richards's experiment once was.

This should not obscure the fact that Richards stands firmly in the line of Matthew Arnold and T.S. Eliot regarding the importance of literature and, more particularly, poetry. Like so many young intel-lectuals of the period, Richards had deep misgivings about a con-temporary world that seemed to have lost its bearings. He, too, saw in poetry an antidote to a spiritual malaise that seemed to pave the way for chaos. If the moral order would indeed fall apart because of the loss of traditional values that he saw around him, we would, Richards suggested, 'be thrown back, as Matthew Arnold foresaw, upon poetry. It is capable of saving us; it is a perfectly possible means of overcoming chaos' (Richards 1926: 83). Poetry, and the arts in general, could save us because it is there that we find what is truly, and lastingly, valuable – what gives meaning to our lives:

> The arts are our storehouse of recorded values. They spring from and perpetuate hours in the lives of exceptional people, when their control and command of experience is at its highest, hours when the varying possibilities of existence are most clearly seen and the different activities which may arise are most exquisitely reconciled, hours when habitual narrowness of interests or confused bewilderment are replaced by an intricately wrought composure.
>
> (Richards [1924] 1972a: 110)

This statement is not in the last place interesting because it so clearly illustrates Richards's view of the creative subject. The keywords are 'control', 'command', 'reconciled', and 'composure'. For Richards, the minds of artists are in control of whatever may have befallen them, they reconcile contradictions, and transcend our usual self-centredness. This command and transcendence originates within the artists themselves: we are offered a perfect picture of the liberal humanist individual or subject.

Because the arts are our storehouse of recorded values, they 'supply the best data for deciding what experiences are more valuable than others' (111). Literary art, then, helps us to evaluate our own experience, to assess our personal life. It is all the better equipped for this because its language is not *scientific* but *emotive*. Scientific language is, for Richards, language that refers to the real world and makes statements that are either true or false. The emotive language of literature, however, conveys a certain type of knowledge which is not scientific and factual but allows us to connect with superior feelings and attitudes.

As I have just noted, practical criticism focuses upon the text and the text alone. Because of this exclusively textual orientation, it was an ideal programme for teasing out all the opposites that for Richards (following Eliot) were reconciled and transcended in poetry, often through the use of irony. 'Practical criticism' – named after the book *Practical Criticism* (1929) in which Richards reported his Cambridge experiments – became a major instrument in spreading the idea that the best poems created a vulnerable harmony – a precarious coherence – out of conflicting perspectives and emotions. As we will see, in the United States this view would develop into the *New Criticism* that in the 1930s and 1940s became the major mode of criticism there.

THE NOVEL AS GREAT ART

So far, we have been almost exclusively concerned with poetry. F.R. Leavis, the other Cambridge academic who would put a – highly personal – stamp on (especially English) literary studies, was, at least initially, no exception. Leavis, too, started out with poetry and also took Eliot's views as his guiding light. In the course of the 1930s he accordingly subjected the history of English poetry to an icy scrutiny in order to separate the wheat from the chaff, in the process relegating a good many English poets of up till then fine repute (including John Milton) to minor status. In particular Victorian poets, standing collectively accused of a 'divorce between thought and feeling, intelligence and sensibility' – a condemnation in which we clearly hear Eliot's 'dissociation of sensibility' – did not fare well (see, for instance, '"Thought" and Emotional Quality', in Leavis 1975: 71–93).

However, his work of the later 1940s, in which he sets out to revalue the English novel, is more pertinent here. Until Leavis changed the picture, fiction had gone largely unnoticed. Novels cannot very well be subjected to the same sort of analysis that we use with poems, especially not the substantial, if not actually sprawling, novels that until the end of the nineteenth century were more or less the rule. But Leavis's discussions of fiction would in any case have departed from the course set out by Eliot and Richards. By the 1940s Leavis had already in his discussions of poetry begun to include a moralistic dimension that is almost completely absent from the work of his American contemporaries, the New Critics. Leavis increasingly comes to judge poems in terms of the 'life' and the 'concreteness' they succeed in conveying. In other words, he begins to discuss content as relatively independent of form while for the New Critics, as we will see below, form and content were inextricably interwoven. While for the New Critics and an ever greater number of affiliated academics a text's form created the ironic maturity of its content, for Leavis form became increasingly of secondary importance. What the literary work should provide was a mature apprehension of authentic life, and certainly not one that was too ironic and therefore emotionally sterile (he was not charmed by the ironies of James Joyce's *Ulysses* (1922), which Eliot had thought a great work of art). Like so many others, Leavis was dismayed by what he saw as the superficiality and commodification of the contemporary world; and, much like Eliot, he looked back to Elizabethan England, when people had led authentic lives as members of an organic community.

For Leavis, authentic representations of life depended on a writer's personal authenticity and moral integrity. As he said in *The Great Tradition* (1948) of the novelists he considered great: 'they are all distinguished by a vital capacity for experience, a kind of reverent openness before life, and a marked moral intensity' (Leavis [1948] 1962: 17). One of Leavis's 'great' novelists, the English writer D.H. Lawrence (1885–1930), had already offered a characteristically provoking illustration of such openness:

> If the bank clerk feels really piquant about his hat, if he establishes a lively relation with it, and goes out of the shop with the new straw hat on his head, a changed man, be-aureoled, then that is life.
>
> The same with the prostitute. If a man establishes a living relation to her, if only for a moment, then that is life. But if it *doesn't*: if it is just for the money and function, then it is not life, but sordidness, and a betrayal of living.
>
> If a novel reveals true and vivid relationships, it is a moral work, no matter what the relationships may consist in.
>
> (Lawrence [1925] 1972a: 129)

Because they believe that because of its scope and its attention to authentic detail the novel can represent life in all its fullness, it is for Leavis and Lawrence superior to whatever the other arts or the human sciences (such as psychology or sociology) may have to offer. It can, moreover, make us participate in that fullness. As Lawrence said: 'To be alive, to be man alive, to be whole man alive: that is the point. And at its best, the novel, and the novel supremely, can help you' (Lawrence [1936] 1972c: 135).

This is an attractive programme for the novel – and for us. Who would not want to live authentically and to defend the forces of life against whatever may happen to threaten it? However, like so many attractive programmes, it falls apart upon closer scrutiny. Who is to define a mature apprehension of life, a vital capacity for experience, or a reverent openness before life? And what about the morals that are felt so intensely? Do we know what exactly constitutes the right set of morals? In any case, given his interest in full representations of life in its totality, Leavis almost inevitably came to focus on the novel. If you want scope, the novel has more to offer than lyrical poetry. So, somewhat belatedly, Leavis brought the novel into the amazing professionalization of the study of English as it had started in the 1920s. (Drama, and in particular Shakespeare, many of whose plays lent themselves to an approach in poetic terms, had already been embraced in the 1930s.) This is not to say that novels had been completely ignored. But Leavis elevated this interest into a programme. Moreover, he significantly expanded its scope, arguing that literary criticism, and in particular criticism of the novel, provided the best imaginable basis for criticizing contemporary culture, anticipating the critique of ideology that much later would come to characterize literary studies. As we will see in the later chapters of this book, literary studies – although broader defined than Leavis ever imagined – is still very strongly engaged in social and cultural critique, albeit in ways of which Leavis would not necessarily approve.

MEANING IN THE UNITED STATES

In the 1930s, the work of Eliot, Richards, and Leavis found a warm welcome on the other side of the Atlantic among a group of poets, including John Crowe Ransom, Allen Tate, Robert Penn Warren, and Cleanth Brooks, who in the middle of that decade initiated a professionalization of American literary studies comparable to the developments in England.

These *New Critics*, as they came to be called (the label derives from the title of Ransom's 1941 book *The New Criticism*), shared the misgivings of their English colleagues about the contemporary world. They, too, saw around them a world driven by a desire for profit in which the so-called triumphs of modern science, in combination with capitalistic greed, threatened to destroy tradition and everything that was not immediately useful – including poetry. Like their English mentors, they turned to an idealized past in which organic unity and social harmony had not yet been destroyed by the industrialization and commercialization of the contemporary world.

The New Critics, then, saw poetry as a means of resisting commodification and superficiality. Because of its internal organization – its formal structure – a poem created harmony out of opposites and tension and thereby presented a vital alternative. In creating coherent wholes out of the full variety and contradictory complexity of life, poetry halted and transcended the chaotic flux of actual experience. As John Crowe Ransom (1888–1974) put it in a 1937 essay titled 'Criticism, Inc.': 'The poet perpetuates in his poem an order of existence which in actual life is constantly crumbling beneath his touch' (Ransom [1937] 1972: 238). In perpetuating such fleeting orders, one of the poet's main strategies was the use of paradox with, as Cleanth Brooks (1906–94) said, 'its twin concomitants of irony and wonder'. By means of paradoxes, 'the creative imagination' achieves 'union'. That 'fusion is not logical', Brooks continues, 'it apparently violates science and common sense; it welds together the discordant and the contradictory' (Brooks [1942] 1972: 300–01).

In this emphasis on paradox – a statement containing contradictory aspects – and irony the New Critics clearly follow Eliot and Richards. They, too, see poems as storehouses of authentic values and as expressing important truths about the complexities of life that no other medium can convey nearly as effectively. This is so, Brooks suggests, because 'apparently the truth which the poet utters can be approached only in terms of paradox' (292), while for Ransom the 'imagination' is an 'organ of knowledge [that] presents to the reflective mind the particularity of nature; whereas there is quite another organ, working by a technique of universals, which gives us science' (Ransom 1938: 156). In some ways, however, they follow their own course. Richards had been seriously interested in the effects of poetry upon its readers. The New Critics exclude both the poet – as Richards had done in *Practical Criticism* – and the reader from their approach to poetry. As a result, they focus

more on the actual *form* of literary works than their English counterparts. In fact, within the context of English and American criticism, their approach to literature might well be considered *formalist*
and it does indeed often go by that label. However, compared to the
European formalists whom I will discuss in the next chapters, their
interest in form is relatively limited. They are not interested in form
for its own sake, but in form as contributing to a text's meaning.
Indeed, as the prominent New Critic W.K. Wimsatt put it, the aim
of literary criticism is 'to give a valid account of the relation between
poetic form and poetic meaning' (Wimsatt 1965: 244).

The New Critics' lack of interest in how the poem affects its
readers does not mean that they denied the special character of
poetic language. As Brooks tells us, 'the poet's language ... is a
language in which the connotations play as great a part as the
denotations' (Brooks [1942] 1972: 295). Moreover, for the New
Critics, too, a poem had to be fully experienced in order to be
effective. 'A poem should not mean, but be,' as they said, echoing
Richards's 'It is never what a poem *says* which matters, but what it
is' (Richards 1926: 3). Reading a poem should be a complete
experience that engages all our faculties and that far exceeds merely
extracting its 'message'. Anything but the entirety of its paradoxes,
opposites, and reconciling ironies is reductive and damaging.

'Close reading' – that is, the focus on the text that Richards and
Leavis had promoted so vigorously in England – became closer than
ever in the hands of the New Critics. With the author's intentions
and the reader's response removed from the scene, the study of
literature restricted itself to analysing the techniques and strategies
that poems used to deliver their paradoxical effects: the system of
checks and balances that creates the diversity in unity that we
experience. Although it probably seems counter-intuitive, from this
perspective it is not the poet – about whose intentions we usually
know next to nothing – but the poem itself that does the deliver-
ing. What organizes the poem – brings its diverse elements
together – is not so much authorial intention as an abstract principle, the principle of *coherence*, which the New Critics assumed
present and active in any 'good' poem. In good poetry – and, by
extension, all good literature – the principle of coherence keeps the
text's paradoxes and possible contradictions in check. Some may
object that this does not make much sense because literary texts do

not spring up overnight and all by themselves in remote and mysterious areas, so it might seem rather perverse to exclude the author from the discussion of a text. But it makes a good deal of practical sense. In some cases we do not even know who the author is, and in many cases we can only guess at their intentions because we have no information. Moreover, when we have that information it does not necessarily illuminate the poem, at least not from the perspective that I am discussing here. As we have seen, these critics assume that good literature is not bound by time and place. It transcends the limitations of its place of origin (including the author) and addresses the complexities of an essentially unchanging human condition. The concrete intentions of the author, or the circumstances that triggered the poem, are therefore mostly or even wholly irrelevant. What does it matter if we know that Poet X wrote this particular poem because he was hopelessly in love with the undeserving Lady Y? The poem in question will be worthwhile only if it does *not* give us all the details but focuses on scorned love in general. In this sense, information about authorial intention or the direct occasion for a work of literature may be damaging rather than helpful.

For humanist critics such as Eliot, Richards, Leavis, and the New Critics, human nature and the human condition have not changed over time and are essentially the same the world all over. Human nature is not black, or white, or brown; it does not speak English or Tagalog; it is not prehistoric, medieval, or postmodern; it does not lean towards deep-sea fishing, pig farming, or business administration. Such details will inevitably feature in a literary work, but they are secondary to what a good poem, novel, or play has to offer.

THE REIGN OF THE CRITICS AND ITS LIMITATIONS

In his 1937 essay 'Criticism, Inc.' the New Critic John Crowe Ransom tells us that criticism 'might be seriously taken in hand by professionals' (Ransom [1937] 1972: 229). Aware that he is perhaps using 'a distasteful figure', he nonetheless has 'the idea that what we need is Criticism, Inc., or Criticism, Ltd.' The essay catches the new professionalism that literary academics on both sides of the Atlantic were not unreasonably proud of and invites us to look at the role that Ransom had in mind for himself and his fellow professionals.

One part of their self-appointed task stands out. As we have seen, for the New Critics and their English colleagues, literature, and in particular poetry, constituted a defensive line against the world of vulgar commerce and amoral capitalist entrepreneurialism that they held responsible for the moral decline of the Western world. But who was to decide which works of literature among the plenitude that the past has left us (and to which the present keeps on adding) actually contain 'the best that has been thought and said in the world', to use Arnold's words again? Who was to expose the – at first sight – attractive poems that because of their limited view and superficial emotions ultimately, even if unintentionally, undermined Arnold's 'culture'?

If literature takes the place of religion, as Arnold had prophesied, then critics are the defenders of the faith. For a period of fifty years the large majority of literary academics on both sides of the Atlantic saw themselves as the elect, as an intellectual and moral elite that had as its central task to safeguard 'life', the fullness of human experience. In the minds of the Leavisites especially, but also those who partly or wholly shared their views, criticism and social critique were so intimately interwoven that they could not be separated from each other. As I have already suggested, the interrelatedness of criticism – even if it now usually goes under other names – and social critique is still a hallmark of English and American literary studies.

But let me return to the specific view of literature that we find among the first generations of literary academics. With hindsight, we can easily see the intimate relationship between their discussions of structure, irony, and so on and a good many indisputably important literary works of the period: Eliot's 'The Waste Land' (1922), Ezra Pound's *Cantos* (1925–60), Virginia Woolf's *To the Lighthouse* (1927), James Joyce's *Ulysses* (1922), William Faulkner's *The Sound and the Fury* (1929), and countless other poems, novels, and plays. What was essentially an early twentieth-century view of literature, formed under the influence of specific historical circumstances, became a prescription for all ages. Predictably, the large numbers of writers who for one reason or another had operated in a different mode (Walt Whitman, for instance, with his long descriptive passages) fell from grace. Literary history was reshaped in the image of the early twentieth century. Whereas we can see the 'irony' that the writers and the critics of the period valued so highly as a defensive strategy in a confusing world of rapid social and technological change, they themselves genuinely believed it to be an infallible sign of 'maturity' and proceeded to demote all texts (and writers) that did not meet the required standard.

We can also see now that the required standard is heavily *gendered*. (This anticipates a much fuller discussion of 'gender' in a later chapter, but it must be mentioned here.) Eliot's 'wit', the 'irony' of Richards and the New Critics, and the 'maturity' of Leavis all serve to underline a shared masculinist perspective. This is not to say that they have no place for female writers – in its first instalment Leavis's 'great tradition' of English novelists includes two male and two female writers. But in a period in which self-discipline (the self-discipline of the poet who refuses to personalize the poem), wit, a controlling irony, and related qualities are all seen as typically male, whereas overt emotions and a refusal to intellectualize experience are seen as typically female, the female writers elected for inclusion in the literary pantheon were admitted because they met a male standard.

Practical criticism and New Criticism have had a lasting influence. Their preoccupation with the text and nothing but the text would live on after their demise, which is perhaps less surprising if we realize that their view of the text falls well within the range of the enormously influential theorization of the work of art – the aesthetic object – proposed by the German philosopher Immanuel Kant (1724–1802), who argued that the true work of art is characterized by a 'disinterested' autonomy, that it is not instrumental and has no purpose except being itself. Even now the textual orientation of the New Criticism in particular is still a force to be reckoned with, although always tempered by other considerations and mostly – but not necessarily – stripped of its largely conservative prejudices. It is, of course, only natural that texts, and not, for instance, landscaping, should play a central role in literary studies. It is less obvious, however – counter-intuitive as it may seem – that *meaning* should be so prominent. In the next two chapters we will look at approaches to literature in which the meaning of individual texts, which in England and America provided the major drive for literary studies, is of – at best – secondary importance.

SUMMARY

English and American literary studies traditionally focus on the *meaning* of literary texts. Practical criticism (the United Kingdom) and New Criticism (the United States) first of all provide *interpretations*, with the New Critics paying particular attention to the formal aspects of literature, which for them also contribute directly to a text's meaning. Within this Anglo-American tradition, literature is thought to be of great importance because in poems, novels, and plays we find 'the best that has been thought and said'. Literature offers the most profound insights into human nature and the human condition that are available to us. Because of its profundity and its authenticity, it offers a vantage point from which to criticize the superficial, rationalized, and commercialized world in which we live. Literary criticism, which seeks out and preserves the very best of what millennia of writing have to offer, thus functions simultaneously as social critique. Finally, in this traditional form literary studies takes *liberal humanism* and its assumptions for granted. It sees the individual – the *subject*, in technical terms – as not determined and defined by social and economic circumstances, but as fundamentally free. We create ourselves, and our destiny, through the choices we make.

SUGGESTIONS FOR FURTHER READING

There is no shortage of books on the English and American literary-critical heritage. Two very accessible and even-handed studies are Chris Baldick's *The Social Mission of English Criticism, 1848–1932* (1983), which has chapters on Arnold, Eliot, Richards, and Leavis, and his more recent *Criticism and Literary Theory 1890 to the Present* (1996), which covers some of the same ground, but also discusses the New Criticism and later developments. Mark Jancovich's *The Cultural Politics of the New Criticism* (1993) is especially interested in what the New Critics saw as their social mission. Garrick Davis's *Praising It New: The Best of the New Criticism* (2008) offers an excellent collection of seminal New Critical essays.

Gerald Graff's *Professing Literature: An Institutional History* (1987) maps the institutionalization of literary studies in the United States while *Masks of Conquest: Literary Study and British Rule in India* (1989) by Gauri Viswanathan offers a fascinating account of 'English' in colonial India.

Eliot's early essays – 'Tradition and the Individual Talent', 'Hamlet', and 'The Metaphysical Poets' – are still worth reading. Those who would like to see the New Criticism in action can also still go directly to the source. Cleanth Brooks's *The Well-Wrought Urn: Studies in the Structure of Poetry* ([1947] 1968) contains a number of now classic essays while his collaboration with Robert Penn Warren in *Understanding Poetry* ([1939] 1976) led to an enormously influential textbook on New Critical interpretation. Leavis's approach to poetry and the poetic tradition comes through vividly in his *New Bearings in English Poetry* (1932) and *Revaluation* (1936); *The Great Tradition* ([1948] 1962) is a good example of his equally uncompromising criticism of the novel.

Finally, English studies features fairly regularly in English and American fiction. For those who want to have a look behind the scenes, I can recommend David Lodge's three novels dealing with 'English' in both England and the United States – *Changing Places: A Tale of Two Campuses* (1975), *Small World: An Academic Romance* (1984), and *Nice Work* (1988) – and A.S. Byatt's *Possession: A Romance* (1990). And for those who want to have an overview, Elaine Showalter's rather caustically titled *Faculty Towers: The Academic Novel and Its Discontents* (2005) looks unsparingly at the absurdities of academic life.

READING FOR FORM I
FORMALISM AND EARLY STRUCTURALISM, 1914–60

In spite of the enormous influence of Eliot, Leavis, and the New Critics, our current perspectives on the study of literature owe perhaps more to continental Europe than to England and America. The continental European tradition of literary studies that is responsible for this begins in Russia in the second decade of the twentieth century, specifically in Moscow and St Petersburg. It finds a new home in Prague in the late 1920s, when the political climate in Russia has become too repressive, and travels to France (by way of New York City) after the Second World War, where it comes to full bloom in the 1960s and begins to draw widespread international attention. It is in France, too, that it provokes a counter-movement that achieves its full force in the 1970s and 1980s and that is still the dominant presence in literary – and cultural – studies.

Like its Anglo-American counterpart, this originally Russian approach to literature initially concentrated on poetry. But that is about all the two had in common. The English, later Anglo-American, line of development and the Russian one had nothing whatsoever to do with each other. The Russians who developed the so-called *formal method* – which gave them the name *formalists* – were totally unaware of what happened in England, while the English and Americans were completely ignorant of the debates that took place in Russia (and later in Prague). It was only when a prominent formalist, the Russian linguist Roman Jakobson (1896–1982), and his fellow formalists began to be translated into English in the late 1950s and 1960s that the English-speaking world began to take notice of their wholly different approach to literary art. But even then the response was slow, no doubt because the formalist approach was so foreign to what Eliot, Leavis, the New Critics, and their ubiquitous heirs saw as the mission of literature and of writing about literature. Significantly, the formalist perspective had to be picked up, assimilated, and further developed by the French before it really made an impact on English and American literary thought.

In what follows I will concentrate on the work of the Russians and look only briefly at some later developments. Relevant here is not historical comprehensiveness but a certain *way* of looking at literature that much later would have a great impact in the English-speaking world.

EARLY FORMALISM

As the phrase 'formal method' will have suggested, the formalists were primarily oriented towards the *form* of literature. That focus on formal aspects does not mean that they could not imagine a possible moral or social mission for literature. As one of them, Viktor Shklovsky (1893–1984), put it in 1917 in an essay titled 'Art as Technique', literature has the ability to make us see the world anew – to make that which has become familiar, because we have been overexposed to it, strange again. Instead of merely registering things in an almost subconscious process of recognition because we think we know them, we look at them once again: 'art exists that one may recover the sensation of life ... The purpose of art is to impart the sensation of things as they are perceived and not as they are known' (Shklovsky [1917] 1998: 18). The result of this process of defamiliarization is that it enables us once again to see the world in its full splendour or, as the case may be, its true awfulness. I should say that this was not a radically new insight. More than a hundred years earlier the English poet Shelley had already claimed that poetry 'lifts the veil from the hidden beauty of the world' – Shelley had not much eye for awfulness – 'and makes familiar objects be as if they were not familiar' (quoted in Scholes 1974: 174). But although the formalists were prepared to recognize this as a not unimportant effect of literature, they initially relegated it to the far background. The social function of literature, either as the repository of the best that had been thought and said, or as one of the great revitalizers (with the other arts) of our perception of the world around us, largely left them cold in the first phase of their explorations. What they wanted to know was how literature works, how it achieves its defamiliarizing effects. For the New Critics the formal aspects of literary works were not unimportant. However, they were first of all interested in the form in which a poem presented itself because a close scrutiny of its formal aspects would reveal the complex of oppositions and tensions that constituted the poem's real meaning. But the formalists were after what they considered bigger game and in order to do so they ignored literature's referential function, the way it directs us to the world we live in, and gave it, even more than the New Criticism had done, an autonomous status – or at least gave the *aesthetic dimension* of literature an autonomous status, as Jakobson qualified their position in 1933.

From their earliest meetings, around 1914, the formalists focused on what Jakobson in 1921 started to call 'literariness' – that which makes a literary text different from, say, a piece in *The Economist* or *Time*. In other words, although they always worked with individual texts, what they were interested in was what all literary texts have in common – a literary common denominator. Seeing the study of literature as a science, they concentrated, like true scientists, on general rules. Whereas practical criticism and the New Criticism focused on the individual meaning of individual texts, formalism sought to discover general laws – the more general, the better.

The secret of 'literariness', the formalists decided, was that in poetry – the initial focus of their interest – ordinary language becomes 'defamiliarized'. While an article in *Time* aims for clarity and will therefore use plain language, poetry subjects language to a process of defamiliarization. It is this linguistic defamiliarization that then leads to a perceptual defamiliarization on the part of the reader, to a renewed and fresh way of looking at the world. How does poetry defamiliarize what I have just called 'plain' language? It employs an impressive range of so-called 'devices'. It uses, for instance, forms of repetition that one does not find in ordinary language, such as rhyme, a regular meter, or the subdivision in stanzas that we find in many poems. But poetry also uses 'devices' that one may come across in non-poetic language (although not with the same frequency) like metaphors and symbols. In so doing, it often also exploits the potential for ambiguity that language always has. Whereas a *Time* article tries to avoid ambiguities because it wants to be as transparent as possible, poetry makes use of all the second (and third) meanings that words and phrases tend to have, plus all the associations they evoke. What all these devices have in common is that they always draw attention to *themselves*: they constantly remind us that we are dealing with language and not with the real world because they signal their own difference from the non-literary language that we ordinarily use (and which we take to represent the world). Advertising agencies are well aware of this. At one time the Heinz company tried to boost its baked beans sales with the brilliant slogan 'Beans Means Heinz', a phrase that inevitably draws our attention to its own language. Because its ingenious play with language catches the eye and makes it stand out among other ads, it probably also effectively served its purpose: to sell more beans. For the formalists, then, poetry is not poetry because it employs time-honoured and profound themes to explore the human condition but rather because in the process of defamiliarizing the language it draws attention to its own artificiality, to the *way* it says what it has to say. As Roman Jakobson said in 1921, poetry is a mode of language characterized by an orientation towards its own form. Or, as he put it in 'What Is Poetry?' (1934):

> Poeticity is present when the word is felt as a word and not a mere representation of the object being named or an outburst of emotion, when words and their compositions, their meaning, their external and inner form acquire a weight and value of their own instead of referring indifferently to reality.
>
> (Jakobson [1934] 1987: 378)

What poetry's orientation upon its own form first allows us to see in a fresh manner is language itself. What that language refers to – what it communicates – is of secondary importance. In fact, if a work of art draws attention to its own form, then that form becomes part of its content: its form is part of what it communicates. (This is obvious in paintings that are completely abstract: since such paintings do not refer us to the outside world, they can only 'be' about themselves. They force us to pay attention to their form, because that is all they have to offer.)

Now the idea of defamiliarization works well enough in the case of poetry and the difficult, wilfully innovative and defamiliarizing Modernist poetry of the formalists' own period perfectly confirmed the validity of defamiliarization as the ultimate criterion in establishing 'literariness'. But unsurprisingly they ran into trouble in their attempts to make the defamiliarizing 'devices' of poetry work for fiction: the most obvious ones – rhyme, for instance – simply do not occur in fiction and the less obvious ones – such as imagery – can also be found, even if not to the same degree, in ordinary usage. It is true that there are novels that in spite of this achieve an impressive degree of defamiliarization. This, for instance, is how Russell Hoban's *Riddley Walker* takes off: 'On my naming day when I come 12 I gone front spear and kilt a wyld boar he parbly ben the las wyld pig on the Bundel Downs' (Hoban [1980] 1982: 1). But such novels are rare. Usually we have to look pretty closely to find real deviations from ordinary language.

FABULA AND SYUZHET

In 1925 Boris Tomashevski (1890–1957), building upon earlier efforts of his colleagues, formulated the fullest formalist answer to the question of how to distinguish the language of fiction from ordinary language. The difference, he argued, is not so much a difference in language but a difference in *presentation*. In order to clarify this he juxtaposed two concepts: *fabula* (introduced by Shklovsky in 1921) and *syuzhet* (or *suzhet*, depending on how one transcribes the Russian alphabet). The *fabula* is a straightforward account of something: it tells us what actually happened. For instance, John Doe kills his cousin Jack to become the sole heir of a fortune and sits back to wait for the demise of his aged and infirm uncle – old J.J. Doe, his cousin's father and only remaining kin – who controls the money. The police work hard at solving the case but fail to do so. J.J. Doe hires a private eye who naturally succeeds where the police have failed. John Doe is arrested and duly sentenced.

These are the bare bones of the sort of story that one finds in countless private eye novels. But this is not how the standard private eye novel, which is usually narrated by the private eye himself (or herself), would tell it. The novel would begin with the private eye being invited by J.J. Doe to come to his mansion to talk about the case. The fact that the murder has been committed by John will not become clear until we have almost reached the end. As in all detective novels, the author manipulates the *fabula* to create maximum suspense. Such a manipulation of the *fabula* creates the *syuzhet* (the story as it is actually told) and it is the *syuzhet* that has the defamiliarizing effect that devices have in poetry: like, for instance, rhyme, the *syuzhet* calls attention to itself. Moreover, it defamiliarizes the events of the story because it actively interferes with the story's chronology. (I will discuss in a moment why we usually do not experience that attention-calling effect when we read, say, a detective novel.) It will immediately be obvious that one and the same *fabula* can give rise to a good many *syuzhets*. That insight became the basis for a book that much later would enjoy widespread influence, Vladimir Propp's *The Morphology of the Folk Tale* (1928), which I will look at briefly because it forms an important link between the formalists and the French so-called 'structuralists' of the 1960s.

FOLKTALES

It struck Propp (1895–1970) that if you looked closer at many Russian folktales and fairytales you found one and the same underlying story. In *Folktale* he tries to show how a hundred different tales are in fact variations upon – in other words *syuzhets* of – what seemed to be one and the same underlying *fabula*. This is a rather free use of the *fabula/syuzhet* opposition, as we will see in a moment, and it must be stressed that Propp was not a formalist. He is not interested in literariness and in many of his tales there is hardly any difference between *fabula* and *syuzhet* as understood in formalist terms. In a simple, chronologically told fairytale without flashbacks or other narrative tricks, the *syuzhet* is identical with the *fabula*. Still, Propp's at the time revolutionary idea that a hundred rather widely varying folk- and fairytales might actually tell one and the same underlying story is clearly inspired by the distinction between *fabula* and *syuzhet*.

How is one and the same *fabula* possible if we have characters who play important roles in some fairytales – a prince, a forester, a hunter, a miller, a good fairy, an evil queen – and yet are wholly absent from others? How could all of these tales possibly be presentations of the same basic story? Propp very ingeniously solves this problem by thinking in terms of *actors* and *functions*, by which he means acts or events that crucially help the story along. Let me try to give an idea how this works. One of the actors that Propp identifies – and which he sees returning in all his tales – is the 'helper'. Since it is not relevant to the function – all that he or she has to do is offer an act of help that keeps the story moving – Propp need not further specify who or what the 'helper' is. The 'helper' can be either male or female, a forester (as in 'Little Red Riding Hood') or a hunter (as in 'Snow White'), old or young, rich or poor, and so on – the possibilities are infinite. In one of his examples Propp illustrates the act of helping with examples from four fairytales. In the first the hero is given an eagle that carries him to another kingdom; in the second he is given a horse that gets him to a similar place; in the third he is presented with a boat; and in the fourth he is given a ring that magically produces a number of young men who carry him where he wants to go. The people who help the heroes are all different, the heroes themselves have different names, and the means of conveyance (if we can call an eagle a means of conveyance) are different. But the actor – and the function of the event – is in each case exactly the same. We might say that various *syuzhet*-elements correspond to one *fabula*-element (if we take the liberty of seeing all the fairytales in terms of one single *fabula*).

Propp distinguishes a limited number of actors (or, in his term, 'dramatis personae') – hero, villain, seeker (often the hero), helper, false hero, princess – and thirty-one functions that always appear in the same sequence. I should add that all thirty-one of the latter do not necessarily make an appearance in every single fairytale. Propp's fairytales get along very well with only a selection, even if the final functions – the punishment of the villain and the wedding that symbolizes a happy ending – are always the same. It is also possible for a fairytale to interrupt itself and start a new, embedded sequence (and another one) or to put one sequence after another. The individual qualities of the characters, however, are always irrelevant. At Propp's level of abstraction only their acts – which derive from the functions – really count. The villain and the helper are unimportant except for what they *do*, and what they do always has the same function in the various tales. This approach in terms of actors – embodied by interchangeable characters – and functions allows Propp to collapse a hundred different *syuzhets* into the skeleton of one single *fabula*. In my example of the detective story, all the different ways in which the story may be told – it could, for instance, begin with a description of the murder without giving away the identity of the murderer – would still have John Doe as the murderer and his cousin Jack as the victim. At Propp's level of abstraction, however, we ignore the characters and concentrate on their function within the story. If we look at Propp's tales from this abstract vantage point we see similarities between them that otherwise would have escaped our notice.

By presenting things in this way, Propp makes us see his folktales as systems in which the functions that he identifies have a specific place. In my discussion of the New Critics I have suggested that they – a decade after Propp – saw the literary work, and in particular the poetic text they were preoccupied with, as a system of checks and balances, with the checks and balances obviously interrelated. In Propp's book the interrelatedness of the various elements of a text is given more emphasis because his clearly defined functions are part of an equally clearly defined chain (there is, after all, only one underlying *fabula*). The 'helper' is always there to offer help, and not to the 'villain', even if what he or she does may vary widely from tale to tale. Each of Propp's folktales, then, contains an underlying *structure* of which the unsuspecting reader will usually not be aware. But if folktales contain such a structure, then maybe other narratives, too, can be made to reveal an underlying structure. That idea would come to dominate literary academia more than thirty years later.

FORMALISM REVISITED

The formalists, too, came to see literature in systemic terms, so that Jakobson and his colleague Yuri Tynyanov (1879–1943) in the same year that Propp published his work could already speak of the study of literature as a 'systematic science'. In its early phase, formalism had seen a poem as the totality of its 'devices': as the footing of a column of devices that were not necessarily related in any way. Apart from that, it had assumed that 'literariness' was the product of the inherent qualities of those devices. Those qualities, and the resulting literariness, could be identified, pointed at. And this is where early formalism went wrong. I have said above that the formalists were primarily interested in generalities. One general rule seemed unassailable: the rule that literariness is created by defamiliarizing devices. But it soon proved impossible to establish rules with regard to those devices. The 'defamiliarizing' potential of certain techniques or ways of presenting things is not an inalienable property. It manifests itself only in the right context. The only rule that can be formulated is that defamiliarization works by way of contrast, of *difference*. Because the early formalists presupposed a too rigid connection between a fixed set of devices and the principle of literariness, they did not see the devices that they regarded as the building blocks of literary texts in their proper light.

They gradually gave up this position when it became clear that to identify the various ways in which literature differed from ordinary language was only a first step towards explaining how literature works. Why is it, for instance, that we do not ordinarily realize how thoroughly we are being manipulated in a detective novel? Could it be that the suspense keeps us from noticing? Or is it that we have become so familiar with the genre that we no longer see what is happening right under our noses? Could the process of familiarization that is responsible for our relative blindness with regard to our environment, including language, be at work within literature itself? The formalists decided that this was indeed the case. What is more, familiarization worked at two levels: that of the single literary work and that of literature as a whole. Now where we find familiarization we may also expect defamiliarization, or at least attempts at defamiliarization, so the formalists started to look for processes of defamiliarization *within* literature – and the literary work – itself.

As was the case with Propp, the more abstract level that this way of looking at things brought into the discussion led the formalists away from 'devices' and in the direction of 'functions'. Let us first look at defamiliarization within one and the same literary text. Imagine a long poem consisting of heroic couplets (iambic pentameters – lines of ten syllables – with the rhyme scheme *aa, bb, cc,* and so on). Carried along by its rather monotonous cadence we suddenly come across two non-rhyming lines of fourteen syllables each. These two lines function to defamiliarize the reading process because they make us stop and think. But this also works the other way around. Imagine a long poem of unrhymed lines of fourteen syllables each in which you suddenly come across heroic couplets. Now the heroic couplets would have the function of making us stop and think. In other words, whether a certain poetic technique serves as a defamiliarizing device depends on the larger background.

To take this a little further, the ability to defamiliarize our perception is not a quality that certain techniques inherently possess, it is all a matter of how a certain technique *functions* within a given literary work, and that function can change from text to text. What counts is the way and the extent to which it *differs* from its environment. It is of course true that certain techniques, like the use of extreme hyperboles, would defamiliarize most literary texts, but it is equally true that in a text filled from the start with extreme hyperboles another hyperbole would not even be noticed. Every imaginable literary technique, then, can have either a familiarizing or a defamiliarizing effect. Everything depends on the way it functions within a given text. Differentiation is the crucial factor. This led to a view of the literary work as a system that establishes a textual environment that is then again and again made new with the help of defamiliarizing devices. From this perspective, it is first of all the system that dictates the actual techniques that will have to be used (long, non-rhyming lines in an environment of heroic couplets; heroic couplets among long non-rhyming lines). The system will, of course, offer a wide range of choice, but it will always demand difference.

Extending this insight to literature as such, the formalists came up with an interesting explanation of literary change. We all know that literature has changed over time. But why? Why do new genres emerge – the novel, for instance – and old ones disappear over the cultural horizon? And why do we find such rather considerable changes within genres themselves? The novel has gone from realism (mid- and late nineteenth century) to modernism (early twentieth century) and postmodernism (1960s and beyond). What is the driving mechanism behind such developments? As Boris Eichenbaum (1886–1959), another prominent formalist, said in 1926 (bracketing the role of individual authors), 'For us, the central problem of the history of literature is the problem of evolution without personality – the study of literature as a *self-formed social phenomenon*' (Eichenbaum 1965: 136). The formalist solution to this problem will not come as a surprise: defamiliarization. Literature as a whole renews itself through the development of, for instance, new genres, while genres in their turn defamiliarize (and thereby change) themselves through, for example, parody – a defamiliarizing strategy because it invariably focuses on peculiarities – and through the incorporation of new materials and techniques taken from other genres or from popular culture.

Acts of defamiliarization will have only a temporary effect: with the passage of time, even the most innovative devices will lose their capacity to catch our attention. The idea that an everlasting dynamic between an inevitable process of familiarization and acts of defamiliarization is the driving mechanism behind literary change – in other words, the driving force in literary history – is ingenious and interesting. It tries to give answers to questions of historical change that the New Critics, with their focus on the words on the page, could not even begin to address. But the formalist answers can only be part of a much larger picture. As the formalists themselves realized in the later 1920s, literature is not wholly autonomous; it is not completely divorced from the world in which it exists. Far-reaching social changes must have had consequences for the course of literary history. With the disappearance of the medieval world of heroic knights and grave quests, for instance, the long narrative poems that presented knights and quests became obsolete. In Miguel Cervantes's *Don Quixote* (1605–15) such a knight, although in some ways still admirable, has become the object of gentle ridicule. Moreover, the mechanism of defamiliarization cannot say anything about the nature of the devices that will be deployed. All it tells us is that change is inevitable. It does not tell us which new course that change will take. Surely the individual author plays a significant role in making a selection from the array of devices that are available or, even better, in creating wholly new ones.

FURTHER DEVELOPMENTS

In the later 1920s the cause of formalism was taken up in Prague, not least because Jakobson had moved there to get away from the political turmoil – and violence – in what had become the Soviet Union. In this brief section I will focus on what, from our vantage point, are the most relevant aspects of the way the Prague (or Czech) structuralists contributed to literary theory.

Most importantly, they further developed the idea that a literary text is a structure in which all the elements are interrelated and interdependent. There is nothing in a literary work that can be seen and studied in isolation. Each single element has a function through which it is related to the work as a whole. The formalists tended to focus on the defamiliarizing elements within literary art – either those elements that distinguished literary texts from non-literature or those that served the process of defamiliarization within those texts themselves. As a result, they paid little attention to all the elements that did not directly contribute to the defamiliarizing process. For the structuralists, however, everything played a role in what a text was and did.

One reason for arriving at this position was that, drawing on new insights in contemporary linguistics, they expanded the formalists' notion of 'function'. In so doing they gave a better theoretical foundation to the idea that literature is concerned with itself while simultaneously explaining how it could also refer to the outside world. As we have seen, for the formalists 'function' has to do with the way textual elements achieve effects of defamiliarization because of their difference from their environment. For the structuralists, the text as a whole – and not just the literary text – has a function too, and it is on the basis of the way a text functions as a whole that we can distinguish between various sorts of texts. A text's function is determined by its orientation. These orientations, worked out exhaustively by Jakobson in his famous 'Linguistics and Poetics' essay of 1960, are basically those of a so-called 'speech act' – they derive from what we do with speech. Let me illustrate some of the possibilities, using speech examples.

One of the shortest sentences in the English language is 'Damn!' Expressing a wide range of emotions – disappointment, anger, surprise, and so on – 'Damn!' is quite often oriented towards the speaker him- or herself. Because everything we say or write may be seen as a message, we could also say that here, perhaps somewhat paradoxically, the message is oriented towards its sender. It has, in Jakobson's terms, an 'expressive' or 'emotive' function. 'Hey, you!', however, is oriented towards the person who is addressed (the addressee) and has what Jakobson calls a 'conative' function. If we tell a friend about the movie we have just seen, or the near-accident we have witnessed, then our 'text' is oriented towards things in the outside world – it refers to the reality in which we both live (what one might call the context) and has a 'referential' function. From this perspective, in terms of orientation, literary texts are oriented towards themselves, but not in the way that 'Damn!' is often oriented towards its 'sender'. Literature focuses on its own *form*; its focus is on the *message* rather than on the sender, the addressee, or any other possible target. It is, in other words, oriented towards the way it presents itself and has a 'poetic' function.

Of course, these orientations almost never occur in a pure form. If I am all by myself 'Damn!' will probably be wholly oriented towards me, but if there are other people around I may very well be trying to catch their attention – to address them obliquely. 'Hey you!' is oriented towards an addressee, but may through its phrasing also express my own feelings about that addressee. Literary texts are oriented towards themselves (they are very conscious of their form and the outside world they would seem to refer to is often fictional and does not exist), but there are few works of literature that we cannot in one way or another make relevant to the world in which we live. In other words, in actual practice texts always have more than one orientation and more than one function simultaneously. What counted for the structuralists was which orientation and accompanying function is *dominant*. This concept of the 'dominant' allowed them a view of literary texts that was a good deal more flexible than that of the formalists: literature referred primarily to itself, but it could also be taken as referring to the outside world, although the referential element, of course, would always have to be subservient to its orientation on the literary code, to the poetic function. (A text would cease to be literature if its dominant orientation shifted from the text itself – its form – to the outside world.) Moreover, as I have just pointed out, from this point of view the whole text functions as a coherent whole, kept together by its 'dominant'. It is a structure in which all elements, whether they defamiliarize or not, work together to create a certain orientation.

In a second move, the Prague group further theorized the idea of defamiliarization and gave it a place in their view of the literary work as a structure. Borrowing from psychological studies of the way our mind processes the infinite number of data that our senses present to it and filters out what seems relevant, the structuralists replaced defamiliarization with *foregrounding* (taken from such perception studies by one of the Russian formalists who had already described its potential for literary studies). Unlike defamiliarization, which would not seem to affect its immediate textual environment, foregrounding has the effect that it 'automatizes' neighbouring textual elements. It draws the reader's attention to itself and obscures whatever else may be going on right beside it. While defamiliarization points to a contrastive, but static, relationship between the defamiliarizing element and the other elements, foregrounding emphasizes the dynamism of that relationship: what one element gains in terms of being foregrounded is lost by the other elements that constitute its background. In other words, just like the idea of a 'dominant', foregrounding implies a perspective that sees a text as a structure of interrelated elements. In contemporary literary criticism foregrounding, with its structuralist orientation, has effectively replaced defamiliarization.

THE AXIS OF COMBINATION

In the late 1950s Roman Jakobson formulated what is probably the ultimate attempt to define the aesthetic function in poetry; that is, the 'literariness' of poetry. I will briefly discuss Jakobson's definition because it is one of the prime examples of the formal, 'scientific', approach to literature that marks continental European thinking about literature from the 1910s until the 1970s. 'The poetic function' – that is, literariness – Jakobson said, 'projects the principle of equivalence from the axis of selection into the axis of combination' (Jakobson [1960] 2000: 38). This is not an inviting formula, but it is less impenetrable than it might seem to be.

Jakobson's definition departs from the simple fact that all words can be classified and categorized. Every time we use language what we say or write is a combination of words selected from a large number of classes and categories. Take, for instance, a bare bones sentence like 'Ma feels cold.' In this sentence we might have used 'Pa' or 'Sis' or 'Bud' or 'John' (and so on) instead of 'Ma' and we might have used 'good', 'bad', 'hot' (and so on) instead of 'cold' without disrupting the sentence's grammar. The alternatives that I have mentioned are grammatically equivalent to 'Ma' or 'cold'. 'Butter feels cold' would definitely be odd, and so would 'Bud feels butter.' The selection process that starts up whenever we are on the point of speaking or writing is governed by invisible rules that make us select words from large classes of grammatically equivalent words: nouns, verbs, adjectives, and so on. However, we also constantly make selections in the field of *meaning*. Here we are on less abstract ground than in the previous example and the starting point is what we actually want to say. Usually there will be more than one way of saying what is virtually the same thing. The most obvious case is that of a word for which there is a perfect synonym. We will have to choose between the two equivalents. Or we can choose from a group of words that is closely related with regard to meaning, for instance: man, guy, fellow, bloke, gent, and so on. Which word we choose may depend on the degree of colloquiality (or dignity) that we want to project or on how precise we want to be: a gent is not only a man, but a specific kind of man. In any case, we make a selection from a number of words that have much in common and may even be roughly identical: they are approximately or even wholly equivalent in meaning. Both with regard to its (grammatical) structure and with regard to meaning (its semantic dimension), language knows all sorts of equivalence. It is this principle of (linguistic) equivalence that poetry borrows from what Jakobson calls 'the axis of selection' and then employs in the 'axis of combination'.

This is also less mysterious than it seems. Jakobson claims that poetry, like all other language use, not only constantly selects items from long lists of words that are in one way or another equivalent to each other, but selects to create equivalences *between* the words it chooses. It can do this by way of alliteration, for instance, which is basically an equivalence between the sounds with which two or more words begin: 'The Soul selects her own Society' (Dickinson 1970: 143) – to quote an Emily Dickinson poem which uses an initial 's' in three of its six words (one of which also ends with an 's'). Or poetry can create equivalences by way of rhyme, in which almost whole words are equivalent to each other (like 'words' and 'nerds'). But it can also do so by way of meter – iambic pentameters, for instance – which creates metric equivalences unknown or rare in ordinary language; by way of grammatical parallelisms, inversions and juxtapositions (which in order to work presuppose equivalence between the two elements involved); and in numerous other ways. This is how Charles Dickens's *A Tale of Two Cities* ([1859] 1949: 1) opens:

> It was the best of times, it was the worst of times, it was the age of wisdom, it was the age of foolishness, it was the epoch of belief, it was the epoch of incredulity, it was the season of Light, it was the season of Darkness.

Parallelism and juxtaposition go hand in hand to create a 'poetic' effect in a prose text.

This develops Jakobson's early formalist work in the direction of structuralism, although it also represents a return to the formalists' hunt for literariness. However, literariness is here not the result of a number of discrete 'devices' that defamiliarize ordinary language, but of the specific organization of literary language which organizes itself along lines different from the organization of other uses of language. Literariness is the result of a specific structural principle – that of equivalence on the axis of combination. It is that equivalence that contributes to a literary text's coherence. Jakobson even suggests that words that are 'similar in sound' are 'drawn together in meaning' (Jakobson [1960] 2000: 48) because of that, but here he is clearly on extremely speculative and shaky ground and not many commentators have been willing to explore this lead. However, as with the formalists, the question of meaning hardly arises. And it is obvious that the principle of equivalence has even less to say about the relative *merit*, the *value* of individual works of literature. A text that is absolutely jam-packed with equivalences is not necessarily great literature. Witness these lines from Stephen Sondheim's 'The Day Off' (from the musical *Sunday in the Park with George*):

> What's the muddle
> In the middle?
> That's the puddle
> Where the poodle did the piddle.

Still, Jakobson's formula stands as one of the most serious – and, I should add, successful – attempts to capture that which makes the bulk of Western literature, and especially poetry, different from the language we use in a recipe for brownies or a letter of complaint to an insurance company.

SUMMARY

In the first half of the twentieth century, Russian and Czech literary theorists worked to develop a theory of *literariness*: what made literary texts different from, for instance, government reports or newspaper articles? In trying to answer this question they focused on the *formal* aspects of literature, on its specific forms and on the sort of language that it employs. The so-called Russian formalists suggested that literature distinguishes itself from non-literary language because it employs a range of 'devices' that have a *defamiliarizing* effect. In a later stage, they saw this principle of defamiliarization also as a moving force within literary history: literature, as an artistic discipline, renews itself by making itself strange again whenever its current forms have become overly familiar and a sort of automatization has set in. Because unfamiliarity is not an inherent quality but depends on contrast – with what is known and has become routine – the emphasis within formalism soon shifts towards the *function* of devices, rather than focusing on any innate qualities they might possess. Central to that function is the idea of *difference*. The successors to the formalists, the Prague structuralists, build on this and begin to see the literary text as a structure of differences. After all, the neutral immediate context that a defamiliarizing element needs in order to stand out is as necessary as that element itself. *Foregrounding* is literally made possible by the existence of a background. Foreground and background – the unfamiliar and the familiar – function within one single structure and together create literary effects. Finally, the literary text distinguishes itself from other texts because we can see it as a message that is primarily oriented towards itself – its own form – and not towards the outside world or its potential readers. Although a literary text will usually also have other orientations – it generally will refer us in one way or another to the real world – this orientation towards itself, its *poetic function*, is dominant.

SUGGESTIONS FOR FURTHER READING

Russian Formalism: History-Doctrine (3rd ed. 1981) by Viktor Erlich is the standard survey of formalism. Peter Steiner's *Russian Formalism: A Metapoetics* (1984) is a very good introduction; somewhat controversially, but quite helpfully, Steiner includes Jakobson and Propp in his discussion. More recent and more thorough is Jurij Striedter's *Literary Structure, Evolution and Value: Russian Formalism and Czech Structuralism Reconsidered* (1989). Tony Bennett's *Formalism and Marxism* (2003) looks at formalism from a Marxist perspective (see Chapter 4).

Boris Eichenbaum's 'Introduction to the Formal Method' and Viktor Shklovsky's 'Art as Technique' are excellent introductions to early formalist thinking. Both are reprinted in *Russian Formalist Criticism: Four Essays* (2nd ed. 2012), translated by Lee T. Lemon and Marion J. Reis. Roman Jakobson's 'Closing Statement: Linguistics and Poetics', the ultimate in attempting to establish 'literariness', appeared originally in Thomas Sebeok's *Style in Language* (1960) and has frequently been reprinted, as for instance in Lodge and Wood (2000). *Readings in Russian Poetics: Formalist and Structuralist Views* ([1978] 2002), edited by Ladislav Matejka and Krystyna Pomorska, collects a number of classic texts while the major texts of Czech or Prague structuralism are available in Paul L. Garvin's *A Prague School Reader on Esthetics, Literary Structure, and Style* (1964).

3

READING FOR FORM II
FRENCH STRUCTURALISM, 1950–75

THE INEVITABILITY OF FORM

Why were the formalists and the Prague structuralists, the French structuralists that I will discuss in this chapter, and, to a lesser extent, the New Critics so preoccupied with the *form* of literary works? Why not concentrate on the *meaning* of a given work of literature, on what it has to tell us? Why waste time on something that would seem to be of secondary importance?

For many readers educated in the Anglo-American tradition, form and structure are not only alien to their interests – they do not read literature to learn about form and structure – but actually threaten the experience of reading. Many readers do not want to hear about form and structure because they seem to undermine the spirituality and freedom of the novel or poem that they are reading. We are dealing here with an underlying humanistic perspective that is uneasy with form and structure because they ultimately seem to diminish our own spirituality and freedom and represent a severely reductionist approach to human beings and their cultural achievements.

Readers who can identify with this may have a point, as will become clear later in this chapter. Form, however, is inevitable. Art cannot do without form. No matter how life-like a novel or a movie may seem, it is the end product of countless decisions involving form. That is even true if we are not talking about fiction or a Hollywood movie, but about their real-life cousins reportage and documentary film. Imagine that we set up a camera on New York's Times Square or in London's Oxford Street, and let it run from dawn till nightfall. We might argue that here we really have a slice of life, the ultimate realism in movie-making: the camera has registered only what happened in that part of Times Square or Oxford Street covered by the lens. (We have, of course, not moved the camera because that would have introduced a new perspective and would have constituted formal interference, no matter how rudimentary.) But we would above all have the most boring film ever made – thousands of cars, taxis, buses, and pedestrians passing in front of the lens. We might have picked out one of these people, a man with a promising grim expression, and followed him with our camera. But in so doing we would immediately have been forced to make decisions on form. We could film the man while following him, and we could occasionally overtake him to film him from the front. We could rent a helicopter and film him from above. Whatever we do excludes all the other options that we have. Even documentaries, then, no matter how true to life they seem, are the end products of long lines of decisions on the way their material should be presented.

LANGUAGE AS A SYSTEM OF SIGNS

Form is clearly inevitable. Whatever we do with images (as in movies) or with language always has a formal dimension. But what about the structure that I have just discussed? After all, structure is not something that we can easily identify. It's all very well to say that all the elements of a text are interconnected and that the various functions of these elements and the relations between them constitute a structure, but that does not really help. However, for the French structuralism that is the main subject of this chapter structure is even more fundamental than form. Form is inevitably bound up with meaning; structure, however, is what makes meaning possible. It is that which enables meaning to emerge. This is an enigmatic claim that clearly needs some explanation. After all, we are not even aware of the structures that supposedly play a role in the creation of meaning. It seems to us that we ourselves create meaning. We do this by saying something, or by making a gesture, or through a work of art, if we happen to have the talent – we create meaning because we want to express something by way of language, music, choreography, painting, film, and a good many other means. Meaning would seem to be produced by you and me, not by an invisible and intangible structure.

Structuralism has its origin in the thinking of the Swiss linguist Ferdinand de Saussure (1857–1913) who in the early twentieth century revolutionized the study of language. Nineteenth-century linguistics is mainly interested in the history of language – for instance, in how French and Italian developed out of Latin, or how English, Dutch, and German developed out of the West-Germanic language that the ancestors of the English, the Dutch, and the Germans shared some fifteen hundred years ago. Linguists studied the origin of individual words (modern English 'way', for instance, derives from Old English 'weg' – and the latter word still has the same meaning in Dutch) and tried to formulate the laws that apparently govern processes of linguistic change. Comparing new and old forms of a language, and using related languages to support their findings, historical linguists were able to discover the rules that govern linguistic transformations and to reconstruct how the various European languages had developed over historical time.

Saussure advocated a completely different angle. Instead of the usual historical, diachronic approach – following language through time – he opted for an ahistorical, and far more abstract, approach. To Saussure, questions concerning the way particular languages changed over particular periods were subordinate to a more fundamental question: how does language work? So instead of focusing on actual instances of language use – spoken or written – Saussure focused on the question of how language works in order to formulate general insights that would be valid for all language use and all languages. I should perhaps point out that this is also different from what grammarians – the other type of linguist around in Saussure's time – used to do. Grammarians wanted to describe the underlying grammatical rules that we automatically follow when we talk or write. So they analysed instances of language use – our individual utterances, which Saussure called *paroles* (plural) – to get at those rules. But Saussure was interested in how language as such works – in what he called *langue* – not in the grammatical matrix of this or that language.

This approach led Saussure – whose work found wider circulation only after it was published in 1915, two years after his death – to the idea that language should first of all be seen as a system of signs (he himself did not use the term 'structure'). Second, those signs are in the first instance arbitrary – after which they have become conventions – and have not taken their specific form because of what they mean, but to be different from other signs. Let me explain this. The 'signs' are simply the words that we use: for instance, 'way', 'yard', 'yarn'. 'Way' is 'Weg' in German and some of us will know that it is 'chemin' in French and 'camino' in Spanish. We need only a very superficial knowledge of a foreign language, or even of a dialect form of our own language, to know that the words we use to refer to the objects around us are different in other languages. From that knowledge it is only a small step to the realization that the link between a word and what it refers to must be arbitrary. Since other languages have different words for what we call a 'way' – and for all our other words – and in spite of that would seem to function perfectly well, we can only conclude that calling a way a 'way' is not a necessity. There is clearly nothing in what we call a 'way' that dictates the particular word 'way'. If that were the case, people everywhere would use 'way'. In fact, if real-world objects dictated our language, obviously we would all speak the same language. As it is, the relationship between the sign 'way' and what it refers to is indeed fundamentally arbitrary – in the sense that 'way' could have been quite different. In fact, since it once was 'weg', it already *has* been different. The arbitrariness, of course, applies only to the *fundamental* relationship between words and what they refer to. In practice, those relationships have become matters of convention. If we want to refer to an object – a table, for instance – we automatically use the word that everybody else uses. When Dr Seuss in 1950 first used the word 'nerd' in *If I Ran the Zoo*, the relationship between 'nerd' and what it referred to was arbitrary. As a matter of fact, if he had not provided illustrations with his story, we would have had a hard time figuring out what to make of 'nerd'. Now it is still arbitrary but also a matter of convention: there is now a standard relationship between 'nerd' and a certain type of person.

If the form of words is not dictated by their relationship with what they refer to, then that form must have its origin elsewhere. Saussure traces the origin of the form of words – of linguistic signs – to the principle of differentiation. New words like 'nerd' take their places among existing words because they are *different*. The whole system is based on often minimal differences: in ways, days, rays, bays, pays, maze, haze, and so on, only the opening consonant is different. Words, then, function in a system that uses difference to create its components. (A more practical way of saying this is that we automatically fall back on difference if we want to coin a word.) As Saussure himself says of all the elements that make up a linguistic system: 'Their most precise characteristic is being what the others are not' ([1915] 1959: 117). This is fairly self-evident. But then Saussure introduces an argument that seems completely counter-intuitive. The principle of difference that gives rise to the signs (words) of which language is made up, he tells us, also gives rise to their *meaning*. The usual assumption might be that the meaning of words derives from what they refer to and that it is the world we live in that gives the words in our language their meaning. However, that cannot be true. After all, if that were the case, we would indeed all speak the same language. Does this mean that Saussure's improbable claim is correct? Are language and the world that we intuitively feel is reflected by that language really so separated from each other as he suggests?

A strong point in Saussure's favour is that form and meaning cannot be separated. If we change 'ways' to 'days' or 'rays', we have not only a new form but a new meaning. In other words, the differential principle not only works to distinguish words from each other but simultaneously distinguishes *meanings* from each other. A linguistic sign – a word – is both form and meaning. Saussure calls the form – the word as it is spoken or written – the *signifier* and the meaning the *signified*. A change in the signifier, no matter how minimal, means a new signified. We must accept that meaning is indeed bound up with differentiation. But is it the full story? Not quite. Here I must introduce another counter-intuitive complication. A sign's meaning, its signified, is *not* an object in the real world, as we tend to think. That is again the way it might easily seem to us, and I have so far spoken freely of that which words refer to, but what they refer to is not the real world – at least not directly. Take a seemingly uncomplicated word like 'tree', which my *American Heritage College Dictionary* (3rd ed.) defines as 'A perennial woody plant having a main trunk and usu. a distinct crown'. This definition makes clear that 'tree' does not refer to any single object in the real world but to a category of objects that may or may not have 'distinct crowns'. The meaning of the sign 'tree' includes oaks, beeches, and chestnuts but also dwarf pines and Douglas firs. Its *signified* is a man-made category, a concept. A little reflection will tell us that this is also true of other signs: love, table, child, field. They all refer to concepts – not unrelated to the real world, but clearly the products of generalization and abstraction. It is those concepts that we then apply in our actual use of language in the real word, where they then have concrete referents. In a phrase like 'That tree over there' the sign 'tree' has an actual referent.

Our intuition that meaning is bound up with the real world is not completely wrong, even if the relationship between meaning and the world is a matter of convention and much less straightforward than we tend to think. But 'bound up with' is a vague phrase. Which of the two is dominant in this relationship? Do the real world and everything that it contains indirectly determine the meanings of our language, or does our language determine our world? To put it more concretely: does the fact that there are chestnuts somehow give rise to the admittedly arbitrary sign 'chestnut', or does the fact that the sign 'chestnut' has somehow come into being allow us to see chestnuts as a separate species among trees? If we had the word 'horse' but not the word 'pony', would we still see ponies as ponies or would we see them as horses, much like all other horses, because our language would not offer us an alternative? If the latter were true, then it might be argued that language precedes thought and constitutes the framework within which thought must necessarily operate. Some theorists, including Saussure, have thought so and have argued that our reality is in fact constituted by our language. If that is indeed the case, then the language we inherit at birth is for all practical purposes an autonomous system that carves up the world for us and governs the way we see it. (It is never quite autonomous because we can tamper with it and, for instance, expand it – witness Dr Seuss's nerd.)

This position which claims that our reality is determined by language is called *linguistic determinism* and I will have occasion to return to it later in this book. To many people, such a position appears unnecessarily radical and turns an interesting insight with a limited range of application into an iron law. We can perhaps agree on two principles, however. If we for a moment forget about the way we use language (or language uses us) and focus on language itself, we can agree that if we see language as a system of signs, then the meanings that arise – the signifieds – are, first, arbitrary in their relationship to the real world and, second, the product of difference in the sense that difference has a crucial, enabling function. Without difference there would be no language and meaning at all. The role that difference plays in its turn implies that meaning is impossible without the whole system of differences: the structure within which difference operates. After all, signs must differ from other signs and they need these other signs to be different. Although meaning is in the first instance produced, or at least enabled, by difference, it is at a more fundamental level produced, or again at least enabled, by the structure – by the *relations* between the signs that make up a language, or, to give this a wider application, between the elements that together make up a given structure. Meaning, then, resides not so much in those individual elements, but rather in the relationships between them. This admittedly improbable claim will be explained further below.

ANTHROPOLOGICAL STRUCTURALISM

These principles are indispensable for an understanding of the various approaches to literature that together constitute the French literary structuralism of the 1960s and 1970s. They are even more indispensable for a proper understanding of the so-called *poststructuralism* that developed after structuralism and that I will introduce in a later chapter. It is, in fact, mainly with an eye on poststructuralism that I have offered such a detailed discussion. Poststructuralism is also the reason why I will begin this overview of French structuralism with a discussion of its first, exclusively anthropological, phase. The anthropological structuralism that was developed in the later 1940s by the French anthropologist Claude Lévi-Strauss has never had much direct relevance for literary studies, but its indirect influence, through its apprehension and adaptation by poststructuralism and poststructuralism's many offshoots, is still immense. So we will first take a detour through an intellectual landscape that may perhaps be rather unfamiliar.

Like all structuralisms, anthropological structuralism is directly indebted to the Saussurean concept of language as a sign system governed by difference. However, anthropological structuralism gave the idea of a system of signs that function in the first instance because they are different from each other a much wider range – already foreseen, incidentally, by Saussure himself – and transposed it from linguistics to anthropology; that is, from the study of language to the study of cultures that from a Western perspective seemed 'primitive'.

The first anthropologist to see the potential of Saussure's analysis of language as a way of approaching the most diverse cultural phenomena was Lévi-Strauss. In the early decades of the twentieth century anthropology was still largely descriptive and functionalist: it sought to record the myths, taboos, rituals, customs, manners – in short, everything that was recordable – of the non-Western cultures that it studied and tried to establish their function. Lévi-Strauss broke with that tradition in two major ways. The first way is indebted to Vladimir Propp's study of Russian fairytales. Transposing Propp's idea to the field of myths, Lévi-Strauss tried to show how the most diverse myths, recorded in cultures that seemingly have no connection with each other, can be seen as variations upon one and the same system of ideas.

More important for our purposes here is that Lévi-Strauss saw the possibilities of Saussure's notion that meaning is ultimately the product of difference for the study of discrete cultural phenomena. For the structuralism that Lévi-Strauss developed in a series of major anthropological publications, the almost countless discrete elements that together make up a culture constitute a sign system. Eating customs, taboos with regard to menstruation, initiation and hunting rites, the preparation of food, the rules underlying so-called kinship relations – in short, everything that has a cultural origin and is not biologically determined – counts as a sign. The discrete bits of culture that we can distinguish are not meaningful in themselves, but draw their meaning from the sign system in which they function and, in particular, from their difference from other signs. As Lévi-Strauss put it in his study of the way masks were used in certain Native American cultures: 'A mask does not exist in isolation; it supposes other real or potential masks always by its side, masks that might have been chosen in its stead and substituted for it' (Lévi-Strauss 1982: 144). What a given element signifies within a culture depends on the system, not on an intrinsic meaning (which it does not have). Masks

> which no one would have dreamed of comparing ... cannot be interpreted each for itself and considered in isolation. They are parts of a system within which they transform each other. As in the case with myths, masks (with their origin myths and the rites in which they appear) become intelligible only through the relationships which unite them.
>
> (Lévi-Strauss 1982: 93)

Just like the relationship between the linguistic sign and its real-world referent, the relationship between a specific cultural phenomenon and what it expresses – its meaning – is arbitrary in the sense that it is determined by convention.

BINARY OPPOSITIONS

However, the relationship between a cultural sign and what it expresses is not necessarily completely arbitrary. Anthropological structuralism is also interested in the question of how our ancestors once, some time during the evolutionary process that gave us the sort of conscious awareness of ourselves and our environment that animals lack, started to make sense of the world in which they found themselves. A very basic mental operation comprises the creation of opposites: some things are edible, others are not; some creatures are dangerous, others are not. Classification in terms of such oppositions, in which the opposites are related to each other because they express either the presence or the absence of one and the same thing (edibility, danger, and so on), seems a natural thing to do, the more so since it would seem to be reinforced by nature itself. Man and woman constitute a binary pair, intimately related yet in a crucial way each other's biological opposite; our right hand and left hand constitute another closely related pair of opposites. Lévi-Strauss's basic assumption is that our primitive ancestors deployed this simple model, or structure, to get a grip on a world that slowly began to appear to them as something separate and alien. For him, the structure of primitive thinking is binary. Having acquired the rudiments of language, our ancestors must have started to categorize their world in very basic terms that always involved a presence and an absence – light/darkness, man-made/natural, above/below, noise/silence, clothes/naked, sacred/profane, and so on. Prehistoric men and women must have organized their experience around such + / – (that is, binary) oppositions.

For Lévi-Strauss, such binary oppositions, the most fundamental of which is that between what is man-made and what is part of nature (between culture and nature), constitute the basis of what we call culture. The basic apprehensions of reality that we find in those oppositions are translated into cultural acts. Once they have found expression in certain rites, taboos, customs, manners, and the like, they are permutated over time until, as often as not, they become completely unrecognizable. In fact, they may appear in completely different and even contradictory guises in different cultures. In some cases, the meanings that were attached to the original opposites and that found expression in their cultural materialization were clearly rooted in the real world: it makes sense to attach a positive value to things that are edible and it also makes sense to attach a negative value to things that will kill you. In other cases, however, those meanings are as arbitrary as the relationship between a linguistic sign and its real-world referent and are based not on factuality (as in the case of edibility), but on what we would call superstition. The standard positive valuation of light and negative valuation of darkness, for instance, ignores the facts that light and darkness are in themselves neutral natural phenomena and that how we value them depends on circumstance. (It is, for instance, much easier to hide from an enemy in the dark.) Meanings attributed to the pair above/below (as in a number of major religions) are even more obviously arbitrary. Cultural signs position themselves somewhere on a sliding scale between pairs of opposites and in so doing express a relationship between two terms, one of which represents a presence while the other represents an absence – a notion that, as we will see, is crucial for the poststructuralism of the 1970s and later.

It should be clear that anthropological structuralism, in spite of its overriding interest in the way the human mind has from the beginning interacted with its natural environment, does not take up a humanist position. Whereas an interest in form is wholly compatible with humanism (as in the New Criticism), structuralism denies that the individuals whose behaviour it studies are autonomous and act and think as they do out of free will. On the contrary: if I were a member of a 'primitive' tribe, my personal contribution to a ritual would take its meaning only from its function in the whole, from its relation to other parts of the ritual, and not from my personal intention. It is, in fact, questionable whether it would be at all possible for me to have a personal intention in a primitive culture in which everything, down to the smallest thing, is governed by assumptions, conventions, and rules of unknown origin that cannot be questioned. Anthropological structuralism, then, takes up a firmly anti-humanist position.

SEMIOLOGY (OR SEMIOTICS)

From the rituals, taboos, customs, and myths of primitive cultures it is only a short step to contemporary culture. After Lévi-Strauss had shown the way, a range of contemporary cultural phenomena came under structuralist scrutiny. In 1957 the French literary critic Roland Barthes (1915–80) – who would later straightforwardly claim that culture is 'a language' – published *Mythologies*, in which he applies a very loose and freewheeling structuralist analysis to the differences between boxing and wrestling and between soap-powders and detergents, to the drinking of wine versus the drinking of milk, to striptease, to the design of the new Citroën, and a wide range of other cultural phenomena. The method (although Barthes is highly unmethodical) is familiar: the activities under scrutiny are taken apart so that their constituent elements – the various signs that make up the structure – become visible, after which Barthes analyses how they acquire meaning because of their difference from the other elements in the chain. His boxers, wrestlers, and strippers do not make personal statements with the motions they go through but these motions are signs that take their meaning from the underlying structure of their activities. The central insights of this cultural structuralism – called *semiology* (a term coined by Saussure) or *semiotics* – have been enormously productive and still play a prominent role in the way we think about how cultures (and all sorts of subcultures) work. Especially the idea that we can see the most unlikely things as signs and study them as parts of a larger sign system in which the meaning of those signs is not inherent in the signs themselves but the product of difference has paved the way for in-depth analyses of virtually everything imaginable. The claim that such sign systems constitute 'languages' should, however, not be taken too seriously. It makes more sense to see them as analogous to language in an important way.

Fashion has been a prominent target of structuralist analysis – in particular by Barthes – because its semiotic character is fairly obvious. In classrooms, where I always wear a jacket, I usually face T-shirts, sweaters, and so on. My jacket is in itself meaningless, as are the T-shirts and sweaters. However, an outside observer could easily draw the conclusion that a jacket clearly 'means' the right to come in at the last moment, to forget your book, to hold long monologues, to sit apart from the others, and to tell them what to read and write – in short, that it means authority or power. And, indeed, it does. But in a good many English schools the students wear the jackets. If I taught at one of those schools and wore a sweater in the classroom, then my sweater would spell authority and the sign 'jacket' would mean lack of power. What we see illustrated here, first, is that jackets and sweaters have no inherent meaning, but that meaning is enabled by difference – in a situation where everybody wears a jacket, jackets are meaningless (in which case it could be their colour, or their cut, that might enable meaning to emerge). Second, the relationship between sign and meaning is arbitrary: exactly the same meaning can attach itself to either jacket or sweater, depending on the circumstances. Third – and here I return to anthropological structuralism – my jacket functions within the relationship between the poles of one of structuralism's basic binary oppositions: that of dominance/submission. It situates itself somewhere between +power (dominance) and −power (submission); right at the +power end of the scale, in fact.

As I have just said, my jacket has no inherent meaning. Even in the first case, with me firmly and self-confidently in that jacket, this particular meaning of 'jacket' is limited to the institutional context. If I meet a couple of my students in a local café my jacket does not give me the right to expose them to a long monologue or to tell them what to drink. The sign 'jacket' acquires meaning only on the basis of difference within a certain context. That meaning here finds a very real basis in the institution's rules, in an underlying relationship of dominance/submission. But often enough the meaning that attaches itself to difference is not at all based on anything substantial. Fashion as a whole is a system in which mere difference, not backed up by rules or institutional power, often suffices to create meaning. Food, too, functions as a sign system – don't we all prepare special meals for guests? In fact, consumer culture as such, which sells us a good many things that we absolutely do not need and usually throw out after we grow tired of them, might be said to sell signs (that we buy only because we attach meanings to them on the basis of their difference from other consumer-signs) rather than products. Once we have been alerted to this sign function of things, we see signs everywhere. Even products that some of us arguably *do* need – cars, for instance – have on top of their practical value an additional sign value that car commercials expertly exploit. The semiological, or semiotic, approach that I am sketching here, and in which the most diverse things (including many of our actions) are seen as signs that have no meaning in themselves but take their meaning from their functions within a given structure – from their relationships with other signs – is still of great importance.

LITERARY STRUCTURALISM

In 1960 Lévi-Strauss, as a logical consequence of his work on myths, proposed a search for the underlying structure of all narratives – not only novels, stories, and other forms of fiction, but reportage, biography and autobiography, travel literature, and so on. The influence of linguistics is obvious in the work of the (mostly French) theorists who took up the challenge. Tzetvan Todorov (b.1939), who uses Boccaccio's late medieval *Decameron* (1351–53) to get at the structure of narrative in general, calls his study *The Grammar of the Decameron* (1969). Barthes tells us that 'a narrative is a long sentence', but the search for a universal 'grammar' of narrative that would reveal how the human mind arranges experience has never been able to live up to its initial promise. Most of the models that have been proposed are far too abstract to be of much use.

A good example of the abstract character of early literary structuralism is provided by an article on 'the logic of possible narratives' that Claude Bremond published in 1966 (later worked out in much greater detail, so that my remarks here do not do justice to his work). Bremond suggests as the basis for a general model of narrative the logical possibilities that any narrative will have. We should distinguish three stages: virtuality, actualization, and realization, which roughly mean the possibility of action, the transition to action – very broadly defined – and the result of action or 'achievement'. Phase one is the default position – a narrative sets up a scene that offers the possibility of action. It should be clear that all narratives do this. Even a description of a totally empty landscape has us waiting for what is going to happen next; that is, for action. In phase two elements are added that set the narrative in motion (+) or they are not added, in which case nothing will happen (–). We will not have much of a narrative if phase two chooses for the minus (–) option, but logically it is perfectly possible (we will see in a moment that this seemingly silly (–) option is highly relevant). If the narrative has been set in motion (the + option), phase three, that of achievement, may either follow or not follow. The transition to action may or may not achieve its objective. The new state of affairs may then function as a new starting-point – that is, a new virtuality – in particular if the action has not been successful. In that case a new cycle will begin: the narrative again has the choice between transition to action (+) and inaction (–) and if it opts for action will again have a choice between achievement (+) and failure (–).

This cyclical model is typical, for instance, of many action movies. In the James Bond series Bond's mission will usually go through at least two such cycles. His first encounters with the forces of darkness will follow a +, +, – pattern: we have potentiality for action, we have the transition to action, but we do not (yet) have achievement because Bond's attempt to get at the master criminal is thwarted. Only the last cycle will be fully positive: Bond achieves his objective and defeats the villain. The villain's end is pretty soon followed by a scene (usually Bond with a young woman) in which we have no transition to action because this is where the movie ends. The minus option of phase two (transition to action) turns out to be highly relevant: narratives conventionally end with zero transition to action.

Bremond's model will perhaps not come as a revelation. We are usually aware that narratives start somewhere, really get going because something happens, end somewhere else, and then may get going again. And we also know that writers, to complicate things, usually interweave a number of such sequences. However, even though the model operates on a high level of abstraction, it allows us to see a pattern – a structure – in the Bond movies, for instance, that otherwise might have escaped us.

NARRATOLOGY

There are a good many far more detailed structuralist studies, using rather different approaches. A.J. Greimas's *Structural Semantics* (1966), for instance, stays fairly close to one of his sources, Propp's study of Russian fairytales. I will focus in the rest of this chapter on what is by general consensus the most influential of all structuralist studies, Gérard Genette's *Narrative Discourse* (published in 1972 and translated in 1980). Genette's type of structuralism, often called *narratology*, is exemplary in its focus on the structure of narration, the way a story – taken in its widest sense – is told. This aspect of literature has for a long time commanded the attention of writers, who after all must take any number of decisions involving the way they are going to tell their story, and it has also drawn a good deal of attention on the part of literary critics (*The Rhetoric of Fiction* by the American critic Wayne Booth, published in 1961, is a brilliant exposé of technical strategies). What distinguishes the structuralist approach to the way stories are told is their systematicity and – inevitably – their focus on the underlying structures that make stories (and thus meaning) possible. The ultimate goal of narratology is to discover a general model of narration that will cover all the possible ways in which stories can be told and that might be said to enable the production of meaning.

Genette's *Narrative Discourse* is a brilliant contribution to narratology, the field that is literary structuralism's lasting legacy, and I will briefly sketch his project to give an idea of the structuralist approach to narration. Although Genette introduces a number of completely new categories, he more often redefines existing categories and insights in terms of *relations*. As he states early in *Narrative Discourse*, 'Analysis of narrative discourse will thus be for me essentially a study of the relationships between narrative and story, between narrative and narrating, and ... between story and narrating' (Genette [1972] 1980: 11). Let me give an idea of how this works by looking at some redefinitions of familiar literary-critical insights.

The first concerns the way in which the chronological *order* of the events and actions of, for instance, a novel (the formalists' *fabula*) is presented in the actual story (the *syuzhet*). We can express the relationship between the chronological order and the narrative order in terms that express their relative positions at a given point. The narration may temporarily lag behind the chronological order of events (which is what we find in a *flashback* – although Genette does not use the term), it may be synchronic with events, or it may run ahead of them (when the narrator speculates about the future, for instance). It may even present unlikely combinations of these possibilities: 'It would happen later, as we have already seen', to quote one of Genette's examples (83). Genette offers a detailed analysis of all the possible relations between the order of events and the order of narration and does so in a technical vocabulary that always calls to our attention that we are dealing with a relationship between two givens ('analepis', 'prolepsis', 'achrony', 'proleptic analepsis', 'analeptic prolepsus').

The second relationship that Genette discusses – *duration* – concerns the relationship between the time an event has taken up in the reality of the narrated world and the time that it takes to narrate that event. In order to avoid disastrous consequences – such as our day-long film – narration must speed things up. Equal duration of event and narration may occasionally create unexpected and arresting effects – 'John walked walked walked walked walked walked walked upstairs' – but this is not the way we can usefully describe a marathon. We usually find equal duration only in the unembellished presentation of dialogue. The question that then arises is how we can map the various possibilities of compression.

The third relationship is *frequency*, which in Genette's scheme of things covers the relationship between the number of times that an event occurs in the world that we are told about and the number of times that it is narrated. It is quite common for events that occur repeatedly to be described only once (a technique for which Genette uses the term 'iterative'). Such a narration might start with,

'We went for a swim every single day, that whole summer', and might then describe who went to the beach, what they talked about, who fell in love with whom, the thunderstorms that gathered on the horizon in the late afternoon, and so on. The reader will understand that this description probably stretches things somewhat – not one single rainy day, that whole summer? – but essentially covers a series of very similar events. Far less common is the reverse situation: an event that occurred only once is narrated repeatedly. But this is also not as strange as it may seem. A single event may be told by different characters from different perspectives, or it may be told by one and the same character at different points in her or his life (in which case we will also expect different perspectives).

Genette's most difficult analyses concern what in traditional literary criticism is called *point of view* and which he complicates considerably. Let me give an example. We all know that when writers sit down to begin a novel they have a wide range of possibilities at their disposal. There are first-person narratives, in which the story is told by an 'I' who is inside the story, and there are third-person narratives in which the narrator would seem to be absent from the story that is being told. However, as a structuralist, Genette does not take as his starting-point the writer who sits behind a desk and considers the available options, but the variations that are offered by the relationships between the various elements that play roles in the way stories are told. This structuralist perspective, in which there is no place for the author, leads him to suggest that, although we usually do not realize it, a third-person narration must have a narrator and that this narrator is always present in the story. This seems an unnecessary manoeuvre – why not simply identify authors as the narrators of their stories? – but it is not so strange as it may seem. Imagine a novel that is told by an invisible third-person narrator and that is set in seventeenth-century New England. That narrator obviously must know the seventeenth-century world that the novel describes. But the reader may not for a second get the impression that the narrator is also very much aware of mobile phones, hard disks, and the Dow Jones Index. In other words, the narrator functions as a continuum of the world that is described rather than as a continuum of the author. Even if we have our doubts about Genette's suggestion, we might well have to accept that the invisible, implied, narrator of a third-person narrative is not identical with the author.

In any case, positing an invisible narrator inside a third-person narrative enables Genette to see first- and third-person narration in terms of the relation between narrator and character and allows him to set up a neat binary opposition. In a first-person narrative the narrator is identical with a character; in a third-person narrative the narrator is not identical with any of the characters. In the first case the narrator tells us about him- or herself (a first person); in the second case the narrator tells us about third persons. Genette calls the first type of narration *homodiegetic* and the second type *heterodiegetic* ('self' versus 'other'). The relationship between narrator and character is intimately bound up with the relationship between narrator and the world that is narrated. A homodiegetic narrator is always involved in the world that is narrated. However, that involvement can be rather marginal. If I am at a party and tell a story about a weird thing that happened to me six years ago, I am, somewhat paradoxically, not part of the world that I am narrating. The course of time has made me *external* to that world. First-person stories will often combine 'external' descriptions, in which the narrator presents a former self, with current events in which the narrator participates and in which the relationship between narrator and the world that is narrated is *internal*. Heterodiegetic (third-person) narrators are not part of the world they narrate, not even if their creator – the author – *is* part of it. In Norman Mailer's *The Armies of the Night* (1968) the main character is Norman Mailer, who is participating in a march on the Pentagon. But for Genette the third-person narrator who always refers to Mailer in the third person – as Norman Mailer – is *not* the author and is therefore external to the narrated world.

Any reasonably experienced reader knows that the relationship between narrator and narrated world is a complicated matter. Even if we are well aware of who is the general narrator of the story or novel we are reading, we may still encounter passages in which the identity of that narrator is far from clear. This is especially the case with what is called free indirect discourse, defined by Dorrit Cohn as 'the technique for rendering a character's thought in their own idiom while maintaining the third-person reference and the basic tense of narration' (Cohn 1978: 100). In free indirect discourse the narrator's descriptive reportage can so gradually give way to the reflections of one of the characters that at a certain point we honestly can no longer say to whom we are supposed to attribute what is being thought or through whose eyes we see what is being described (with whose point of view we are dealing, in traditional terms). Are we still directly dealing with the narrator or have we slipped into the perspective of one of the characters? ('He realized that they would have to part, but he would always love, adore her, and remember the dimple in her chin.') One of Genette's lasting contributions to the way we talk about literature is his introduction of the term *focalization* for dealing with this complication of the relation between narrator and the world that is being narrated. (Genette derived the term from a New Critical source: Cleanth Brooks and Robert Penn Warren's (1943) notion of 'focus of narration'.) If the narrator has indeed given way to the perspective of one of the characters – even if that perspective is still described for us by the narrator – the narration takes place through a *focalizer*. 'Focalization' then allows Genette to draw broad distinctions between various types of narrative.

This only scratches the surface of Genette's structuralist narratology. It will be obvious, however, that the relationships I have sketched here and the others that Genette identifies can be further broken down and refined into a highly sophisticated analytical apparatus. Genette's narratology focuses and directs the way we look at texts. It allows us to map how exactly actual stories are embedded in other stories, or how focalization shifts during the course of a story, to mention only two of its benefits, and it can assist in the interpretation of complex texts. In fact, we know that it can do so because *Narrative Discourse* is not only a work of structuralist literary theory but a brilliant dissection of the narrative strategies of Marcel Proust's *À la Recherche du temps perdu* (*Remembrance of Things Past*; 1913–27), which functions as Genette's main textual source. But it is the reader who through a close reading operation must apply the model to the text under consideration and who is ultimately, in the absence of authorial control, left alone with the text. Genette exhaustively maps the possibilities, the endless combinations of relational positions, that the narrative form offers; the actual business of interpreting the literary text is left to the reader.

SUMMARY

Taking its cue from linguistics and – in its analyses of culture and its institutions – from structuralist anthropology, structuralism focuses on the conditions that make meaning possible, rather than on meaning itself. For the New Critics, who were also interested in structure, the organic structure that they assumed to be present in every successful text – and that produced that text's complex meaning – was ultimately the result of conscious intention, even if they preferred to deal with the words on the page. But for structuralism such intention remains well beyond the horizon. It tries to map the structures that are the actual carriers of meaning and the various relationships between the elements within those structures. Structuralism in literary studies may, for instance, examine the underlying structure of a specific genre, such as the detective novel; it may try to reduce the at first sight enormous diversity of characters that we meet in stories and in novels to a limited number of roles that always occur in fixed relations to each other; or it may study the narrative aspects of texts (and of film, historical writing, commercials, and other cultural products that make use of narration) in order to systematize the *narratological* possibilities – the narrative strategies – that are available to a writer (or a director). David Lodge speaks very appositely of 'the characteristic structuralist pursuit of explanatory models with which masses of literary data may be classified and explained' (Lodge and Wood 2000: 137).

SUGGESTIONS FOR FURTHER READING

Robert Scholes's *Structuralism in Literature: An Introduction* (1974) and Jonathan Culler's *Structuralist Poetics: Structuralism, Linguistics and the Study of Literature* (1975), despite their ages, are still good introductions to structuralism, with Scholes also satisfyingly accessible. Two classic introductions to structuralism have fairly recently been reissued in new editions: John Sturrock's *Structuralism* (2nd ed. 2003) and Terence Hawkes's *Structuralism and Semiotics* (2nd ed. 2003). Jonathan Culler's massive and wide-ranging *Structuralism* (2006) collects practically all important structuralist contributions to the humanities and the human sciences. Specifically focused on narratology are two other classics: Dorrit Cohn's excellent *Transparent Minds: Narrating Modes for Presenting Consciousness in Fiction* (1978) and Shlomith Rimmon-Kenan's *Narrative Fiction: Contemporary Poetics* (1983). Other good introductions to narratology are Mieke Bal's *Narratology: Introduction to the Theory of Narrative* (2nd ed. 1997) and Monika Fludernik's *An Introduction to Narratology* (2009). David Herman's *The Cambridge Companion to Narrative* (2007) aims specifically at those who have little or no prior narratological experience.

The best, although admittedly not easy, example of narratological criticism is still Gérard Genette's *Narrative Discourse* ([1972] 1980). Examples of structuralist analyses of specific genres are Tzvetan Todorov's 'The Typology of Detective Fiction' from 1966 (found in both his *The Poetics of Prose* (1977) and Lodge and Wood 2000), his *The Fantastic: A Structural Approach to a Literary Genre* ([1970] 1975), and Will Wright's *Sixguns and Society: A Structural Study of the Western* (1975).

4

POLITICAL READING

CLASS, GENDER, AND RACE IN THE 1970s AND 1980s

What the major approaches to literature that I have so far discussed have in common is that they focus strongly on literature itself. Richards's practical criticism and the New Criticism limit themselves in their search for a text's meaning to the 'words on the page'. Formalism is primarily interested in what makes literature different from other ways of using language and in the literary reasons for literary-historical change. Structuralism seeks to establish the structures that underlie narratives and make meaning possible. Conspicuously absent is a serious interest in what many literary academics would now consider the very important issues of the *historical situatedness* (or historical embedment) and the *politics* of literary texts.

To what extent is a literary text the product of the historical period in which it was written? The world has gone through enormous socio-economic and political changes in the last millennium. Isn't it reasonable to expect those changes to turn up in our literature? And isn't it at least plausible to assume that those changes have somehow affected the way we experience things? Can the human condition have remained essentially the same? And what sort of view of politics do we find in a given text? Does the text support the socio-economic and political status quo or does it take an openly or more implicitly critical stance?

Before the late 1960s – the years that function as a watershed in this book – such questions were thought to be irrelevant or even detrimental to reading and interpretation by the large majority of English and American literary academics. With only a few exceptions, critics had not much use for historical context and even less for politics. In this chapter on literature and politics I will focus on three major modes of political criticism that became a forceful presence in Anglo-American literary studies in the course of the 1970s: Marxism, feminism, and criticism that concerns itself with racial relations. In Marxist criticism *social class* and *class relations* function as central instruments of analysis; in feminist criticism the concept of *gender* is the crucial critical (and political) instrument; while in criticism concerned with racial relations the fundamental category is, of course, *race*. I should point out that the 1960s-to-1980s versions of these critical approaches, to which I will limit myself in this chapter, are by current standards rather traditional. If I may allow myself a Genettian 'prolepsis', literary theory and criticism would go through great changes under the impact of the literary-theoretical upheavals of the later 1970s and the 1980s, which witnessed the spectacular rise of so-called *poststructuralism*. Still, the fairly traditional characters of the Marxist, feminist, and race-oriented criticism that I will look at here in no way diminishes their importance: traditional perspectives still play an important and valuable role within the world of literary studies. It must be kept in mind, however, that there are newer versions of these and other critical approaches that have assimilated the poststructuralist thought that I will discuss in the next chapter and which continue political criticism from somewhat different perspectives. For strategic reasons, which will become clear in my discussion of feminism, I will first discuss Marxist literary criticism.

THE POLITICS OF CLASS: MARXISM

To discuss Marxism in the early twenty-first century may well seem strangely beside the point. After all, since the fall of the Berlin Wall in 1989, one self-proclaimed Marxist regime after another has been forced to consign itself to oblivion. And the officially Marxist political parties that for a long time were a serious force in Western European politics have either disappeared or have become marginal.

However, Marxism as an intellectual perspective still provides a useful counterbalance to our propensity to see ourselves and the writers whom we read as completely divorced from socio-economic circumstances. It also counterbalances the related tendency to view the books and poems we read as originating in an autonomous mental realm, as the free products of free and independent minds.

Marxism's questioning of that freedom is now considerably less sensational than it was in the 1840s and 1850s when Karl Marx (1818–83) began to outline what is now called Marxist philosophy, although it is still controversial. When he noted, in the Preface to *A Contribution to the Critique of Political Economy* ([1859] 1970: 3), that the 'mode of production of material life conditions the general process of social, political, and intellectual life', the Victorian upper class, if aware of this line of thought, would have been horrified. And they certainly would have been outraged by the conclusion that followed: 'It is not the consciousness of men that determines their existence, but their social existence that determines their consciousness.'

What does it mean that the 'mode of production' conditions 'the general process of social, political, and intellectual life'? If people have heard about Marxism, they usually know rather vaguely that it is about how your social circumstances determine much, if not all, of your life. This seems reasonable enough. If you work the night shift in your local McDonald's, for instance, you are unlikely to fly business class to New York City for a week in the Waldorf Astoria or to bid on the next Rembrandt that comes up for sale. But this sort of determinism is perfectly compatible with the idea that we are essentially free. Certain politicians would tell you to get an education, get rid of your provincial accent, buy the right outfit, and start exuding self-confidence. In other words, you have options, like everybody else, and all you have to do is make the right choices and start moving up the social ladder.

This was not what Marx had in mind. Marxist theory argues that the way we think and the way we experience the world around us are either wholly or largely conditioned by the way the economy is organized. Under a medieval, feudal regime people will have thought and felt differently from the way we think and feel now, in a capitalist economy – that is, an economy in which goods are produced (the 'mode of production') by large concentrations of capital (old-style factories, new-style multinationals) and then sold in a free, competitive, market. The *base* of a society – the way its economy is organized, broadly speaking – determines its *super-structure* – everything that we might classify as belonging to the realm of culture, again in a broad sense: education, law, but also religion, philosophy, political programmes, and the arts.

This implies a view of literature that is completely at odds with the Anglo-American view of literature that goes back to Matthew Arnold. If the way we experience reality and the way we think about it (our religious, political, and philosophical views) are determined by the sort of economy we happen to live in, then clearly there is no such thing as an unchanging human condition. On the contrary, with, for instance, the emergence of capitalism some centuries ago, we may expect to find a new experience of reality and new views of the world. Since capitalism did not happen overnight we will not find a clean break but we certainly should find a gradual transition to a new more-or-less collective perspective. The term 'collective' is important here. If the economic 'base' indeed determines the cultural 'superstructure', then writers will not have all that much freedom in their creative efforts. They will inevitably work within the framework dictated by the economic 'base' and will have much in common with other writers living and writing under the same economic dispensation. Traditional Marxism, then, asserts that thought is subservient to, and follows, the material conditions under which it develops. Its outlook is *materialist*, as opposed to the *idealist* perspective, whose claim that matter is basically subservient to thought is one of the fundamental assumptions of modern Western culture: we tend to assume that our thinking is free, unaffected by material circumstances. In our minds we can always be free. Wrong, says Marxism. Minds aren't free at all; they only think they are.

Capitalism, Marxism tells us, thrives on exploiting its labourers. Simply put, capitalists grow rich and shareholders do well because the labourers who work for them and actually produce goods (including services) get less – and often a good deal less – for their efforts than their labour is worth. Labourers have known this for a long time and have organized themselves in unions to get fairer deals. What they do not know, however, is how capitalism *alienates* them from themselves by seeing them in terms of production – as production units, as objects rather than human beings. Capitalism turns people into things; it *reifies* them. Labourers, as Marx himself said, must 'sell themselves' and are, essentially, 'a commodity'. Negotiations about better wages, no matter how successful, do not affect (let alone reverse) that process. However, this process of rei- fication is not limited to labourers. The capitalist mode of produc- tion generates a view of the world − focused on profit − in which ultimately all of us function as objects and become alienated from ourselves.

IDEOLOGY

This leads inevitably to the question of how it is possible that we can be so blind to the real state of affairs around us and so terribly delude ourselves. It also leads to the question of how it is possible that apparently some people are *not* deluded. The answer given to this second question by one important movement within Marxism − so-called 'Western' Marxism − is that we always have a certain margin of freedom. To put that in the terms usually employed in the debates over such issues as freedom of action and thought: within Western Marxism there is room for human agency and subjective consciousness; that is, for action and thought that have their origins in ourselves and are not wholly determined by forces over which we have no control. As a consequence, the superstructure − including, of course, literature and culture in general − also enjoys a certain measure of independence (a point that Marx himself makes). But to return to our (almost) collective delusion − for Marxism, we are blind to our own condition because of the effects of what it calls *ideology*. We should not confuse the Marxist use of 'ideology' with the way we often use the term: as referring to a set of beliefs that people *consciously* hold − beliefs of which they are aware and which they can articulate. We can, for instance, speak of the ideology of the free market − referring to a series of arguments that defend free enterprise against state intervention − and of the commu- nistic ideology that gave the state total control over production. For Marxists, however, the term is much more encompassing.

In Marxist usage, ideology is what causes us to misrepresent the world to ourselves. As I have just said, for Marxism, the basis of any society is its economic organization, which then gives rise to certain social relations – for instance, the class relations between capitalists and workers in nineteenth-century capitalist economies. This socio-economic base then conditions the cultural superstructure. However, there are forces at work that prevent us from seeing this: for instance, the liberal humanist idea that we are essentially free and can remain free as long as we can think. For Marxists, ideology is not so much a set of beliefs or assumptions that we are aware of – although most of them would include consciously held beliefs and assumptions in their definition of the term – but, more importantly, that which makes us experience our life in a certain way and makes us believe that that way of seeing ourselves and the world is *natural*. In so doing, ideology distorts reality in one way or another and falsely presents as natural and harmonious what is artificial and contradictory – the class differences that we find under capitalism, for instance. If we succumb to ideology, we live in an illusory world, in what Marxists have often described as a state of *false consciousness*. As we will see later, the idea that we are blind to our own condition is in more than one way still vitally important for literary studies.

How is ideology able to hide authentic reality from us? One very influential answer was given in the 1960s by the French Marxist philosopher Louis Althusser (1918–90). Althusser's first thesis regarding ideology is that 'Ideology represents the imaginary relationship of individuals to their real conditions of existence' (Althusser 1971: 153), which roughly corresponds with what I have just said: ideology distorts our view of our true 'conditions of existence'. His second thesis connects ideology with its social sources. For Althusser, ideology works through so-called 'ideological State apparatuses', which, although they may have their own sub-ideology, are all subject to the ruling ideology (from the Marxist perspective, the State is not neutral, but actively supports the capitalist order). Althusser's ideological State apparatuses include organized religion, the law, the political system, trade unions, the educational system, the media – in short, all the institutions through which we are socialized and other organizations that have in one way or another been co-opted by those institutions. Ideology, then, has a *material* existence in the sense that it is embodied in all sorts of material practices. Althusser mentions some of the practices that are part of 'the *material existence of an ideological apparatus*, be it only a small part of that apparatus: a small mass in a small church, a funeral, a minor match at a sports club, a school day, a political party meeting, etc.' (158). The list of material ideological practices could be almost infinitely expanded. What is clear is that ideology is waiting for us wherever we go, and everything we do and everything in which we engage are pervaded by ideology. This leads Althusser to the following conclusion: 'It therefore appears that the subject acts insofar as he is acted by the ... system' (159). While we believe that we are acting out of free will, we are in reality 'acted by the ... system'. We recognize in this formulation the anti-humanist structuralist anthropology of Lévi-Strauss. Because within such a perspective there is no room for freedom, Althusser does not attribute the unequal distribution of wealth that we find within capitalist societies to the manipulations of 'a small number of cynical men' (154). The driving mechanism behind ideology is not the self-interest of those who profit from the way a given society has economically organized itself. Those who profit are as blind as everybody else. (Marx, who had argued that the ruling class has its own interests adopted by the general public through the workings of ideology, would not necessarily have agreed.)

But if that is the case, where does ideology come from and how has it acquired its immense influence? To answer these questions, Althusser draws on the writings of the French psychoanalyst Jacques Lacan (1901–81), whose work I will discuss in more detail in the next chapter. For Lacan, the processes that we go through when we grow up leave us forever incomplete. Aware of that deep lack – although we cannot name it – and yearning for completion and wholeness, we turn to ideology, the more so since it constantly 'hails and interpellates' (addresses) us as 'concrete subjects' – as if we are whole already. In so doing, it may 'interpellate' us in the different social roles that we play, or, as Althusser would say, the different 'subject positions' that we occupy. One and the same woman could be interpellated as a mother, as a member of a particular church, as a doctor, as a voter, and so on. The way ideology addresses us creates those subject positions for us; yet simultaneously those positions are already familiar to us because they are part of what we know. Ideology is not a set of political views, but offers a fundamental coherence and stability, tied up with a specific socio-economic order. Ideology invites us to accept an image of ourselves that is deeply tempting; and because we want to be tempted, it convinces us that we are whole and real, that we are the 'concrete subjects' we want to be. No wonder, then, that we see whatever ideology makes us see as natural, as belonging to the natural, harmonious order of things.

Althusser's analysis paved the way for explorations of the way ideology works in literature. Colin McCabe and other British critics showed how, for instance, the objective realism of the mid-nineteenth-century English novel is not so objective after all. They argued that novels like Charlotte Brontë's *Jane Eyre* (1847) and George Eliot's *Middlemarch* (1871–72), which present their characters as essentially free, even if not all of them make use of that freedom, 'hail' us just as ideology hails us. Such novels invite their readers to become part of a world that is essentially free and to look over the shoulders of people who make autonomous decisions. They create a specific subject position for their readers and give them the illusion that they, too, are free. Just like ideology, such novels give their readers the idea that they are complete: they make them believe that they are free agents and in that way make them complicit in their own delusion.

HEGEMONY

Although Althusser's analysis led to valuable insights in the various ways in which literature can conspire with, and simultaneously deceive, its readers, a good many Marxist critics felt uneasy with the deterministic character of his view of ideology. As we have seen, Althusser would seem to leave no room at all for autonomous, non-ideological thought or action. With the publication of the writings of the Italian Marxist Antonio Gramsci (1891–1937) in the early 1970s, a modified concept of ideology became available. Gramsci, writing in the 1930s, is fully aware of the power of ideology, which leads to '[t]he "spontaneous" consent given by the great masses of the population to the general direction imposed on social life by the dominant fundamental group' (Gramsci [1971] 1998: 277). This consent is '"historically" caused by the prestige (and the consequent confidence) which the dominant group enjoys because of its position and function in the world of production' (277). Gramsci's explanation of the power of ideology has the merit of allowing us to resist what he calls the *hegemony* – the domination of a set of ruling beliefs and values through 'consent' rather than through 'coercive power'. Gramsci's 'hegemony' is far less inescapable than Althusser's ideology, even if it, too, establishes and maintains itself through 'civil society' and employs cultural means and institutions. Under hegemonic conditions the majority – usually a large majority – of a nation's citizens has so effectively internalized what the rulers want them to believe that they genuinely think that they are voicing their own opinion, but there is always room for dissent. Gramsci's hegemony, although it saturates society to the same extent as Althusser's ideology, is not airtight and waterproof. We can catch on to it and resist its workings with counter-hegemonic actions even if we can never completely escape its all-pervasive influence.

In the United Kingdom, the important Marxist critic Raymond Williams (1921–88) emphasized this aspect of Gramsci's thought. For Williams, 'hegemony is not singular … its own internal structures are highly complex, and have continually to be renewed, recreated and defended … they can be continually challenged and in certain respects modified' (Williams [1980] 1996: 22). Although the economic 'base' and its 'mode of production' are still important factors, the idea that the 'base' completely determines the cultural 'superstructure' is too simple: 'no mode of production, and therefore no dominant society or order of society, and therefore no dominant culture, in reality exhausts the full range of human practice, human energy, human intention' (26). Marxist critics who follow Williams's more flexible notion of ideology – such as the cultural materialists whom I will discuss in Chapter 7 – see literature as an important vehicle for ideology, but they are very attentive to the dissenting voices and views that literature may also present.

MARXIST LITERARY STUDIES

This discussion of ideology and hegemony will have made clear that a Marxist perspective leads to an approach to literature that is significantly different from the approaches I have discussed so far. As we have just seen, Marxists may differ on the extent to which the cultural superstructure is determined by the socio-economic base. Marx himself, for instance, is on record as leaving the arts a good deal of leeway – the development of the arts, for him, did not

necessarily immediately reflect changes in the economic arrangement and the relations between classes – while the so-called 'vulgar
Marxists' of the inter-war period saw a direct cause–effect relationship between the socio-economic base and literature, and saw the
writer as directly conditioned by his or her social class. All Marxist
critics agree, however, that in the study of literature the social
dimension is absolutely indispensable. Writers can never completely
escape ideology and their social background, so the social reality of
the writer will always be part of the text.

A central question in Marxist approaches to literature concerns
the reliability of literary texts as social 'evidence'. If Charles
Dickens's *Great Expectations* (1860–61) and George Eliot's
Middlemarch (1871–72) are conditioned by the capitalist society of
Victorian England, what, then, are we going to find in these
novels: a true picture of Victorian England or an ideologically distorted reflection? In short, is it possible for writers or for literary
texts – this is a crucial distinction, as we will see – to offer objective
insights (as Marxists see them): to present history as a never-ending
struggle between antagonistic classes for economic and social gains
and to present contemporary reality as only the latest instance of
that struggle?

Over time, Marxist critics have proposed different answers to this
question, although most have been inspired by the notion – first
formulated by Friedrich Engels in 1888 – that the meaning of a
literary work must be seen as independent of the political (and
ideologically coloured) views of its author. This by now familiar
strategy of separating text and author does, however, not separate
the text from social reality (as the formalists and the literary structuralists did). On the contrary, the idea is that if we remove the
author from the picture – or at least the author's political views –
we might get an even better picture of the real world of class conflicts and political tension. This idea has the great merit that it
allows Marxist critics to read the work of even the most reactionary
authors against the grain of their political views so that their work,
too, can be appreciated from a Marxist perspective. The Hungarian
critic George Lukács (1885–1971), the most prominent Marxist
critic of the inter-war period, for instance, holds the novels of
Walter Scott, the French novelist Honoré de Balzac (1799–1850),
and the Russian Leo Tolstoy (1828–1910), none of them known

for progressive views, in high regard. In fact, Lukács vastly prefers the panoramic novels of such conservative writers to the fragmentary, avant-garde products of the sometimes fiercely leftist artists of the 1920s because it is only in the wide-ranging panorama, and in the merging of individual life stories with the larger movements of history, that the reader is confronted with the historical truth. The work of art must 'reflect correctly and in proper proportion all important factors objectively determining the area of life it represents' and must, moreover, 'so reflect these that this area of life becomes comprehensible from within and from without, re-experienceable' (Lukács 1970: 30). And great literary art succeeds in doing this:

> Achilles and Werther, Oedipus and Tom Jones, Antigone and Anna Karenina: their individual existence ... cannot be distinguished from their social and historical environment. Their human significance, their specific individuality cannot be separated from the context in which they were created.
>
> (Lukács [1957] 1972: 476)

The narratives in which these characters appear are to some extent independent of their authors' political convictions and accurately reflect historical reality. They effectively overcome their authors' ideological limitations and they do so because they offer a total overview of all the social forces involved, approaching the dialectical thinking in terms of the total social process that Marxism demands.

For the British and American Marxist critics of the 1970s, and 1980s, usually influenced by Althusser and his grim view of an enormously powerful ideology, texts do not so easily allow us a view of an undistorted reality. I have already mentioned that, following Althusser, critics sought to demonstrate that the great realistic novels of the nineteenth century, just like ideology, address ('hail') their readers and make them complicit in their own ideological delusion. Ideology is seen as such a strong presence in the text that we more or less have to break down its resistance to get at a truer picture of the reality the text pretends to present, although in a somewhat mysterious way the text itself also facilitates that process. As Althusser says in his 'Letter on Art' (1966), which also addresses literature, 'art makes us *see* ... the ideology from which it is born, in which it bathes, from which it detaches itself as art, and to which it *alludes*' (1971: 204). An important influence on critics of the period (especially British ones) was the French critic Pierre Macherey's *A Theory of Literary Production* (1966; translated in 1978). For Macherey, too, literary works are pervaded by ideology. So in order to get beyond a text's ideological dimension we will have to begin with the cracks in its façade, with those sites where the text is not fully in control of itself (a lack of control summarized in the title of one of Macherey's later essays: 'The Text Says What It Does Not Say'). In order to expose a text's ideology, interpretation must paradoxically focus on what the text does *not* say, on what the text *represses* rather than *expresses*. We find what the text does not say in gaps, in silences where what might have been said remains unarticulated, and in 'disparities which point to a conflict of meaning'. Literature, as Macherey puts it, *reveals* the vulnerability of ideology (see Macherey [1966] 1978: 59–60). The text might almost be said to have an unconscious to which it has consigned what it cannot say because of ideological repression. Macherey finds the cracks in the text's façade not in its major themes, which are fully controlled by ideology, but in textual elements that are only tangentially related to the main theme (or themes), in the text's 'margins'. Here is where we see ideology, with its suppression of contradiction and exclusion of what is undesirable, actually at work. And since in a literary text the work of ideology is never completely successful, we will find 'the inscription of an *otherness* in the work'. Literary criticism then 'brings out a *difference* within the work by demonstrating that it is *other than it is*' (78).

This leads to a way of reading literature that is completely different from that of the English and American critics of the 1920s and beyond whom I discussed in the first chapter. Macherey and like-minded critics in the United Kingdom, such as Terry Eagleton, were not interested in what makes a text coherent but in what makes it incoherent, in what does not fit or is absent for obscure reasons (see, for instance, Eagleton's analyses of a number of canonical texts in his *Criticism and Ideology* of 1976a).

Let us have a brief look at the British critic Catherine Belsey's Macherey-inspired reading of a number of Sherlock Holmes stories in her *Critical Practice* (1980). Their author, Arthur Conan Doyle (1859–1930), presents his detective hero as unerringly penetrating, a man gifted with a brain that can solve any riddle. The 'project' of these stories – to make everything subject to scientific analysis, as Belsey puts it – would seem to promise a true and unflinching picture of reality. However, if we look closely at the reality that the stories present, we see that their presentation of the real world is strangely deficient. As Belsey demonstrates, the women in these stories and their social position are not subjected to analysis at all. They remain mysterious and opaque. The silence of these stories with regard to their female characters reveals the working of a patriarchal ideology in which the males take centre stage and the women are taken for granted. They may, at best, provide an occasion for Holmes's intellect to dazzle us.

This may well raise a question: do we need a theoretical concept like ideology to find what other readers might have discovered without its help? In fact, Macherey's own analyses of the fiction of Jules Verne raise the same question. However, we should not underrate the added value of this approach. Whereas a more traditional critic might suppose that in the Holmes example we are dealing with a personal blindness or an unwillingness on the part of the author to present a truer picture of late nineteenth-century or early twentieth-century reality, for Marxist critics the omission is not personal at all, but points directly to an impersonal cluster of beliefs and values with an immense social influence. It is this ideology that is the real target of literary investigation, and the aim in this particular case is not to show up Doyle's personal shortcomings, but the differences between ideology and the real world. Through the politics of the text – its ideological dimension – Marxist criticism addresses the politics of the world outside the text.

BAKHTIN

Although perhaps more formalist than Marxist, the work of the Russian critic Mikhail Bakhtin (1895–1975) has more links with the discussion above than with the formalism and structuralism discussed in earlier chapters. Moreover, Bakhtin's work came to the English-speaking world very late, long after its publication in Russian, and was absorbed into the exchanges on literary theory as they then took place. In his first book to be published in English, *Rabelais and His World* (written in the early 1940s and first translated in 1968), Bakhtin argues that in the fiction of the French writer François Rabelais (1494?–1553) we find an opposition between a folk culture characterized by spontaneity and laughter, in the spirit of carnival, and an official culture that in both its religious manifestation (the Church) and in its worldly ones (the period's feudal institutions) was not only repressive but essentially life-denying in its negative attitude towards the bodily functions that folk culture did not work hard to hide from sight. Seeing the annual carnival as the epitome of folk culture, Bakhtin celebrated the 'carnivalesque' in Rabelais, and in early modern culture in general. His positive valuation of the carnivalesque was picked up especially by those critics who saw its potential as a site of resistance against contemporary forms of repression, in particular patriarchy (see below) and the reign of consumer capitalism. These critics found instances of a carnivalesque undermining of (male) authority – an undermining from below through comic reversals or outright laughter – in a wide range of texts.

Bakhtin's seminal contribution to contemporary literary theory, the essay 'Discourse in the Novel', dates from the early 1930s but remained virtually unknown in the English-speaking world until it was published in *The Dialogic Imagination: Four Essays* in 1981. In this essay Bakhtin argues that the novel, as a literary genre, is inherently plural; that is, it always presents a plurality of 'voices'. Since novels with only a single character are exceedingly rare, this seems fairly self-evident. But that is not what Bakhtin has in mind. The presence of a variety of characters who all articulate themselves in different ways is 'a mere diversity of voices', not the 'heteroglossia' that is his real interest here. For Bakhtin, a natural language – Russian, English, etc. – is not a seamless unity but a compound of a large number of 'languages': 'social dialects, characteristic group behavior, professional jargons, generic languages, languages of generations ... languages of the authorities, of various circles and of passing fashions' (Bakhtin 1981: 263) and so on. And all of these 'social and historical voices populating language, all its words and all its forms ... are organized in the novel into a structural stylistic system that expresses the differential socio-ideological position of the author and the heteroglossia of the epoch' (300). Unlike poetry, in which he sees a unity of style, the novel – '[e]very novel' – is 'a *hybrid*', even if it is 'an intentional and conscious hybrid, one artistically organized' (366). Whatever the intention of their authors, novels are arenas, sites where diverse and often competing discourses and ideologies live together in a not necessarily peaceful coexistence. Language itself – every word, every phrase – comes laden with a history that testifies to this. Whatever 'object' language wants to address is 'already as it were overlain with qualifications, open to dispute, charged with value ... It is entangled, shot through with shared thoughts, points of view, alien value judgments and accents. The word, directed toward its object, enters a dialogically agitated and tension-filled environment' (276–77).

When 'Discourse in the Novel' found its way into the debate on literary theory in the early 1980s, it was immediately harnessed to the cause of the poststructuralist 'decentring' (see the next chapter) that had by then become the hottest topic in literary criticism (and especially American literary criticism). But compared to the views of, say, Roland Barthes or Jacques Derrida, Bakhtin's 'dialogism' is, as we will see, fairly traditional, even if it offered new insights in the social and historical dimensions of language and the specific character of fiction. For Bakhtin, the novel still constitutes a unity kept together through intentional artistic organization. It is a work of art whose creation 'demands enormous effort: it is stylized through and through, thoroughly premeditated, achieved, distanced' (366). To stress this may seem unnecessary, even puzzling, but the following chapters will make clear why it makes sense to emphasize that Bakhtin's work belongs with the more traditional criticism that has been discussed thus far.

THE POLITICS OF GENDER: FEMINISM

It is now obvious that it does not make much sense to consider the literature that over the ages has been produced by female writers without taking into account the social realities that female authors have had to face. For one thing, for a very long period women were not really supposed to receive an education. It is, of course, possible to become a writer without a formal education – a fortunate circumstance to which we owe a number of great women writers – but clearly the odds are against members of any group that is discriminated against in this way. The work of female writers has so obviously been under a number of serious historical constraints that it is now hard to understand why the odds they faced were virtually ignored in literary discussions (except by some of these writers themselves: Virginia Woolf, for instance). The answer surely has to do with the general blindness of (male-dominated) Western culture to its treatment of women as second-rate citizens. Moreover, as long as within literary studies interest was virtually limited to the 'words on the page' (Richards, Leavis, the New Criticism), to the underlying structures that made literary meaning possible (the French structuralists), or to ideology and the class struggle as mediated through literary texts (traditional Marxist criticism), the plight of women writers drew little attention.

Most critics now believe that it is impossible to cordon off a given field of interest or study neatly from the rest of the world. For better or for worse, everything seems somehow related to everything else. With regard to the social position of women, and therefore also with regard to the field of female writing, that view is to a large extent due to the feminist movement that began to gain momentum in the 1960s. Curiously, even Marxism, with its wide-ranging historical theorizing, had largely ignored the position of women. With hindsight, this oversight is all the more incomprehensible since some of its key concepts – the struggle between social classes, the blinding effects of ideology – might have been employed to analyse the social situation of women.

The feminist movement, then, put socio-historical circumstances as a determining factor in the production of literature firmly on the map. Feminism was right from the beginning involved in literary studies, and for good reasons. Kate Millett's trailblazing *Sexual Politics* (1970), for instance, devotes long chapters to the attitudes towards women that pervade the work of prominent twentieth-century authors such as D.H. Lawrence (1885–1930) and Henry Miller (1891–1980). Both were held in high regard by many critics for their daring and liberating depictions of erotic relations. Millett, however, showed that the attitude of their male characters towards women was not so emancipated after all: most of the male characters that she examined – and especially those of Miller – were denigrating, exploitative, and repressive in their relations with women. Feminism saw very clearly that the widespread negative stereotyping of women in literature and film (and we may now add the internet) constituted a formidable obstacle on the road to true equality. At least as important is that in the work of the male writers she discusses Millett finds a relationship between sex and power in which the distribution of power over the male and female partners mirrors the distribution of power over males and females in society at large. In other words, in terms of power, acts that we usually think of as completely private turn out to be extensions of the public sphere. The private and the public cannot be seen as wholly separate – on the contrary, they are intimately linked. Since this is the case, Millett argues, the private sphere is, just like the public realm, thoroughly political: it is a political arena where the same power-based relations exist as in the public world. Feminism and feminist criticism are profoundly political in claiming that the personal and the political cannot be separated. They are also political in the more traditional sense of trying to intervene in the social order with a programme that aims to change existing social conditions. Feminism seeks to change the power relations between men and women that prevail under what in the late 1960s and the 1970s was usually called *patriarchy*, a term that referred to the (almost) complete domination of men in Western society (and beyond).

FEMINIST LITERARY STUDIES

In its first phase, feminist literary studies focused on 'the woman as reader' and on 'the woman as writer'. The American feminist critic Elaine Showalter, from whom I am borrowing these formulations, put it as follows in her 1979 essay 'Towards a Feminist Poetics':

> The first type is concerned with ... woman as the consumer of male-produced literature, and with the way in which the hypothesis of a female reader changes our apprehension of a given text, awakening us to the significance of its sexual codes ... Its subjects include images and stereotypes of women in literature, the omissions of and misconceptions about women in criticism, and the fissures in male-constructed literary history.
>
> (Showalter [1979] 1985b: 128)

When feminist criticism focuses on 'the woman as writer' it concerns itself with woman as the producer of textual meaning, with the history, genres and structures of literatures by women. Its subjects include the psychodynamics of female creativity; linguistics and the problem of female language; the trajectory of the individual or collective literary career; literary history; and, of course, studies of particular writers and works.

(Showalter [1979] 1985b: 128)

The first type of feminist criticism asks questions of the following kind. What sort of roles did female characters play? With what sorts of theme were they associated? What are the implicit presuppositions of a given text with regard to its readers? (Upon closer inspection many texts clearly assume that their readers are male – just like those commercials in which fast cars are presented by seductive young women.) Feminist critics showed how often literary representations of women repeated familiar cultural stereotypes. Such stereotypes included: the woman – fast car or not – as an immoral and dangerous seductress; the woman as eternally dissatisfied shrew; the woman as cute but essentially helpless child; the woman as unworldly, self-sacrificing angel; and so on. Since the way female characters were routinely portrayed had not much in common with the way feminist critics saw and experienced themselves, these characters clearly were *constructions*, put together – not necessarily by the writers who presented them themselves, but by the culture to which they belonged – to serve a not-so-hidden purpose. If we look at the four examples I have given we see immediately that female independence (in the seductress and the shrew) gets a strongly negative connotation, while helplessness and renouncing all ambition and desire are presented as endearing and even admirable. The message is that dependence leads to indulgence and reverence while independence leads to dislike and rejection. The desired effect – of which the writer clearly need not be aware – is a perpetuation of the unequal power relations between men and women.

GENDER

To put what I have just sketched in somewhat different terms, this type of feminist criticism leads to a thorough examination of *gender* roles. Gender has to do not with how females (and males) really are, but with the way that a given culture or subculture sees them; how they are culturally *constructed*. To say that women have two breasts is to say something about their biological nature, to say something about what it is to be female; to say that women are naturally timid, or sweet, or intuitive, or dependent, or self-pitying, is to construct a role for them. It tells us how the speaker wants to see them. What traditionally has been called 'feminine', then, is a cultural construction, a *gender* role that has been culturally assigned to countless generations of women. The same holds for masculinity, with its connotations of strength, rationality, stoicism, and self-reliance. Like femininity, traditional masculinity is a gender role that has far less to do with actual males than with the wishful thinking projected on to the heroes of Westerns, hard-boiled private eyes, and British secret agents. Masculinity, too, is a cultural construction. We can see this, for instance, in one of the traditional representations of homosexuality, in which maleness and masculinity are uncoupled. Although homosexuals are male, they are often portrayed as feminine; that is, as lacking masculinity.

Feminism, then, has right from the beginning focused on gender because a thorough revision of gender roles seemed the most effective way of changing the power relations between men and women. Since no one in their right mind will want to give serious power to a person who must be timid, dependent, irrational, and self-pitying because she is a woman, the effort to purge the culture of such gendered stereotyping is absolutely crucial. Feminism has politicized gender – by showing its constructed nature – and put it firmly on the agenda of the later twentieth century. Moreover, after its initial focus on the gendered representation of women (and men) in Western culture, it has very effectively widened the issue and shown how often seemingly neutral references, descriptions, or definitions are in fact gendered, and usually according to the same pattern. A masculine gendering is supposed to evoke positive connotations; a feminine gendering is supposed to evoke negative ones. Feminism has shown how this binary opposition – to use the structuralist term for such pairs – is pervasively present in the way we think about nature, emotion, science, action (or non-action), art, and so on.

THE WOMAN AS WRITER

The textual focus that we find in studies of how literary representations of women are gendered also characterizes attempts to establish a specifically female tradition – or specifically female traditions – in writing by women. A famous example with regard to the specificity of nineteenth-century female writing is Sandra Gilbert and Susan Gubar's *The Madwoman in the Attic: The Woman Writer and the Nineteenth-Century Literary Imagination* (1979). For Gilbert and Gubar, the limitations – social and otherwise – that a nineteenth-century female writer faced led to 'an obsessive interest in these limited options'. In the work of these writers that interest expressed itself in an 'obsessive imagery of confinement that reveals the ways in which female artists feel trapped and sickened both by suffocating alternatives and by the culture that had created them' (Gilbert and Gubar 1979: 64). An example is 'the madwoman in the attic' of Gilbert and Gubar's title: the supposedly mad wife that Jane's employer and future husband Rochester keeps locked in the attic in Charlotte Brontë's *Jane Eyre* (1847). Predictably, then, the attempt to establish a female literary tradition fairly soon led to calls for a specifically female form of literary studies, for ways of reading and theorizing that could tell us how typically female experience has been reflected in literature written by women over the ages.

Female literary studies focused on specifically female themes, genres, even styles, but also on the origins and development of larger female traditions. The female focus of this search for a female literary tradition has greatly benefited literary studies in general. It has rediscovered forgotten female authors, rehabilitated ignored ones, and in its efforts to let women speak for themselves unearthed much writing of a personal nature, such as letters, travel journals, and diaries, that has contributed to a redefinition and expansion of the literary field. Feminism has expanded the canon, rehabilitated such forgotten genres as that of the 'sentimental', domestic novel, and, within the larger literary tradition, constructed a dynamic canon of writing by women.

The rediscovery and rehabilitation of authors raises the question: why did they disappear from sight in the first place? What eliminated these women writers from the race to lasting literary fame? At first sight the answer seems obvious: reviewers and critics must have found their work lacking in quality, as not up to the standards required for admission to the literary pantheon. But that leads to further questions: what exactly were those standards, who established them, and who were the people who put the work of these female writers to the test? There is an easy general answer to the last two questions: male critics and male reviewers. And so another issue suggests itself: could maleness have been a factor in literary judgements in general? Is it possible that the whole issue of literary value is in some way gendered? Couldn't, for instance, T.S. Eliot's preference for impersonality, for irony, and for a sort of stoic resignation be seen as typically masculine rather than generally valid? Couldn't it be possible that the odds have been against female writing all along, not only with regard to opportunities for writing but also with regard to that writing's evaluation? Under the pressure of feminist scrutiny, reviewers, critics, and literary academics have in the last thirty years been forced to recognize their masculinist prejudices and have, for instance, accepted forms of literary criticism in which the personal experience of the (female) critic is brought to bear upon a text in order to illuminate passages that might otherwise remain obscure.

For the defenders of impersonality in literary matters, such practices are downright irresponsible – if not typically feminine, too. Feminism has been hard on the impersonalists. In their use of autobiographical material, female academics have followed a trend set earlier by female writers such as the American poets Sylvia Plath (1932–63) and Adrienne Rich (1929–2012). Since the mid-1960s women writers, drawing on their personal experiences, have increasingly brought female sexuality, female anguish, childbirth, mothering, rape, and other specifically female themes into their work. Still, the feminist criticism and writing that I have so far discussed are in some ways fairly traditional, for instance in their view of the subject. In this (mostly American) feminist criticism of the 1970s and 1980s the female subject, like its male counterpart, is essentially free and autonomous. Once the social and cultural restraints on women have been lifted, women will be as autonomous and self-determining as men. Moreover, in its earlier stages, this feminism assumes that it speaks for all women, regardless of culture, class, and race. This is undeniably more modest than liberal humanism's (male) assumption that it speaks for all of humankind, but it still ignores the often rather different experience of women who, unlike virtually all early feminists, are not white, heterosexual, and middle class. As early as 1977 the African-American critic Barbara Smith argued that black women writers were ignored by academic feminism ('Towards a Black Feminist Criticism'; reprinted in Showalter (1985a)). In the wake of Smith's article and of bell hooks's acclaimed *Ain't I a Woman? Black Women and Feminism* (1981) more and more groups of women – African-American women, Chicana women, lesbian woman – began to assert identities of their own and to create separate feminist literary traditions. Smith had in 1977 already taken that initiative with regard to black female writing, arguing that writers like Zora Neale Hurston, Alice Walker, and Toni Morrison presented black women who with their folk memories, their special skills (midwifery, for instance), and their intimacy with the natural world were clearly distinct from white women. As a result of these developments, American feminism and the feminist literary studies that it had produced began to fragment along lines of ethnic and sexual identity, while its liberalist perspective was also submitted to severe critique.

MARXIST FEMINISM

A similar fragmentation would ultimately destabilize a specifically British offshoot of feminism: Marxist feminism. From a Marxist perspective, history is dominated by a struggle between social classes that will end only when a truly classless society has been achieved. Given the fact that throughout history women have been collectively denied important rights, it was almost inevitable that a Marxist feminism would emerge that saw women as constituting a seriously underprivileged class. Moreover, many Marxist concepts, especially as these were redefined by Louis Althusser, seemed greatly relevant. In particular Althusser's definition of ideology and his concept of interpellation, which explains how ideology addresses us in a certain role and draws us into a conspiracy that is ultimately aimed at ourselves, proved useful for feminist literary studies and film studies. As we have seen, for Althusser we experience ourselves as complete and whole individuals ('concrete subjects') only through the internalization of ideology. Ideology is what actually gives us what we experience as our individuality. Althusserian feminism examines how literary texts, films, or commercials 'hail and interpellate' their readers or their audience and 'position' them with regard to gender. Into what position does a text, a film, a rock video, or a commercial try to manoeuvre us through specific strategies of narration, specific shots, images, and other forms of representation? How does it persuade a female audience to accept a liberal humanist ideology that so clearly disadvantages them? But Althusserian feminism is by no means the whole story. We also find a British Marxist feminism that, in Ruth Robbins's words,

> is interested in the material conditions of real people's lives, how conditions such as poverty and undereducation produce different signifying systems than works produced and read in conditions of privilege and educational plenty. This kind of approach is likely to be most interested in the content of a literary text as symptomatic of the conditions of its production.
>
> (Robbins 2000: 13)

However, after its heyday in the early 1980s, Marxist feminism, too, was increasingly charged with being insensitive to *difference*, and came to be seen as the product of a white academic elite (with its standard middle-class background) and as unacceptably neglectful of the specific social problems – and the way these had been given literary expression – of women who did not belong to the white heterosexual middle class. Black Marxist feminists, for instance, were quick to point out that black female writers had to cope not only with biases based on gender but with an equally crippling racial bias, and that an approach that failed to take race into account would never be able to do justice to the work of such writers.

Like virtually everything else in literary and cultural studies, feminism and feminist criticism have undergone the impact of the enormous attention that in the last thirty years has been given to the ways we are different from each other.

THE POLITICS OF RACE

The third political instrument of analysis is that of race. Until the twentieth century, the literatures written in the various Western languages were overwhelmingly the product of white writers, male and female. That picture began to change in the inter-war years. In the 1920s African-American writing, flowering in the so-called 'Harlem Renaissance', became almost overnight a permanent force within the field of US literature, and in the1930s and 1940s writers hailing from France's African and Caribbean colonies became a presence on the French literary scene. With the emergence of a black literary presence race entered the agenda of literary studies. In one sense it also entered literature itself – in the sense that it was now presented from the perspective of non-white writers. Racial discrimination is a recurrent theme in African-American writing, from the fiction and poetry of the Harlem Renaissance, via Ralph Ellison's *Invisible Man* (1952), whose theme is that racial prejudice makes blacks invisible as individuals, to the novels of the Nobel Prize-winning (1993) Toni Morrison. In another sense, however, race was not a new theme at all but had been there all along. As we will see in Chapter 8, race seen through the eyes of Western writers had always been part of Western literature, but its presence had gone largely unnoted, at least by Western readers.

With the idea of *négritude* – which might be translated as 'negro-ness' – French-speaking black writers like Aimé Césaire (originally from Martinique) and especially Léopold Senghor (from Senegal) in the 1940s and 1950s introduced and developed the idea that lit-erature written by Africans was not merely thematically different from Western literature (in its emphasis on race) but *intrinsically* different, because Africans, no matter where they lived, were dif-ferent from whites. 'Negritude' has been variously defined – at one point Senghor equates it with 'feeling', for instance; at another he sees it in terms of a reverent attitude towards life and a desire to find harmony in an integration with the cosmos – and has been severely criticized by both African and African-American writers. But the Harlem Renaissance and the development of 'negritude' mark the beginnings of African-American and African or, as the case may be, Caribbean self-definition in the face of a Western racism and a Western system of colonial oppression that had denied (and continued to deny) substance and validity to non-white cul-tures and cultural expressions, all of which were considered far inferior to the great achievements of Western culture. Inevitably, that process of self-definition involves a critique of Western repre-sentations of Africans and African-Americans, representations that usually repeat the stereotypes that have, for instance, legitimized colonization. That self-definition and the critique of Western representations stand at the beginning of the interrogation and contestation of Europe's colonial enterprise and its legacy that is now called postcolonial studies, a relatively new field of literary, cultural, and political enquiry that will be discussed in Chapter 8.

The mordant critique of colonialism that we find in the 'negritude' movement – in his *Discourse on Colonialism* we find Césaire stating that Hitler already spoke through those who defended colonial oppression and exploitation (Césaire [1955] 1997: 79) – found a highly articulate and influential supporter in Frantz Fanon (1925–61), a psychiatrist from Martinique who became involved in the Algerian resistance to French colonialism. Fanon merits attention here not only because he called attention to the debilitating psychological effects of colonialism upon the colonized, which is a major theme in postcolonial studies, but because in *The Wretched of the Earth* (originally published in French in 1961) he outlines a theory of what we might call colonial literature – that is, the literature of the colonized. In that theory he distances himself from 'negritude'. The idea that all blacks would have essential features in common for him mirrors the homogenization that blacks have always suffered at the hands of white culture: 'The Negroes of Chicago only resemble the Nigerians or the Tanganyikans in so far as they were all defined in relation to the whites' (Fanon [1961] 1963: 216). Instead of a homogeneous 'negritude', he stresses the importance of national culture for 'the native intellectual'. Fanon distinguishes three phrases in the cultural – including the literary – relations between colonized and colonizer. In the first phase the native intellectual takes pride in demonstrating that 'he has assimilated' – that is, mastered – 'the culture of the occupying power'. In the second phase, 'the native is disturbed; he decides to remember what he is' (222). He goes back to his own people, immerses himself in the native culture, and the 'rhyming poetry' of the first phase gives way to 'the poetic tom-tom's rhythms' (226). In the third phase, the 'fighting phase', the intellectual and the writer will break out of this immersion, turn into 'an awakener of the people', and produce a 'fighting literature, a revolutionary literature, and a national literature' (223). For Fanon, writing in 1961 – when much of Africa was still under colonial rule – national cultures and literatures played a crucial role in the process of liberation. The poststructuralist theorizing which emerges in the 1970s and the postcolonial theory which then follows in the 1980s take a rather dim view of the idea of 'nation', of the so-called nation-state, which they primarily see in terms of oppression. In the historical context in which Fanon is writing, however, the sort of revolutionary nationalism and the corresponding national culture that he has in mind seem almost inevitable, if only for the 'psycho-affective equilibrium' of the colonized.

Fanon's view of the differentiation of African writing – which is united only in its desire to resist colonialism – has set the tone for later theories of African, Caribbean, and African-American writing. Abandoning the idea of a pan-African cultural identity that we can find among all African peoples and among the African diaspora in the Americas, critics have emphasized the specific identity of all the various literatures that black writers have created. The Caribbean mixture of languages and populations has, for instance, led a number of Caribbean writers to try to theorize Caribbean literature in terms of cross-cultural exchanges. Writers such as the Guyanese novelist Wilson Harris and the Barbadian poet Edward Brathwaite have argued that the literature of the region must be seen as the product of interlocking cultural traditions, of 'creolization', as Brathwaite called it in *Contradictory Omens: Cultural Diversity and Integration in the Caribbean* (1974), a study in which he argues that various black and white cultures, and, to a lesser extent, Indian and Chinese cultures, have in a continuous process of exchange created a Caribbean identity and culture. In the later 1980s and 1990s the 'hybridity' that is the result of such processes would become a major theme in postcolonial studies.

AFRICAN-AMERICAN LITERARY STUDIES

The development of African-American criticism, which emerged after the mid-1960s when black studies entered the university curriculum and when the so-called Black Arts movement got under way, to some extent runs parallel to that of feminist literary criticism. A major objective was to rediscover and rehabilitate forgotten African-American writers; that is, to have them recognized as serious contributors to the American literary heritage. A second objective was to establish a specifically African-American literary tradition, a tradition that formally distinguished itself from white American writing. The recovery and promotion of forgotten or neglected writers has been successful: all anthologies of American literature now present many African-American writers who were absent from their pre-1980s editions. But the search for a specific African-American literary aesthetic has led to perhaps less definitive results. Although we do now indeed speak of an African-American literary tradition, the question of how this tradition hangs together is still debated. What many African-American texts have in common is the overriding theme of racial discrimination, but it is less easy to say what they have in common in terms of form rather than theme.

In the 1960s the Black Arts movement, in the spirit of *négritude*, posited a 'black aesthetic' that expressed a pan-African, organic, and *whole* sensibility. Led by important writers such as the poet and playwright Amiri Baraka, it focused on creative and political writing and on political intervention through theatrical and other performances. Around the mid-1970s, African-American literary academics began to turn from sensibility to form and to seek the 'blackness' of African-American literature in its specific strategies and use of language. (The idea that African-American literature could be formally distinct from white American literature is plausible: if we look at the American music scene, we immediately recognize musical forms and genres that are distinctly African-American or that derive from African-American sources.) A number of critics, the most prominent of whom is Henry Louis Gates, Jr, began, in Gates's words, 'to chart the patterns of repetition and revision among texts by black authors'. Gates continues: 'Accordingly, many black authors read and revise one another, address similar themes, and repeat the cultural and linguistic codes of a common symbolic geographic. For these reasons, we can think of them as forming literary traditions' (Gates 1992: 30).

This approach, which combines thematic and formal interests, has led to interesting results. Central to African-American writing is this practice of repetition and revision which Gates calls 'signifyin(g)', a term which refers to the trickster figure of the 'signifying monkey' of African-American – and more generally African – folktales. A 'black text echoes, mirrors, repeats, revives, or responds to in various formal ways' a textual world of other black texts. Signifiyin(g) is 'this process of intertextual relation ... the troped revision, of repetition and difference' (Gates 1987: 2). In the black vernacular tradition 'signifying' has a range of meanings related to the trickster aspect of this 'signifyin' monkey'. In African-American culture in general, Gates tells us, 'black rhetorical tropes, subsumed under signifying, would include marking, loud-talking, testifying, calling out (of one's name), sounding, rapping, playing the dozens, and so on' (Gates [1989] 1998: 904). 'The dozens' – a form of verbal duelling that is an ultimately affectionate exchange of inge-nious insults – illustrates Gates's argument that '[t]he Afro-American rhetorical strategy of signifying is a rhetorical act that is not engaged in the game of information giving' (905). Tracing this particular practice to the oral roots of African and African-American literature – in which verbal skills were of course paramount – Gates sees in the 'dozens' one of the elements that are reworked time and again by black writers, just like black musicians borrow riffs from each other and from earlier generations of musicians and rework them. The example of 'the dozens' and the trickster connotation of signifying should not create the impression that we find the practice of signifying only in contexts that are ultimately not very serious. The poet T. Tenton Fortune's poem 'The Black Man's Burden', which for Gates 'signif[ies] … upon Kipling's "White Man's Burden"' (908) – the white race's 'duty' to bring 'civilization' to other peoples through colonial rule – sufficiently demonstrates the seriousness of signifying: 'What is the Black Man's Burden / Ye Gentile parasites / Who crush and rob your brother / Of his man-hood and his rights?' (For a book-length discussion of 'signifyin(g)' practices, see Gates 1988.)

Beginning in the 1980s, we also find another major line of enquiry for African-American criticism: what we might call the *construction* of blackness, the ways in which the dominant white culture and its literary products had over the ages *constructed* black males and females as different from their white counterparts. Just like women had to live up to the feminine gender roles created by a male-dominated society, black males and females were confronted with the cultural demands implied by the constructions of black maleness and black femaleness that white society imposed upon them. By means of these constructions, white society practically forced black males and females to live up to the stereotypes that it had itself created. In order to acquire insight into the nature of these highly discriminatory social constructs, African-American criticism analysed representations of black characters – and of blackness in general – in 'white' literature (or in Jewish-American literature, as in Bernard Malamud's *The Tenants* (1971), in a which a Jewish and an African-American writer entertain a volatile relationship in a condemned and otherwise deserted New York tenement).

Like the more traditional forms of feminist criticism, until the 1980s African-American criticism worked with a view of the subject that was not really different from that of white, liberal humanist criticism. Although far more sensitive to social constraints – and particularly those of race and class – than the average white critic, black critics also saw the subject – black or white – as essentially free and as an autonomous moral agent, able to transcend the limitations imposed by time, place, and colour. Marxist critics once again were the exception. From a Marxist perspective, the relations between the white majority and the black minority could be rewritten in terms of class relations, with the black minority kept subservient by ideology. In a brief discussion of Alice Walker's *The Color Purple*, bell hooks argues that the novel's heroine, who ends as a successful entrepreneur, stays within an individualist, capitalist framework and is therefore not fully liberated: 'Breaking free from the patriarchal prison that is her "home" when the novel begins, she creates her own household, yet radical politics of collective struggle against racism or sexism do not inform her struggle for self-actualization' (hooks [1992] 1997: 222). Like feminism, African-American criticism was strongly affected by the emphasis on difference that emerged in the course of the 1980s. African-American feminists came to see it as male-dominated and focused on specifically male issues, and increasingly pursued their feminist agenda, only to find, like the white feminists, that further fragmentation – for instance, lesbians pursuing yet another agenda – waited down the line.

READERS READING

There is no dearth in literary-critical approaches that focus on the text – its meaning (the New Criticism), its form or structure (the formalists and structuralists), its politics (the criticism discussed in this chapter). But what about us, the readers? How do we figure in all this? I.A. Richards was genuinely interested in us, but after

Richards interest in how readers read was for a long time marginal. This changed in the 1960s and 1970s with the rise of so-called reader-response criticism in Germany and the United States. Since this was soon pushed to the background, if not actually eclipsed, by the developments that will be discussed in the next chapters, I shall offer only a brief outline here.

Reader-response critics mostly start from the phenomenological position that since we cannot with absolute certainty know that we know the outside world, we must focus on how that world appears to our senses and is constituted by our consciousness. We must focus on how we experience the world. We can similarly focus on how a text is experienced, 'processed' by its readers. In Jonathan Culler's deft formulation, which in spite of its brevity covers its various strands, reader-response criticism 'can thus take the form of a description of the reader's progressive movement through a text, analyzing how readers produce meaning by making connections, filling in things left unsaid, anticipating and conjecturing and then having their expectations disappointed or confirmed' (Culler 2011: 137). Reader-response critics focused, for instance, upon the way in which an individual reader experiences a text, charting that process with the help of psychological or psychoanalytic models – see, for instance, *5 Readers Reading* (1975), based on actual readers' responses, by the American critic Norman Holland (b.1927) – or conducted empirical psychological research involving usually brief texts and groups of readers who were asked to fill out detailed questionnaires. Other critics, such as Stanley Fish (b.1938) in *Is There a Text in This Class? The Authority of Interpretive Communities* (1980), argued that readers' responses are to a large extent shaped by the 'interpretive community' to which they belong. Such an 'interpretive community' – a concept proposed by Fish in an earlier article – can be defined as a group whose individual members share a set of values and cultural assumptions that guide their interpretive acts and thus determine the text's meaning for them.

With Fish, who after an early interest in purely individual reader's responses had moved to the collective responses of his interpretive communities, we come close to the work of the two most prominent German reader-response critics, Hans-Robert Jauss (1921–97) and Wolfgang Iser (1926–2007). For Jauss, readers always approach texts from a historically determined perspective and place the text, during the actual reading process, against a (largely aesthetic) 'horizon' of expectations, which then constitutes the basis for interpretation and evaluation. With new generations of readers and perhaps because of the impact of momentous historical events, that 'horizon' will continue to change and it is the critic's business to chart and describe each successive horizon. For Iser, too, the text will be experienced in similar ways by otherwise diverse readers. But that is because he sees the text as actively involved in directing the reader's response. Any text, Iser argues, has an 'implied reader' – not an actual, real-life reader, but 'a textual structure anticipating the presence of a recipient without necessarily defining him'. We have 'the reader's presence without in any way predetermining his character or his historical situation'. The text offers 'a network of response-inviting structures' (Iser 1980: 34) that guides all readers, irrespective of their individual situation, in what is roughly the same direction.

Although initially reader-response criticism, with its focus on the reader, drew a good deal of attention, its various strands, which presupposed a stable text and mostly expected responses to one particular text to stay within a fairly narrow bandwidth, soon no longer seemed adequate. The new so-called 'poststructuralist' theories that also emerged in the late 1960s and in the 1970s would make it look traditional before it had really established itself.

SUMMARY

Literary texts always have a political dimension in the sense that on closer inspection they can be shown to take specific stances with regard to social issues, either through what they say or through what they do *not* say – through the elision of certain themes or topics. Marxist critics are especially interested in issues of class and social exploitation and are specifically attentive to the cultural mechanisms – and their literary versions – that keep people unaware of their exploited status. Literary feminism has called our attention to the pervasive male bias that we find throughout Western history. It has rediscovered forgotten or marginalized female writers and established a history of writing by women; it has expanded the literary field by including in its interests the sort of personal writing that we find in letters, diaries, and journals; and it has shown how writing by women is thematically marked by the historically difficult position of female authors. A third important political category, on a par with class and gender, is that of race. African, Caribbean, and African-American authors and critics have demonstrated the pervasive presence of racial prejudice in Western writing. Like feminism, African-American criticism has rediscovered forgotten or marginalized writing. It has sought to establish a specially black tradition in writing that is not only thematically but in its recurring tropes different from writing by white Americans. Finally, after decades of neglect, there is a renewed interest in how readers actually read, in how readers process texts and attribute meaning to them in the act of reading.

SUGGESTIONS FOR FURTHER READING

MARXIST CRITICISM

Good starting points are Moyra Haslett's *Marxist Literary and Cultural Theory* (1999), which offers an overview of the field, and Drew Milne's *Reading Marxist Literary Theory* (2001). Terry Eagleton's *Marxism and Literary Criticism* (1976b) is a good and brief introduction to the work of major twentieth-century Marxist literary theorists, all of whom – and more – are represented in Eagleton and Milne's *Marxist Literary Theory: A Reader* (1995). Raymond Williams's *Marxism and Literature* (1977) shows us a very influential Marxist critic in action. Arguing that we must see literature in 'material' terms, Williams elucidates not only the basic Marxist notions but also Gramsci's 'hegemony' and his own notion of 'structures of feeling'. In *Marxism and Literary History* (1986) John Frow examines the literary criticism of Pierre Macherey, Terry Eagleton, Fredric Jameson, and others. Eagleton's *Ideology: An Introduction* (1991) takes us through the 'ideology' debate from a Marxist perspective. One of the major contributions to that debate, Louis Althusser's 'Ideology and Ideological State Apparatuses' – originally in *Lenin and Philosophy and Other Essays* (1971) – is quite accessible, in spite of its title, and has been widely reprinted, fairly recently in Rivkin and Ryan (2004). Tony Bennett's *Formalism and Marxism* ([1979] 2003) is a good introduction to the Althusserian criticism of Macherey. An interesting and eminently readable example of the application of the notion of ideology to a specific literary genre is Stephen Knight's *Form and Ideology in Detective Fiction* (1980), which reads classics like Agatha Christie and Raymond Chandler as representatives of liberal humanist ideology. A selection of Bakhtin's major work has been republished in Pam Morris's *The Bakhtin Reader* (2009), while Alistair Renfrew's *Mikhail Bakhtin* (2013) is a recent introduction by a prominent Bakhtin scholar.

FEMINISM CRITICISM

Ruth Robbins's *Literary Feminisms* (2000) is a good and lucid overview. In *Practising Feminist Criticism: An Introduction* (1995) Maggie Humm offers very accessible readings of a wide range of texts combining a feminist perspective with a second one (psycho-analytic, Marxist, poststructuralist, lesbian, and so on). There is an abundance of excellent and often rather hefty collections of essays and anthologies, such as: Gill Plain and Susan Sellers's *A History of Feminist Literary Criticism* (2007), whose essays range from medieval feminist criticism to postcolonial feminist criticism and feminism and queer theory; Sandra M. Gilbert and Susan Gubar's *Feminist Literary Theory and Criticism: A Norton Reader* (2007); Robyn Warhol-Down and Diane Price Herndl's *Feminisms Redux: An Anthology of Literary Theory and Criticism* (3rd ed. 2009); and Mary Eagleton's *Feminist Literary Theory: A Reader* (3rd ed. 2011). Other useful and fairly recent books are Mary Eagleton's *A Concise Companion to Feminist Theory* (2003) and Ellen Rooney's *The Cambridge Companion to Feminist Literary Theory* (2006). But to return to criticism, *Feminist Readings, Feminists Reading* (1989) edited by Sara Mills *et al.*, offers a number of different feminist approaches to Charlotte Brontë's *Jane Eyre*, Alice Walker's *The Color Purple*, and other popular texts. Marleen S. Barr's *Alien to Femininity: Speculative Fiction and Feminist Theory* (1987) looks at science-fiction writing from a feminist perspective, while Sally R. Munt's *Murder by the Book? Feminism and the Crime Novel* (1994) offers a leftist/feminist critique of fairly recent female crime writing.

The seminal text of black feminist criticism is Barbara Smith's 'Towards a Black Feminist Criticism' ([1977] 1985). Barbara

Christian's *Black Feminist Criticism: Perspectives on Black Women Writers* (1985), Hazel Carby's *Reconstructing Womanhood: The Emergence of the Afro-American Woman Novelist* (1987), Susan Willis's Marxist *Specifying: Black Women Writing the American Experience* (1987), and Mary Helen Washington's collection *Invented Lives: Narratives of Black Women (1860–1960)* ([1987] 1989) illustrate the emergence of a forceful black feminist criticism in the mid-1980s. Cheryl Wall's *Changing Our Own Words* (1989) and Henry Louis Gates's *Reading Black, Reading Feminist* (1990) are good and very useful collections of black feminist criticism. For a more general black feminism, see the work of bell hooks – *Ain't I a Woman? Black Women and Feminism* (1982), *Black Looks: Race and Representation* (1992) – Audre Lorde's *Sister Outsider: Essays and Speeches* (1984), Patricia Hill Collins's *Black Feminist Thought: Knowledge, Consciousness and the Politics of Empowerment* (2nd ed. 2000), and Jacqueline Bobo's *Black Feminist Cultural Criticism* (2001). Valerie Lee's *The Prentice Hall Anthology of African American Women's Literature* (2006) presents all major voices in the field, while Barbara Christian's highly influential work was collected in *New Black Feminist Criticism, 1985–2000* (2007).

AFRICAN-AMERICAN CRITICISM

Houston A. Baker, Jr's *Long Black Song: Essays in Black-American Literature and Culture* (1972) collects early but still worthwhile essays in a then developing field. Robert Stepto's *From Behind the Veil* ([1979] 1991) is a classic of African–American criticism, dealing with black literature from slave narratives to Ralph Ellison's *Invisible Man* (1952). *Blues, Ideology, and Afro-American Literature: A Vernacular Theory* (1984) by Houston A. Baker, Jr sees the black literary tradition as shaped by the conditions of slavery and in interaction with the blues. Henry Louis Gates, Jr's *Figures in Black: Words, Signs and the 'Racial' Self* (1987) and his *The Signifying Monkey* (1988) together constitute what is probably the most successful effort to theorize a specific African-American writing tradition. *African American Literary Criticism, 1773–2000* (1999), edited by Hazel Arnett Ervin, and Winston Napier's *African American Literary Theory: A Reader* (2000) enable us to follow the development of African-American criticism. *The Cambridge Companion to the African American*

Novel, edited by Maryemma Graham (2004), offers a good overview, as does Hazel Arnett Ervin's *The Handbook of African American Literature* (2004). In *Icons of African-American Literature: The Black Literary World* (2011) Yolanda Williams Page brings together a comprehensive collection of essays dealing with themes, concepts, and individual authors.

READER-RESPONSE CRITICISM

The Return of the Reader: Reader-Response Criticism (1987) by Elizabeth Freund is a reader-friendly introduction, as is Todd F. Davis and Kenneth Womack's *Formalist Criticism and Reader-Response Theory* (2002), while *Reader-Response Criticism: From Formalism to Post-Structuralism* (1980), edited by Jane P. Tompkins, gathers important material and comes with a lengthy and excellent introduction by the editor. A more recent collection edited by James L. Machor and Philip Goldstein, *Reception Study: From Literary Theory to Cultural Studies* (2001), brings the history of reader-response criticism up to the twenty-first century. *Literary Reading: Empirical and Theoretical Studies* (2006) by David S. Miall, who has a long-standing interest in emotional responses to literature, pays particular attention to the empirical side of reader-response research.

THE POSTSTRUCTURALIST REVOLUTION
DERRIDA AND DECONSTRUCTION

INTRODUCTION

I have already suggested that the late 1960s and especially the 1970s – when Jacques Derrida's *Speech and Phenomena* (1973) and *Of Grammatology* (1976) appeared in English translation – can be seen as a sort of watershed in English and American criticism, and in the previous chapter more than once I said that the political criticism that I discussed there is rather 'traditional' in comparison with later developments – not only within the field of politically oriented literary studies, but within literary studies in general. But how can the Marxist criticism, the feminist criticism, and the race-oriented criticism that I discussed be 'traditional' when so many literary academics viewed them as dangerously radical? There is no doubt that within the context of the 1970s they *were* radical. However, they also, each in their own way, continued certain traditions. Non-Marxist feminism and black criticism basically work with a liberal humanist view of the individual: the subject is ultimately free, self-determined rather than other-determined (by social background, class, economic position, and so on).

This liberal humanist form of feminist and black criticism is of course extremely sensitive to the various ways in which women and blacks – both men and women – have over the ages been limited in their options (to say the least) because of discriminatory social forces. However, it believes that ultimately the subject is a free moral agent. It also believes that the 'best' that has been thought and said over time is of timeless significance. Marxist criticism and the Marxist version of feminist and black criticism deny that such autonomous individuals exist. We have seen how in Althusser's explanation of the workings of ideology 'the subject acts insofar as he is acted by the ... system'. Just as in structuralist anthropology, Althusser's subjects are genuinely convinced that they entertain a certain belief because they choose to do so while in reality a pre-existing structure acts through them. Marxist criticism also assumes that the Marxist analysis of history as a struggle of social classes for domination and that Marxist concepts such as alienation and ideology essentially reflect the world as it is and has been. Although their assumptions are completely at odds with each other, both liberal humanism and Marxism are convinced that, intellectually, they have solid ground under their feet. Both think not only that their view of reality is correct but, more fundamentally, that it is possible to *have* an accurate and true view of reality.

Strange as it may seem, the idea that it is possible to have a true view of the world is now 'traditional' within literary studies. Although this does not necessarily mean that it is wrong, it is – for many critics and theorists working today – an untenable proposition. For them, the idea that it is truly possible to *know* the world is theoretically unfounded. That idea, which is called *essentialism* because it claims that we can know the *essence* of things, is the main target of the *poststructuralist* thinkers whom I will discuss in this chapter and Chapter 6. As I have just said, the poststructuralist arguments against essentialism seem convincing to many critics writing today. But certainly not to all of them. On the contemporary critical scene we still find liberal humanist criticism, both in its New Critical or Leavisite form and in its feminist or African-American form, and we still find 'traditional' forms of Marxist criticism. We also find a good many critics who are willing to accept that absolutely true knowledge of the world is out of reach, but who, in spite of that, keep on working with traditional assumptions. Accepting that their assumptions no longer have the status they used to have, they present them as a programme, or even as merely a point of departure, as a perspective that will still say useful and illuminating things about literary texts. All the time, they are fully aware that that perspective is questionable and not the last word. The contemporary literary-critical world is a fascinating mixture of the old, the new, and the old in new guises (which does not imply a negative judgement). But let us now turn to the poststructuralism that had such an enormous impact on the way we study literature.

POSTSTRUCTURALISM: THE CRETAN PARADOX AND ITS ALBANY SOLUTION

Poststructuralism is a continuation and simultaneous rejection of structuralism – not only literary structuralism but even more so the anthropological structuralism of Lévi-Strauss. I will first discuss the poststructuralism of the French philosopher Jacques Derrida (1930–2004), or *deconstruction*, as it is often called, because it was the first version of poststructuralism to reach the United States. Spreading from there, it had an enormous impact on English and American literary studies in general. Discussing Derrida, by the way, is not without its risks. As David Ayers puts it in his recent (and excellent) *Literary Theory: A Reintroduction*, 'While it is not difficult to para-phrase Derrida's work, it is almost impossible to do so without vio-lating the ethos of that writing and offending professional Derrideans' (Ayers 2008: 133). After Derrida, I will look at the various post-structuralist positions for which deconstruction paved the way in the English-speaking world, even if they do not always derive directly from Derrida's writings. By the late 1970s other poststructuralist thinkers, notably the French historian Michel Foucault (1926–84), had caught the attention of literary academics. In the chapters that follow the discussion of poststructuralism I will look at the major approaches to literature that have been made possible by post-structuralism and that currently still dominate literary studies.

Poststructuralism is unthinkable without structuralism. As I have already suggested, it continues structuralism's strongly anti-humanist perspective and it closely follows structuralism in its belief that lan-guage is the key to our understanding of ourselves and the world. Still, although it continues its anti-humanism and its focus on lan-guage, poststructuralism simultaneously undermines structuralism by thoroughly questioning – 'deconstructing' – some of its major assumptions and the methods that derive from those assumptions.

Poststructuralism continues structuralism's preoccupation with language, but its view of language is wholly different from the structuralist view. As we have seen, structuralism applied originally linguistic insights to culture in general, and literary structuralism applied them to literary texts. The idea of an underlying structure and the principle of differentiality could apparently be successfully transferred from the field of language studies to the study of a wide range of human activities – perhaps even all human activities, at least as far as the specific form they take is concerned. Structuralism, then, takes language very seriously. But it also takes language very much for granted. It knows that there is no natural link between a word and that to which it refers. It does, however, not really examine the possible consequences of that gap between language and the world. That is, on the one hand, not so strange. We all know, to repeat what I said in Chapter 3, that other languages use other words to refer to, say, a house, a tree, or a dog. Rather amazingly, that does not appear to undermine our confidence in our own language. We might ask ourselves whether French wine or German beer is better than the wine or beer produced in our own country, or whether their cars are more elegant or solid, but we never consider the possibility that the language of the French or the Germans might fit the world better than ours. Our own language is so natural to us that it almost never occurs to us that maybe our confidence in language is misplaced.

On the other hand, we have for a long time been aware that language can be extremely slippery. Think of famous classical paradoxes such as the paradox of the Cretan who says that all Cretans always lie. If all Cretans always lie, then the Cretan's statement must be true – but he himself simultaneously proves it untrue, because although he is a Cretan he has at least for once not lied. It is, of course, possible to disentangle the various threads that go into the making of paradoxes. Here the problem is that it is a Cretan who makes the statement. With a speaker from Albany, New York, the claim would simply be true or false. The problem arises only because the speaker is a member of the group – the category – to which his statement refers, so that he himself is included in whatever claim he makes. Still, language can apparently lead us into strange impasses. Paradoxes such as the Cretan paradox show us that what we need for at least one kind of statement is an outside perspective, an outside point of reference: a person from Albany, New York, so to speak. So if we want to say something about language, we ideally want a perspective outside language to say it. With language, however, there is no outside perspective. We can speak about language only with the use of language. No matter what we say, we are always inside. The structuralists never address this problem, operating as if they themselves are never part of structures, as if there is a position outside language and other structures. They never consider the possibility that because there is no outside – objective – perspective on language, whatever they say must be somehow caught up in language or that – in a worst-case scenario – the structures they find, far from being objectively present, are mere subjective projections.

THE ILLUSION OF PRESENCE

The fact that we can never step outside language in order to speak about it is, at least at the theoretical level, a problem. There is, however, another problem with language that is potentially far more serious. As I have just pointed out, whatever language we have learned to speak in our infant years always seems totally natural to us and always seems to fit the world in which we live. But what *is* this 'naturalness'? Or rather, how is it possible that we *experience* as completely natural what we *know* to be arbitrary: the link between language and reality? Why doesn't that arbitrariness permanently bother us? The answer is pretty simple: the arbitrariness does not bother us because we see language as only an instrument, as something that makes it possible for us to do something: to express ourselves. Just as it does not really matter whether we write with a pencil, a felt tip, or an old-fashioned fountain pen, or which colour ink we use, the language we use does not really matter, because we use it only to express something that is *prior* to language: something that exists in our minds before we resort to language to give it shape in words. We know beforehand what we want to say and then choose the words we want to say it with. This is the basis of the confidence we feel in language: the certainty that we know what we know, that we are in direct, immediate touch with ourselves and can then put into words what we know and feel. We know what is so to speak *present* to us and therefore undeniably true.

Why this emphasis on being in direct, immediate touch with ourselves? Imagine you are standing at a street corner, waiting for the lights to change, and somebody comes up from behind and knocks you out. You regain consciousness in a totally dark and apparently soundproof room. You have no idea what has happened or where you are. You cannot be sure of anything. The room may not even be dark because, for all you know, you may have been blinded. So what *do* you know? The only thing you really know for sure is that you are scared to death, that you are apparently able to experience that feeling, and that you can think about your predicament. You know these things for sure because your feelings and thoughts are *present* to you. Presence, then, is the basis of the last pieces of true knowledge that you have and language allows you to convey that knowledge to the outside world. This (according to him, misguided) trust in the combination of presence and language is what the French philosopher Jacques Derrida has called *logocentrism*.

Our trust in language is based upon what happens – or what we think happens – when we actually use it. It is manifestly not based on hearing others speak: we know from experience that hearing them does not necessarily bring us in touch with *their* authentic situation – they may be lying, for instance, or mistaken, or may not be able to explain what they want to say. And our trust is certainly not based on writing: writing may be as unreliable as speech, and as unintelligible, and it does not even offer us the opportunity of finding out the truth if we fail to see it. When people are talking to us, we can interrupt them and ask questions if we don't understand what they are saying, and we can watch them closely for tell-tale signs if we suspect that they are lying. Although we can never be totally sure that we have access to what they think – the authentic truth behind the words they use – we have a better chance to get to the bottom of things than we have with writing.

ABSENCE

The Western philosophical tradition and more popular Western thought have always put more faith in the spoken than in the written word, which has traditionally been regarded as a *supplement* (Derrida's term) to speech. But is the spoken word reliable? To get to the heart of the matter, are the words that we speak reliable? 'No', says Derrida, from whose writings the essence of what I have just said is derived. Let me summarize his main arguments. First of all, Derrida tells us, language is inherently unreliable. As we have seen, language operates on the basis of differentiation. What enables words to refer to whatever they refer to is their difference from other words, not a direct link to their so-called referents. However, those words function within a linguistic system (a language) that never touches the real world. There is no single word that is the way it is because it cannot be another way, because its shape is wholly determined by its referent (not even almost instinctive 'words', such as exclamations of pain; these, too, differ from language to language). If we would have such a word, that word would then be wholly subservient to an object in the real world and would constitute an absolute fixed and 'true' element within the linguistic system, so that we might then possibly build more and more words around it and in that way anchor language firmly in the real world. Reality would then determine the shape of our language. As it is, however, we have to work with meanings that are produced with the help of 'difference' and do not directly derive from the world to which they refer. In language we find only differences without positive terms, as Saussure put it. As a result, Derrida claims, words are never stable and fixed in time.

First of all, because the meaning we see in words is the product of difference, that meaning is always contaminated. Think of a traffic light: we all know the 'meaning' of red, amber, or green. But it never occurs to us that those meanings are not 'pure'. When we see red we do not consciously think of amber and green, but one might argue that amber and green are in a sense present in red. Together, the three constitute a differential structure and it is the structure – including amber and green – that gives red its meaning. After all, in other contexts, red may have a completely different meaning. The red of red roses has for centuries stood for love, and most certainly not for 'stop'. The red of traffic lights, then, carries the 'traces' of amber and green within it, and is not pure, unadulterated red. Derrida argues that the same holds for words: every single word contains traces of other words – theoretically of all the other words in the language system:

the movement of signification is possible only if each so-called 'present' element, each element appearing on the scene of presence, is related to something other than itself, thereby keeping within itself the mark of the past element, and already letting itself be vitiated by the mark of its relation to the future element, this trace being related no less to what is called the future than to what is called the past, and constituting what is called the present by means of this very relation to what it is not.

(Derrida [1982] 1996: 32)

You might say, Derrida tells us, that the process that gives words meaning never ends. The words we say or read never achieve stability, not only because they are related to, and take part of their meaning from, the words that have just preceded them, but because their meaning is always modified by whatever follows. The word that is next to the word we are looking at, or a word later in the same sentence, or even paragraph, will subtly change its meaning. Meaning, then, is not only the product of difference but always subject to a process of deferral.

The 'present' of a word we speak is therefore not the *true* present, which forever eludes language: 'spacing' and 'temporization' intervene. Derrida captures this in a self-coined term, *différance*, that contains both the idea of difference and the process of deferral of meaning. In the terms used in Chapter 3, Derrida destabilizes the relationship between *signifier* and *signified*. The *signifier* – the word we hear or read – is stable enough, but what it signifies – the *signified* – is, according to Derrida, subject to an inherent instability, a condition that frustrates all attempts at definitive interpretation, at genuine understanding.

But there are more barriers to authoritative interpretation. We all know that linguistic instability exists at another level: the meaning of words may change over time, for instance, and phrases that once contained vivid metaphors may now have lost their metaphorical edge. Who thinks of an actual crack in the phrase 'at the crack of dawn'? For Derrida, linguistic change occurs even in the here and now, as the result of what he calls 'iteration'; that is, of repetition, of using the same linguistic 'mark' in a new context.

The iterability of the mark does not leave any of the philosophical abstractions ... intact ... Once it is iterable, to be sure, a mark marked with a supposedly 'positive' value ('serious', 'literal', etc.) can be mimed, cited, transformed into an 'exercise' or into 'literature', even into a 'lie' – that is, can be made to carry its other, its 'negative' double.

(Derrida [1977] 1988: 61)

For Derrida, 'iterability alters', and because it 'alters' it 'unavoidably generates' 'undecidability', as the posthumanist critic Cary Wolfe, whom we will meet later, put it recently (Wolfe 2010: 12). From Derrida's perspective, then, language never offers finite meaning. This does not mean that it presents utter vagueness, a blur. What we have 'is always a *determinate* oscillation between possibilities' (Derrida [1977] 1988: 148), but that does not bring us closer to definitive meaning. (The idea of iterability would later be productively applied in postcolonial criticism – with respect to the way the colonized mime the colonizers – and in so-called queer theory.) Speech, then, turns out to be as deficient as its traditional supplement, writing. Speech, too, needs supplementation, needs 'that which alone makes up or makes good some otherwise irremediable lack in what purports to be perfectly autonomous and self-sufficient', as the British philosopher and critic Christopher Norris formulates it (Norris 2007: 20). But whatever we might put forward in the way of supplementation will again have to be supplemented. Everything we could possibly think of is subject to this logic of supplementarity:

Through this series of supplements there emerges a law: that of an endless linked series, ineluctably multiplying the supplementary mediations that produce the sense of the very thing they defer: the impression of the thing itself, of immediate presence, or originary perception. Immediacy is derived. Everything begins with the intermediary.

(Derrida quoted in Culler 2011: 12)

This sets up a confrontation between the authentic 'truth' we want to express – that which we feel we know – and the slippery medium that we must use to express it; that is, if that authentic truth is really there. That truth is, of course, what structuralism had already rejected. To recapitulate its argument briefly: we are always part of a structure; to be more precise, we figure in a number of overlapping structures. We inevitably articulate, through whatever we do or say, the structures of which we are part. And since the structures were there before we appeared on the scene, it is more appropriate to say that the structures speak through us than to claim that we say or do things that have their origin within us. Derrida has as little use for that authentic knowledge inside us as the structuralists have. Like the structuralists, he rejects the idea of 'presence', or 'voice' (the voice of a speaker in touch with his or her authentic being). For Derrida, too, we cannot express what is authentically present to us because with the act of expression authenticity, the 'absolute present', disappears. In fact, 'the disappearance of natural presence' is 'that what inaugurates meaning and language' (quoted in Culler 2011: 12–13). So in comparison with structuralism, we may still be worse off. From a structuralist perspective we may at least know what we are saying. Because we articulate the structures that speak through us what we say does not originate in us, but it is stable and, in principle, also knowable. With poststructuralism, we lose that cold comfort. In the absence of presence (a phrase that should now make sense), all that is left is a language that is subject to *différance*. Authenticity and truth are impossible because there is nothing that can escape language. As Derrida puts it, 'il n'y a de hors-texte' – there is nothing that is outside-text – because for the human species everything is always mediated by language (Derrida [1967] 1976: 158).

In both writing and speaking true meaning is always deferred. Even if we did have an authentic self that knows things prior to and outside language, we would become the victims of language's inherent unreliability as soon as we would start to speak. We could never fully control the meaning of what we say. The independent 'play' of language that no one can stop is the origin of a surplus meaning that plays havoc with whatever meaning we intended. We might say, then, that what appears to us as meaning derives not from the intention of the speaker – or writer – but from our own intervention in language's flow of meaning: the momentary stop we put on the dissemination of meaning. Traditionally, we have ascribed that stop to a speaker or writer, positing an autonomous subject in full control of its own intentions and of language. As Roland Barthes put it in his 'The Death of the Author', in which he argues against such control: 'To give a text an Author is to impose a limit on that text, to furnish it with a final signified, to close the writing' (Barthes [1968] 2000: 149). But for Derrida and Barthes the text has no closure. Their literary text is not an organic whole, as the New Critics assumed, but an endless network, spreading in all directions.

BINARY OPPOSITIONS REVISITED

It is clear now why we accept what we say as natural and truthful: we are misled by the illusion of presence, by what Derrida calls a 'metaphysics of presence'. But how can the written word mislead us? How can we fail to see that written language generates all that excess meaning that we do not know how to handle?

Poststructuralism's answer is that language, following the culture at large, inevitably sets up centres of meaning that give it stability and stop the potentially infinite flow of meaning that all language use generates. If there is a centre, there is also that which does not belong to it, that which is marginal. Setting up a centre automatically creates a hierarchical structure; it creates order. *Deconstruction*, as Derrida's way of reading texts came to be known, first of all undertakes to bring to light the tension between the central and the marginal in a text. As the American critic Barbara Johnson described it: 'The deconstruction of a text does not proceed by random doubt or arbitrary subversion, but by the careful teasing out of warring forces of signification within the text' (Johnson 1980: 5).

Such hierarchies between centre and margin (or periphery) take the form of binary oppositions (one of poststructuralism's most obvious debts to structuralism). Texts introduce sets of oppositions that function to structure and stabilize them. Quite often these oppositions are implicit or almost invisible – they may be hidden in a text's metaphors, for instance – or else only one of the terms involved is explicitly mentioned. That explicit mention, then, evokes the other, absent term. There is a wide range of such oppositions, with some of them pretty general, while others are more culture bound. Rather general sets of oppositional terms include good/evil, same/other, truth/falsehood, presence/absence, masculine/feminine, thought/feeling, mind/matter (or body), nature/culture, pure/impure, and so on. A notorious oppositional set within Western culture is white/black. One of these terms always functions as the centre – it is *privileged*, in poststructuralist terms, and accorded a *natural* status. Some terms have always been privileged – good, truth, masculinity, purity, whiteness – while others may be found in either the centre or the margin. In literary history we find texts that privilege 'thought' and 'rationality', but in the work of the Romantic poets 'feeling' occupies the centre.

As I have just suggested, the privileging of certain terms can easily escape our notice. Take, for instance, fairly recently coined words such as 'discman' and 'gameboy'. The second, non-privileged and inferior term is even absent here. We may never have realized it, but 'discman' and 'gameboy' set up an opposition between masculine and feminine. Why is a 'discman' not a 'disc-woman' or a 'discgirl'? Why is a 'gameboy' not a 'gamegirl'? In all probability the companies in question used the 'man' in 'discman' and the 'boy' in 'gameboy' to give their products a positive image that would boost sales. In both cases we have an implicit binary opposition in which the masculine term is the privileged one.

But why should we worry about language if it turns out to be so easy to stop the flow of excess meaning by setting up structures of binary oppositions? We should worry because those oppositions are usually intimately tied up with negative stereotyping, repression, discrimination, social injustice, and other undesirable practices and might even be said actively to perpetuate them – after all, the oppositions speak through us. And so deconstruction sets out to deconstruct them, to demonstrate that they are not natural but rather *constructions*. Next to that, deconstruction argues that in binary oppositions we find not only an oppositional relationship between the two terms involved but a strange complicity. Take, for instance, the seemingly wholly natural – that is, not constructed – opposition light versus darkness. Arguably, light needs darkness. If there were no darkness, we would not have light either, because we would not be able to recognize it for what it is. Without darkness, we would in one sense obviously have light – it would be the only thing around – but we would not be *aware* of light. We would not have the *concept* of light, so what we call light (which implies our awareness that there is also the possibility of non-light) would not exist. One might argue, then, that the existence of darkness (that is, our awareness of non-light) creates the concept of light. Paradoxically, the inferior term in this oppositional set – if we assume, because of its cultural connotations, that darkness is the inferior term – turns out to be a condition for the opposition as such and is therefore as important as the so-called privileged term. The two terms in any oppositional set are defined by each other: light by darkness, truth by falsehood, purity by contamination, the rational by the irrational, the same by the other, nature by culture. Here, too, the attribution of meaning is made possible by difference. If there were no purity, we would have no concept of impurity and would not deplore it (if we do). Once difference – the relationship between two such terms – has given rise to meaning, we privilege one pole of the oppositional axis and condemn the other. Even if the terms involved seem at first sight wholly neutral – light/darkness, for instance – our metaphorical operations will set up a positive and a negative pole. Some privilegings will strike most of us as wholly reasonable – good versus evil, or truth versus falsehood – while others have done incalculable damage – white versus black, the masculine versus the feminine. But whatever the effect of binary oppositions, they are constructions that always have their origin in difference. To analyse and dismantle them, as I have just done, means to 'decentre' the privileged term, to show that both terms exist only because of difference and that they are, as often as not, in themselves wholly neutral.

Derrida is fully aware that his own language, whether spoken or written, is subject to *différance*. He also knows that it cannot escape the centring effects that language, because of its countless connotations, always has. Even radical critiques of language have to make use of the medium they criticize in order to communicate. The critique undermines the language that it uses, but that language, because of its centring effects, simultaneously undermines the critique. Derrida, you might say, is caught in the middle: he cannot use language, but he also cannot *not* use language. He finds himself not in an either/or position – we can and do use language because it is reliable or we cannot and do not because it isn't – but in a both/and position: we cannot trust language but we must still use it.

LITERARY DECONSTRUCTION

Deconstruction takes its name from Derrida's practice: his strategy of analysing and dismantling texts or, more usually, parts of texts in order to reveal their inconsistencies and inner contradictions. At the heart of deconstruction is the effort to dismantle the cover-ups that texts use to create the semblance of stable meaning: their attempt to create 'privileged' centres – implicit or explicit binary oppositions – with the help of all sorts of rhetorical means.

Because deconstruction's point of departure is that language is by definition uncontrollable, it expects to find unwarranted privilegings in all texts. No matter whether a text is literary or non-literary, it can always be deconstructed and can be shown to rely for its internal stability on rhetorical operations that mask their origin in difference and also mask the surplus meaning that is the result of *différance*. Deconstruction tries to demonstrate that the apparent either/or patterns of texts mask underlying both/and situations and to reveal those texts' fundamental undecidability. In literary terms, a text never achieves *closure* – which literally means that its case can never be closed: there is no final meaning; the text remains a field of possibilities. In Jeremy Hawthorn's apt formulation: 'Thus for Derrida the meaning of a text is always unfolding just ahead of the interpreter, unrolling in front of him or her like a never-ending carpet whose final edge never reveals itself' (Hawthorn 1998: 39).

In some ways, deconstructionist reading practice resembles the New Critical reading for juxtapositions, tensions, inversions, and the like. Just as the New Criticism did, deconstruction depends on close reading. However, while the New Critics emphasized the ultimate coherence of what they considered successful literary works (coherence being one of their touchstones), deconstructionist criticism seeks to expose the centring operations by means of which a false coherence is brought about. It then goes on to decentre the centres that it finds and, by implication, the whole text that it has under scrutiny. In so doing, it reveals that the text is far more complex than it initially seemed to be and usually makes that text more interesting. It does not impose its own meaning on the text, but points out where and how the text works against what at first sight would seem to be its meaning. In her reading of Herman Melville's *Billy Budd* (1891, first published in 1924), in which a young sailor (Billy) is hanged because he has inadvertently killed the master-at-arms Claggart, who has falsely accused him, Barbara Johnson sees a series of binary oppositions:

the fate of each of the characters is the direct reverse of what one is led to expect from his 'nature'. Billy is sweet, innocent, and harmless, yet he kills. Claggart is evil, perverted, and mendacious, yet he dies a victim. Vere [the captain in charge of the ship] is sagacious and responsible, yet he allows a man whom he feels to be blameless to hang.

(Johnson 1980: 82)

However, the relations between these opposites, and the characters that embody them, turn out to be complex and paradoxical: 'Claggart, whose accusations of incipient mutiny are apparently false and therefore illustrate the very double-facedness they attribute to Billy, is negated for proclaiming the lie about Billy which Billy's act of negation paradoxically proves to be the truth' (86). It is not only that the opposites shift within the structure; they also would seem to collapse into each other. Either/or turns into both/and. Johnson concludes that in *Billy Budd* we have a 'difference' that effectively prevents closure.

Derrida's own reading of the very short story 'Before the Law' by Franz Kafka (1883–1924) emphasizes the same lack of closure. In Kafka's story a man arrives at the door that gives access to the law. He is not allowed to enter but hears from the doorkeeper that he may perhaps enter later and had better not use force because there are many more doors, and many more doorkeepers who are even more powerful than this first one. He waits all his life and finally, just before he dies, asks the doorkeeper why he is the only one who has sought admittance. Answering that this particular door was meant for him only, the doorkeeper shuts the door on the dying man. Derrida sees the story as exemplifying *différance*:

After the first guardian there are incalculably many others, perhaps without limit, and progressively more powerful and therefore prohibitive, endowed with the power of delay. Their potency is *différance*, an interminable *différance* ... As the doorkeeper represents it, the discourse of the law does not say 'no' but 'not yet', indefinitely.

(Derrida [1985] 1987: 141)

In a similar way, the discourse of any given text, even if it seems at first sight far more accessible than Kafka's enigmatic story, also forever tells us 'not yet' in our search for definitive meaning.

Deconstruction has come in for a good deal of criticism. It has been argued, for instance, that ultimately all deconstructionist interpretations are similar, because they always lead us to *différance*, to the impossibility of final meanings. Although this is true, it disregards the fact that before a deconstructionist reading arrives at that point, it has first uncovered the structures that operate in a text and shown us how these structures can be dismantled by making use of elements of the text itself. In the process, texts are subjected to the closest scrutiny, and hidden hierarchical relations – relations of power, which always exist within binary oppositions – are brought to light.

To other critics of deconstruction, its intellectual underpinnings – Derrida's critique of logocentrism – seem extremely far-fetched. You might, for instance, grant Derrida's original point of departure and agree that language is based on difference and hovers over the world without ever touching solid ground, but reject his conclusions: why would that invariably lead to a surplus of meaning that fatally affects the texts we produce? We all know of misunderstandings and misreadings, but we can also point to countless examples of successful communication. So maybe that surplus of meaning – assuming that it exists – is a good deal less damaging than the deconstructionists would have us believe. M.A.R. Habib, in his *Modern Literary Criticism and Theory*, suggests that 'it is only against a simplistic and positivistic understanding of truth, meaning, presence, and subjectivity that [Derrida's] notions of trace, difference, and writing can articulate themselves' (Habib 2008: 111). The American philosopher John Searle, one of Derrida's most outspoken critics, has voiced a similar criticism in even stronger terms, speaking of 'Derrida's ignorance of the current philosophical commonplace that concepts are in general quite loose at their boundaries' (Searle [1994] 2005: 140). In any case, from a so-called pragmatic perspective language would seem to do its work reasonably well. However, even for those critics who prefer a pragmatic position, deconstruction has its uses. It is, for instance, perfectly possible to approach the sets of opposites that deconstruction habitually finds from a modified humanistic perspective. Such a humanism might argue that although ideally free and rational agents, in practice we are to a considerable extent determined by, for instance, our cultural environment. For a humanist, the revelation that the sets of opposites that we can discover in texts always serve to inflict injustice upon the 'inferior' term (the 'feminine' and the 'non-white', for instance) can only be a step towards a better world in which the full humanity of every single human being is recognized and respected.

Such adaptations of deconstruction, and of poststructuralism in general, are particularly useful for those critics – feminists, African-American critics, Marxist critics – who want to be politically effective. The endless play of *différance* will affect whatever we say. There is no getting away from *différance* and infinite uncertainty. But for politically motivated criticism uncertainty is a poor starting-point. If I want to achieve certain political ends there is not much help in the thought that all meanings – including the values that have led to my political stance – are merely the result of difference and have no solid foundation. From a politically activist perspective, deconstruction may even seem positively evasive.

IMPLICATIONS

What are the implications of the poststructuralist deconstruction of our faith in language, of its dismantling of 'presence' and of the privileged centres that the language sets up?

First, poststructuralism breaks with structuralism in an important way. While for the structuralists the structures they described were objectively present in the texts they dealt with, for Derrida such a structure is an arrangement produced by a reader who has temporarily stopped the infinite flow of meanings that a text generates. For Derrida, a text is not a structure, but a chain of signs that generate meaning, with none of these signs occupying a privileged, anchored (and anchoring) position. Language is 'a system where the central signified, the original or transcendental signified, is never absolutely present outside a system of differences', as he put it in his seminal essay 'Structure, Sign, and Play' (Derrida [1970] 2000: 91).

Second, because of its deconstruction of language, post-structuralism is far more wide-ranging than structuralism. Western philosophy, for instance, is based on the idea that we possess a faculty called 'reason' that, with the help of its obedient servant language, can get to know the world. Derrida argues that language is not obedient at all and has repeatedly exposed the figurative nature of seemingly rigorous philosophical language.

Third, poststructuralism has important consequences for the way we see ourselves. I have just mentioned 'reason' and earlier I discussed 'presence'. We usually assume that 'reason' and the way we are 'present' to ourselves have nothing to do with language. 'Reason' and 'presence' are aspects of a unique 'me' that merely uses language as an instrument. As the beagle Snoopy – from the *Peanuts* comic strip – once put it when he woke up right under an enormous icicle that had formed overnight on the roof of his doghouse: 'I am too *me* to die'. As we have seen, the structuralists already objected to that 'me'. If we want to express ourselves, we must always use a linguistic structure that was already in place before we arrived on the scene and we invariably express ourselves within the context of cultural structures that were also already in place. The poststructuralists accept that the individual subject is to a large (although never knowable) extent the product of linguistic and cultural structures (even if their exact nature can never be established). As Roland Barthes wrote in 1970 with regard to reading: 'This "I" which approaches the text is already itself a plurality of other texts, of codes which are infinite, or, more precisely, lost (whose origin is lost)' (Barthes [1973] 1990: 10). Moreover, since for the poststructuralists all structures are inherently unstable, mere temporary arrangements within chains of signification that are literally infinite, the subject, too, is only a temporary arrangement – an interruption of the flow of meaning. If we appear to be stable, we appear so because at an unconscious level we have set up oppositions, because out of both external and internal differences we have constructed oppositions and have then privileged certain poles. Simultaneously we have, in the case of internal differences, of internal conflicts, repressed and denied the undesirable poles – and have perhaps even externalized them, projected them on to others, which would boost both ourselves and the appearance of stability. But in reality we are inherently unstable and, like language itself, without a centre. Since there is no centre, there is no structure: we are, as Barthes suggested, made up of a 'plurality of other texts'. Of course, this is not how we experience ourselves and it is a view of the subject that is certainly not uncontested, but it is fair to say that the liberal humanist subject, with its self-determination, moral autonomy, coherence, and an essential, trans-historical core, has since the 1970s been a major target for poststructuralist critique.

Fourth, the interpretation of literary texts will never lead to a final, definitive result. Like structures, interpretations are mere freeze-frames in a flow of signification. For Eliot, Richards, Leavis, and the New Critics, the literary text had timeless significance because it put us in touch with what I have called the 'human condition'. Literature, unlike other uses of language, referred to vital, unchanging truths and values. For the poststructuralists, literature can do no such thing. Like all other forms of language, it is subject to the effects of *différance*. There is, however, one important difference between literature and other forms of language use: there is a category of literary texts that confess to their own impotence, their inability to establish *closure*. To Derrida and to poststructuralists in general, such texts are far more interesting than texts that try to hide their impotence, such as philosophical texts or realistic novels that claim to offer true representations of the world. If deconstruction deals with literary texts that present themselves as realistic, it will show how their seemingly realistic surface is an effect of suppression and of the suggestion they create that their readers are unified (whole) and in control of the text they are reading – either through the superior knowledge that the text allows us to have or through the ironic position that we are supposed to take up.

Since literary texts, realistic or otherwise, generate an infinite flow of meaning, interpretation is a matter of the reader. We have arrived, as Roland Barthes put it somewhat dramatically in 1968, at 'the death of the author', which simultaneously is 'the birth of the reader' (Barthes [1968] 2000: 150). For poststructuralist critics, text and reader interact to produce fleeting and always different moments of meaning.

SUMMARY

Poststructuralism is unthinkable without structuralism, but in its radical questioning of the structuralists' faith in language and in objective analysis it seriously undermines structuralism's achievements. In its deconstructionist form, primarily associated with Jacques Derrida, it focuses on language and argues that language, even if we have no alternative, is a fundamentally unstable and unreliable medium of communication. Because we rely on language in articulating our perception of reality and in formulating our knowledge of that reality, human perception and knowledge are fundamentally flawed. In a related move, poststructuralism argues that we have no genuine knowledge of our 'self', and that our identity, too, is prey to the indeterminacy of language. The deconstructionist criticism that bases itself upon these and other arguments shows how the instability of language always undoes the apparent coherence of literary texts. As the prominent deconstructionist critic J. Hillis Miller remarked, 'Deconstruction is not a dismantling of the structure of a text but a demonstration that it has already dismantled itself' (Miller 1976: 341).

SUGGESTIONS FOR FURTHER READING

Jonathan Culler's *On Deconstruction: Theory and Criticism after Structuralism* (1982) is thorough but relatively difficult. More recent and quite accessible introductions are Christopher Norris's *Deconstruction: Theory and Practice* (3rd ed. 2002), Catherine Belsey's *Poststructuralism: A Very Short Introduction* (2002), and James Williams's *Understanding Poststructuralism* (2005). *Derrida: A Very Short Introduction* (2011) by Simon Glendinning is a brief and lucid introduction to Derrida's philosophy. *Deconstruction: A User's Guide* (2000), edited by Nicholas Royle, presents essays that apply deconstruction to a wide range of subjects, from literature to technology and weaving. Jacques Derrida's own writings are notoriously difficult. However, '*Différance*', in the opening section of his *Margins of Philosophy* (1982), is a reasonably accessible discussion of this central concept. Another text that might serve as an introduction to Derrida's critique of logocentrism is the much-reprinted 'Structure, Sign, and Play in the Discourse of the Human Sciences' (1970), which may be found in Lodge and Wood (2000). Roland Barthes's 'The Death of the Author' and 'From Work to Text', which focus on literary writing, must also be recommended. Originally published in *Image–Music–Text* (1977), the essays are also available in *The Rustle of Language* (1986), and the former is reprinted in Lodge and Wood (2000). For an early critique of deconstruction, and a riposte, see M.H. Abrams's 'The Deconstructive Angel' (1977) and J. Hillis Miller's 'The Critic as Host' (1977), both of which are reprinted in Lodge and Wood (2000). Miller's reply illustrates the extravagant side of deconstructionist theory and interpretation.

Deconstructionist readings of texts are never easy, but Derrida's discussion of Kafka's 'Before the Law' ([1985] 1987) is fairly accessible and gives a good impression of his interpretative practice. Another good starting-point is Barbara Johnson's discussion of Melville's *Billy Budd*, mentioned briefly above, which is to be found in her *The Critical Difference* (1980).

6

POSTSTRUCTURALISM CONTINUED
FOUCAULT, LACAN, FRENCH FEMINISM, AND POSTMODERNISM

FOUCAULDIAN POWER

Poststructuralism is subversive. It deconstructs all those binary oppositions that are central to Western culture and that give it its sense of
uniqueness and superiority. In deconstructing those oppositions it
exposes false hierarchies and artificial borders, unwarranted claims to
knowledge and illegitimate usurpations of power. In deconstructionist
criticism, however, the dismantling of oppositions and the exposure
of hidden hierarchies and relations of power are generally limited to
the text at hand. Although the interrogation of power on a wider
scale is implicit in Derrida's deconstruction of logocentrism – the
belief that language gives us access to truth – the interest in power
and its workings that dominates the poststructuralist criticism of the
1980s and 1990s derives mainly from the work of Michel Foucault.

During his career as a historian Foucault (1926–84) wrote books
on the history of psychiatry, the origin and rise of clinical medicine,
the evolution of biology and economics, the emergence of the
modern prison system, and other important social developments
that originated in the late eighteenth and early nineteenth centuries – the so-called Enlightenment period – before turning to the
history of 'sexuality' (not in its biological manifestations but as
processed by culture) in his last books. In the earlier books he

focuses on what he sees as the Enlightenment desire to establish the procedures by which our societies regulate themselves on a rationalized and orderly basis. Foucault seeks to expose the way power was at work in the seemingly 'objective' vocabularies and diagnostic terms developed by the various branches of the budding human sciences as these constituted themselves in the course of the nineteenth century. For Foucault, these new sciences – which included psychiatry, criminology, medicine, and (human) biology – and the social policies that emerged from them are essentially repressive. He argues that the increased regulation and surveillance that characterized these policies, which at least in theory aimed to improve things, ultimately have led to a self-imposed submission to social control. The new human sciences have turned out to be straitjackets that, strangely enough, we seem happy to put on.

PANOPTICISM

In a section called 'Panopticism' in his book *Discipline and Punish: The Birth of the Prison* (1975; translated in 1977), Foucault gives a succinct account of how in early modern society leprosy and the plague – both highly contagious diseases – were dealt with. Lepers were simply excluded from social intercourse to minimize the risk of infection. However, with regard to the plague, which always affected large numbers of the population, other measures were necessary. And so seventeenth-century society did its utmost to contain the disease by confining people to their houses once it had manifested itself. But such a drastic measure demands constant surveillance: 'Inspection functions ceaselessly. The gaze [of surveillance] is alert everywhere' (Foucault [1975] 1977: 195). This imprisonment by way of precaution is, for Foucault, typical of how in the modern world the individual is constantly monitored, inspected:

> This enclosed, segmented space, observed at every point, in which the individuals are inserted in a fixed place, in which the slightest movements are supervised, in which all events are recorded ... in which the individual is constantly located, examined and distributed among the living beings, the sick and the dead – all this constitutes a compact model of the disciplinary mechanism.
>
> (Foucault [1975] 1977: 197)

The 'political dream' of the plague is 'the penetration of regulation into even the smallest details of everyday life' (198). It must not be thought that in such attempts to confine the plague one powerful group of citizens controls another, powerless one. There is, with regard to power, not a 'massive, binary division between one set of people and another' (198), but a distribution of power through many channels and over a large number of individuals.

It is the detailed regulation and constant surveillance that were mobilized against the plague that in the nineteenth century begin to be applied to 'beggars, vagabonds, madmen, and the disorderly' – in short, 'the abnormal individual'. The instrument that the authorities responsible for this use is 'that of binary division' – the binary oppositions with which we are familiar: 'mad/sane; dangerous/ harmless; normal/abnormal' (199). Foucault's metaphor for this new sort of social regulation is that of the *Panopticon*, a type of prison designed by the English philosopher Jeremy Bentham in the late eighteenth century. This ideal prison consisted of a ring of cells that was built around a central point of observation from which one single guardian could survey all the cells – which were open to inspection – on a given floor.

However, the prisoner cannot see the supervisor. He never knows if he is being watched. This, for Foucault, is the 'major effect' of the Panopticon:

> to induce in the inmate a state of conscious and permanent visibility that assures the automatic functioning of power. So to arrange things that the surveillance is permanent in its effects, even if it is discontinuous in its action; that the perfection of power should tend to render its actual exercise unnecessary; that this architectural apparatus should be a machine for creating and sustaining a power relation independent of the person who exercises it; in short, that the inmates should be caught up in a power situation of which they themselves are the bearers.
>
> (Foucault [1975] 1977: 201)

'A real subjection is born mechanically from a fictitious relation' (202), Foucault concludes in a formulation that strongly resembles Althusser's definition of ideology as a representation of the 'imaginary relationship of individuals to their real conditions of existence' (see Chapter 4). For Foucault, the Panopticon stands for the modern world in which we, its citizens, are 'the bearers' of our own figurative, mental, imprisonment. As with Althusser, we are complicit in our own confinement.

This may at first sight not seem very plausible. Aren't the various Western democracies supposed to be free and tolerant? Let me therefore offer a simplified account of Foucault's argument with respect to psychiatry and violent crime. Before psychiatry entered the scene, a murder was simply a murder: an act that needed no further explanation beyond the obvious ones – profit, revenge, and the like – and that could be summarily punished. But with the advent of psychiatry, the focus began to shift from law enforcement and the meting out of punishment to the underlying reasons for the criminal act. In other words, the focus shifted from the law to the character of the criminal. Before too long, psychiatry had diagnosed one or more specifically criminal personalities. With the introduction of the idea of criminal personalities we have a wholly new situation: it must be possible for an individual to have a criminal personality without actually having committed a violent crime. (We must, after all, assume that people who commit such a crime because they have a criminal personality already had that personality before they committed the crime.) But this must lead to the conclusion that there may be potential murderers among the people we know: one of them could have a criminal personality. What began as a psychiatric diagnosis leads to general suspicion and surveillance. We suspect others just as they suspect us: all of us are subject to the 'gaze' of surveillance. Moreover, such diagnoses usually lead to self-surveillance: we become the 'bearers' of our own imprisonment.

Another 'personality' that is discovered in the nineteenth century is that of the homosexual. In this case, too, what seemed to be discrete sexual acts are traced back to an underlying, unchanging, homosexual nature. Given the strongly negative connotations surrounding this new 'personality', young males must have started to monitor themselves and, if necessary, to repress undesirable feelings. Foucault argues that over the last two centuries an army of psychiatrists, doctors, sociologists, psychotherapists, social workers, and other self-appointed guardians of 'normality' has sprung up to create a stifling apparatus of social surveillance in which, as we will see in a moment, language plays a major role. But let me first look briefly at a novel that may make this seem more plausible.

Although it predates Foucault's work, Ken Kesey's *One Flew over the Cuckoo's Nest* (1962) describes a truly Foucauldian world. The novel takes place in a mental institution that is run by a woman ('Big Nurse') whose weapons are surveillance and inspection. The patients regularly take part in group sessions in which they must reveal their problems – ostensibly for therapeutic purposes but in reality because the humiliation of public confession keeps them subservient and in line. One of the major surprises of the novel is that many of the inmates have not been committed at all, but have come to the institution on a wholly voluntary basis. They have had themselves committed because the outside world's insistence on 'normality' and its definition of normality have convinced them that they are abnormal and need treatment. They have, in other words, subjected themselves to the authority of the human sciences. They have, first of all, accepted and completely internalized a *discourse* about normality – a term I will explain below – for which the human sciences are mainly responsible; second, they have literally turned their minds and bodies over to one of its institutions. The only 'patient' who is sure that he is absolutely sane has escaped this 'discourse' about normality because he has never gone to school or church – two of Althusser's state apparatuses. Ironically, unlike most of the others, he is not free to leave.

DISCOURSES

Why do we accept this 'panoptical' state of affairs – a world in which we are under constant surveillance and, even more importantly, in which we constantly monitor ourselves for signs of abnormality or even mere strangeness? Foucault attributes this to the 'power' that is at the heart of discourses, a term I will explain in a moment. This power clearly has much in common with Althusser's 'ideology' and Gramsci's 'hegemony' because it, too, rules by consent. In the example of *One Flew over the Cuckoo's Nest* the 'patients' who have had themselves committed genuinely believe that they are misfits and need treatment. They defer, one might say, to the power of psychiatric discourse. Foucault's power, just like 'ideology' or 'hegemony', derives its strength from the fact that we deeply believe what it tells us. In fact, just like Althusser's ideology, it gives us a sense of belonging and contributes to our well-being:

> If power were never anything but repressive, if it never did anything
> but to say no, do you really think one would be brought to obey it? What
> makes power hold good, what makes it accepted, is simply the fact that
> it doesn't only weigh on us as a force that says no, but that it traverses
> and produces things, it induces pleasure, forms knowledge, produces
> discourse.
>
> (Foucault 1980: 119)

We obey power, are loyal to it, even to the point of policing and
repressing ourselves, because it makes us feel what we are. What is
unclear is the extent to which we can resist power. Foucault certainly allows more room for resistance than Althusser:

> We must make allowance for the complex and unstable process whereby
> discourse can be both an instrument and an effect of power, but also a
> hindrance, a stumbling-block, a point of resistance and a starting point
> for an opposing strategy. Discourse transmits and produces power; it
> reinforces it, but also undermines and exposes it, renders it fragile and
> makes it possible to thwart it.
>
> (Foucault 1980: 100–01)

On the other hand, we also find Foucault arguing that resistance is
the means by which power further strengthens itself. Sometimes
Foucault would seem to take up an Althusserian position, which for
all practical purposes rules out resistance; at other times he would
seem to favour a more Gramscian view, which sees resistance –
counter-hegemonic views and actions – as a realistic possibility.

In any case, power works through *discourses* and *discursive forma-
tions*. In its policing of 'abnormal' behaviour the power of the
human sciences derives from what they claim to be *knowledge*; it
derives from their claims to expertise. Such a cluster of claims to
knowledge is what Foucault calls a 'discourse'. To be more precise,
a discourse is a loose structure of interconnected assumptions scat-
tered over writings, cultural artefacts, social practices, and the like,
that makes knowledge possible. In his *The Archaeology of Knowledge*
([1969] 1972) Foucault tells us that a discourse is 'a series of sentences or propositions' and that it 'can be defined as a large group
of statements that belong to a single system of formation' – a so-
called *discursive formation*. Thus, he continues, 'I shall be able to

speak of clinical discourse, economic discourse, the discourse of natural history, psychiatric discourse' (Foucault [1969] 1972: 107–08). A given discourse, say that of sexology in the nineteenth century, establishes a field – in this case that of sexual relations and inclinations – within which 'propositions' about sexuality can be formulated that could not be formulated without it: the creation of the field makes it possible to relate phenomena that seemed discrete and unconnected. Such a discourse, then, produces claims to knowledge and it is these claims – which we accept – that give it its power. There is then an intimate relationship between knowledge and power. Knowledge is a way to define and categorize others. Instead of emancipating us from ignorance, it leads to surveillance and discipline. Occasionally, it seems to lead to more positive results. To stay with the field of sexuality, the 'discovery' that there are men who have a 'homosexual personality' has led to disciplining and stigmatizing, but may also be said to have contributed to the creation of homosexual communities, to solidarity at the personal level, and even to collective action at the political level. Foucault is aware of this, but it is not easy to determine whether he sees such a '"reverse" discourse' (his term) as an instance of successful resistance. A reverse discourse, after all, makes use of the same vocabulary and of the same categories that the discourse itself uses, and thus creates at least the impression that it confirms that discourse's validity. On the other hand, in his later work Foucault seems to hold out the possibility that we shake off the straitjacket of discourses and seriously engage in 'the endeavor to know how and to what extent it might be possible to think differently, instead of legitimating what is already known' (Foucault 1985: 9).

POWER/KNOWLEDGE

Foucault's view of the relationship between knowledge and power is not uncontested. It is absolutely undeniable that in the past false claims to knowledge have served as instruments of power, of social suppression. Take, for instance, the supposed inferiority of women and coloured people, which endless generations of white males have accepted as factually true, as part of their knowledge of the world. Looking back, we see that we are dealing with binary oppositions that power (in this case the power of white males) turned into factual knowledge. Historically, so-called knowledge has in countless cases reflected a relation of power between a subject (the 'knower') and an object (that which the 'knower' knows or studies) rather than what we would call 'truth'.

When I use the term 'false claim', as I have just done, the implication is that there are also correct claims to knowledge. For Foucault, however, that distinction is dubious and the more radical critics who followed his lead in the 1980s and 1990s even rejected it completely, arguing that what was accepted as 'truth' depended first of all on the discursive power of the ideological interests involved. In any case, Foucault is not much interested in establishing which discourses, or parts of discourses, are false and which are true, nor in any individual agency active in their rise to power. His focus is on the set of rules, the *discursive formation*, that governs a discourse and holds it together. His type of history – which he terms 'genealogy' – must first 'account for the constitution of knowledges, discourses, domains of objects etc. without having to make reference to a subject' (Foucault [1969] 1972: 117). Here we see that Foucault operates on the dividing line between structuralism and poststructuralism. Just like, for instance, Genette with regard to narrative, he is interested in underlying principles: in the rules and the conditions that make it possible for 'propositions' to acquire the status of knowledge. These rules determine what counts as knowledge with regard to the field in which they operate and thus – as in the case of clinical medicine or psychiatry – establish bodies of 'knowledge' that apply to us all. Because of their claims to expertise, such discourses then go on to determine the way we talk and think about the field in question (sexuality, for instance, or mental illness) and as often as not persuade us to keep ourselves and others under constant surveillance. Like language in general, they operate independently of any individual intention and perpetuate themselves through their users. Since we are all instruments of the discourses that we have internalized, we ourselves constantly reproduce their power, even in our intimate relations.

At this point a question may well be raised: what relevance does this have for literary studies? The answer is that the idea of discourses as vehicles for power has been immensely productive in the study of literature (even if in Foucault's work literature seems somehow able to transcend discourses). Foucault locates power firmly in language, and language is the business of literary studies. I should perhaps emphasize again that Foucault, in discussing the role of discourses, is not thinking of individuals who abuse certain discourses to gain personal power (although that certainly happens) and that he is also not thinking of a central source of power – the state, for instance – that uses discourses cynically to manipulate us and keep us under control (even if that, too, certainly happens). The state's servants believe in such discourses just as much as we do. Discourses work like Gramsci's hegemony and Althusser's ideology: we internalize them so completely that they even 'induce pleasure'. Discourses organize the way we see the world for us. We live and breathe discourses and because of that function unknowingly as links in a good many power chains, submitting to power but also wielding it.

Deconstructionism is certainly not blind to the fact that language is tied up with power – its dismantling of binary oppositions testifies to that. Foucault, however, places language in the centre of *social* power – rather than textual power – and of social practices. The social role of language – including literature – and its hegemonic power is the starting-point for the various trajectories within literary studies that I will discuss in the chapters that follow.

POSTSTRUCTURALIST PSYCHOANALYSIS

In my discussion of Louis Althusser's explanation of the enormous power of what he calls ideology (see Chapter 4) I briefly mentioned the French psychoanalyst Jacques Lacan (1901–81). In contemporary literary theory and criticism Lacan's work is often evoked to explain how power works – why the individual – the subject – is so extraordinarily susceptible to power. Clearly, we need to look more closely at Lacan. However, a discussion of Lacan's psychoanalytic work cannot take place in a historical vacuum: in order fully to appreciate how it fits into a larger discussion of poststructuralism, we have to see it in relation to the work of the founding father of psychoanalysis – Sigmund Freud (1856–1939) – which it both continues and revises. I will, then, first look briefly at some of Freud's most fundamental assumptions – not least because they have given rise to a specific mode of literary criticism that deserves attention in a book such as this.

In Chapter 4 I discussed approaches to literature that read texts not primarily for their humanist meaning (as in Chapter 1), or for their form (as in Chapters 2 and 3), but for their *politics*. Seen from that perspective, a literary text is not in the first place the product of an individual author, but rather the product of a much larger culture that speaks through the writer and conveys political messages of which the writer may be completely unaware. There is, however, still another mode of criticism in which writers are taken to be largely, or wholly, unaware of their texts' deeper meanings. This criticism takes its inspiration from psychoanalysis, initially that of Freud, and later from other versions, too, including that of Lacan.

Freud's psychoanalysis presents a view of the subject that is radically at odds with the liberal humanist view of the subject as an ultimately free, coherent, and autonomous moral agent. For Freud, new-born babies live in an instinctual world dominated by 'oceanic' desires and feelings in which there is no distinction between the baby itself, its mother, or the larger world. Everything radiates from the centre – that is, the baby itself – and is geared towards fulfilling its boundless desires (for breastfeeding, for instance). Gradually, however, the awareness breaks through that this supposed physical and emotional continuity between baby, mother, and world is an illusion. As a result, the baby experiences a severe sense of loss which, in its turn, produces *desire* – now used in a more general sense.

In a second phase, the baby, now a young child, goes through a further separation from the mother, who for a while has functioned as the primary focus of 'desire'. During this so-called 'Oedipal' stage, which we go through when we are still toddlers, little girls begin to be aware that they lack a penis, as a result of which they develop a sense of inadequacy, and little boys, aware that their mother lacks a penis, begin to suspect that they might lose theirs (which Freud calls a fear of castration). It is this fear that persuades the little boy to give up what Freud takes to be his erotic interest in his mother (in the Greek myth that Freud draws upon Oedipus unknowingly marries his mother – hence Freud's use of the term 'Oedipal'). The little boy knows that he is in direct competition with his father and is on his way to a confrontation that he must lose – with the fearsome implication of castration. If you cannot beat them, join them; and so the little boy decides to be like his father – simultaneously accepting social authority – and (with a considerable time lag) directs his erotic interest towards other women. The little girl, as disappointed by her mother's lack of a penis as by her own, turns to her father – who possesses one – and will eventually give up her desire for a penis and want a baby instead. The Oedipal stage turns both boy and girl into future heterosexual adults.

Freud's account of the little girl's development has understandably infuriated many feminists (see, for instance, Kate Millett's *Sexual Politics* (1970)). What concern me here, however, are the effects of these early developments that we supposedly have all gone through. In our first years, we must again and again give up longings and desires either because we are forced to realize that they are impossible or because their realization would take us into forbidden territory. Those desires, however, do not disappear, but take refuge in a part of our mind that is beyond our conscious control: the *unconscious*. In later life, too, we may find that we have to repress desires because they are unacceptable. Although our conscious mind vigorously polices the border with the unconscious – whose unfulfilled desires and pain always want to remind us that they are still there – the unconscious has ways of getting past its vigilance. It first of all manifests itself in unguarded moments – in slips of the tongue, for instance, or in unintended puns, or in our dreams. But the unconscious also slips through, according to Freud, in language that we see as figurative – symbols, metaphors, allusions, and the like. The unconscious can, for instance, hide a repressed desire behind an image that would seem to be harmless – a trick that Freud called *displacement* – or it can project a cluster of desires on to an image in a manoeuvre that Freud called *condensation*: for instance, a dream figure can combine characteristics of a number of people we know. The language that we use may always have hidden meanings of which we ourselves have no conscious awareness. If we repress our hatred for a person who usually wears red, we may accidentally say 'dead' instead of 'red' in a conversation, or we may dream that a red car is flattened in a traffic accident.

Psychoanalytic criticism focuses on such 'cracks' in the text's façade and seeks to bring to light the unconscious desires of either the author or the characters that the text presents. It does not ignore what the text ostensibly would seem to be about, but its real interest is in the hidden agenda of the language that the text employs. The proposition that the language of a literary work has both a conscious and an unconscious dimension and that the unconscious elements must find ways to get past the censorship exercised by its conscious dimension has been very attractive to Marxist critics, for instance. Arguing that no text could possibly do justice to the full totality of the social world, they are particularly interested in what the text has left out – repressed, if you will. I will return to this point after an equally brief look at Lacan.

LACAN

In the last forty-odd years Freudian psychoanalysis has been criticized for its anti-feminism, but even more for its claims to universal validity. Freud's suggestion that the Oedipal model is of all times and all places has become increasingly controversial. As a consequence, many psychoanalytically interested critics have turned to Jacques Lacan, whose work avoids the fixed developmental scheme that Freud proposed and instead proposes a *relational* structure that allows for difference.

Lacan, too, sees the transition from infancy to childhood as absolutely crucial. For him, the pre-Oedipal infant lives in what he calls the *Imaginary*. In this state, in which the child cannot yet speak, it is subject to impressions and fantasies, to drives and desires, and has no sense of limitations and boundaries; as in Freud, it simply does not know that its body is not the world. It lives in a state of immediacy and experiences a sort of blissful wholeness that later impossibilities and prohibitions will destroy. Via the *mirror stage* (to which I will return in a moment) the child enters the *Symbolic*: it enters the world of *language* in which the *Real* – the real world that we can never know – is symbolized and represented by way of language and other representational systems that operate like language. (We can never know the Real because it can never be fully represented – it is beyond language.) This entrance into the Symbolic necessitates an acceptance of the language and of the social and cultural systems that prevail in the child's environment. It implies a loss of that state of immediacy and the acceptance of limitations and prohibitions. Lacan calls the massive configuration of authority that works through language the *nom du père*, the name of the father, in recognition of the patriarchal character of our social arrangements. The same recognition leads him to speak of the *phallus* as the signifier that signifies that patriarchal character. (Note that he avoids the term 'penis' because in Lacan's conception of things male dominance is a cultural construction and not a biological given. The phallus is thus always symbolic.) Hence the term *phallocentric*, which is of feminist origin and denotes the (false) assumption that maleness is the natural, and in fact only, source of authority and power.

Let me return for a moment to the 'mirror stage'. In this stage we are confronted with the 'mirror' image that the world gives back to us. But that image, just like the image that we see in an actual mirror, is a distortion that leads to a 'misrecognition'. Still, that misrecognition is the basis for what we see as our identity. For Lacan, we need the response and recognition of *others* and of the *Other* to arrive at what we experience as our identity. Our 'subjectivity' is construed in interaction with 'others'; that is, individuals who resemble us in one way or another but who are also irrevocably different. We become subjects – that is to say, ourselves – by way of the perspectives and views of others. We also become subjects under the 'gaze' of the Other or 'great other' (*grande autre*). This 'Other' – 'the locus from which the question of [the subject's] existence may be presented to him' (Lacan 2001: 148) – is not a concrete individual, although it may be embodied in one (father or mother, for instance), but stands for the larger social order, for what we call 'reality'. (We do, of course, also have an 'other' right inside us, in our unconscious.) We become subjects through a literal subjection to an existing order. Since our identity is constituted in interaction with what is outside of us and reflects us, it is *relational* – a notion that introduces the idea of difference into the process of identity construction. The relational character of identity suggests that the structure in which we happen to find ourselves more or less creates us as subjects and thereby situates us as individuals. However, since the social and personal configuration in which we find ourselves at a given point will inevitably change, identity is not something fixed and stable; it is a *process* that will never lead to completion. Identity is not only subject to constant change; it can also never be coherent. First, we have been forced to consign many of our pre-verbal fantasies, drives, and desires to our unconscious; second, since our identity is construed in interaction and does not originate in ourselves, it always depends on 'others'. Finally, since we have left behind whatever is pre-verbal and have entered – and subjected ourselves to – the realm of language, identity can be said to be a linguistic construct: we are constructed in language. That language, however, is not our own.

With the transition from the Imaginary to the Symbolic, in which we submit to language and reason and accept 'reality' as it is, we lose that feeling of wholeness, of undifferentiated being, that, again as in Freud, will forever haunt us. Because we do not have access to this pre-verbal self, or to the Real that that self was not yet divorced from, we live ever after with a lack. With Lacan, too, this loss of our original state results in *desire*, in an unspecific but deep-felt longing that can never be fulfilled, but can only (temporarily) satisfy itself with symbolic substitutes. Even what we call 'love' is only a substitute.

Lacan's view of the conscious and the unconscious is even better suited to feminist and Marxist adaptations than Freud's. Freud sees the repression that leads to the formation of the unconscious in terms of the nuclear family, even if he is aware that that family is embedded in a much larger social order (he speaks of the 'prevailing cultural super-ego'). Lacan, however, sees that repression as the direct effect of entry into the social order. For Lacan, there is a direct connection between the repressive character of language and culture and the coming into being of the unconscious. We may expect everything that is ideologically undesirable within a given culture to have found refuge in the unconsciousness of its members. If we see 'ideology' in psycho-analytic terms – that is, as the conscious dimension of a given society – then we may posit an unconscious where everything that ideology represses – social inequality, unequal opportunity, the lack of freedom of the subject – is waiting to break to the surface. We may then examine the language that ideology uses for tell-tale cracks in its façade. The social unconsciousness will, just like our individual unconsciousness, succeed in getting past the censor. This is the presupposition of the literary-critical practice of Pierre Macherey and the British and American critics who followed his example (see Chapter 4).

As I have already suggested in my discussion of Althusser (also in Chapter 4), Lacan's psychoanalytic model has also been invoked to explain the hold ideology has over us. Ideology gives us the illusion that it makes us whole; it would seem to neutralize the desire that results from our entry into the Symbolic. Lacanian criticism sees this repeated on a smaller scale when we read literary texts. In the process of reading, we enter into a complex relationship with a text in which we allow it to master us, to fill our lack. Lacanian critics are interested in the ways in which narrative structures and rhetorical operations take advantage of this rather one-sided relationship between text and reader. However, although Lacanian psychoanalysis has led to classic interpretations such as Shoshana Felman's (1982) reading of Henry James's *The Turn of the Screw* (1898), it has perhaps been more influential on the level of theory. We have already seen how it can be invoked to theorize the power of ideology, and in Chapter 8 we will see how Lacan's thesis that we develop our identity by way of 'others' can be used to analyse the underlying relations between colonizer and colonized.

FRENCH FEMINISM

From the mid-1970s onwards we see encounters between feminism and poststructuralist thought. Given the French origin of poststructuralist thinking, it is not surprising that French feminists were the first to see the potential of poststructuralist concepts and arguments for feminist critiques of the patriarchal social order.

An early and influential claim for the relevance of binary oppositions for feminism is 'Sorties', an essay published in 1975 by the French writer and literary critic Hélène Cixous (b.1937). 'Sorties' begins with a dramatic question (in a larger type than the rest of the essay): '*Where is she?*' and then presents the following list:

Activity/Passivity,
Sun/Moon,
Culture/Nature,
Day/Night,
Father/Mother,
Head/Heart,
Intelligible/Sensitive,
Logos/Pathos.

(Cixous [1975] 2000: 264)

'Thought', Cixous continues, 'has always worked by ... dual, *hier-archized* oppositions.'

Superior/Inferior,
Nature/History,
Nature/Art,
Nature/Mind,
Passion/Action.

(Cixous [1975] 2000: 264)

For Cixous, everything is related to the man/woman opposition:

In philosophy woman is always on the side of passivity. Every time the question comes up; when we examine kinship structures; whenever a family model is brought into play; in fact as soon ... as you ask yourself what is meant by the question 'What is it'; as soon as there is a will to say something. A will: desire, authority, you examine that, and you are led right back – to the father ... And if you examine literary history, it's the same story. It all refers back to man, to *his* torment, his desire to be (at) the origin. Back to the father. There is an intrinsic bond between the philosophical and the literary ... and phallocentrism.

(Cixous [1975] 2000: 265)

We see in these passages the influence of structuralism (binary opposites in general and kinship structures in particular), deconstruction (the reference to logocentrism), and Lacanian psychoanalysis ('phallocentrism'). Cixous integrates these sources in the argument that the male/female opposition is central to Western culture (if not all cultures) and is pervasively present in all sorts of oppositions that at first sight have nothing to do with either males or females. The inferior term is always associated with the feminine, while the term that occupies the privileged position is associated with masculinity. For Cixous, this never-ending privileging of the masculine, which results from what she calls 'the solidarity of logocentrism and phallocentrism', damages us all, females and males alike, because it curbs the imagination and is therefore oppressive in general. '[T]here is no *invention* possible', Cixous argues, 'whether it be philosophical or poetic, without the presence in the inventing subject of an abundance of the other, of the diverse'

(269). But where to start dismantling this repressive male/female opposition?

In her 1975 essay 'The Laugh of the Medusa', Cixous suggests that laughter, sex (if not policed by patriarchal heterosexuality), and writing may have liberating effects. Aware that writing usually serves the consolidation of patriarchal power, Cixous proposes what she calls *écriture féminine* – that is, a feminine or female writing that will escape the restrictions imposed by 'the phallocratic system':

> It is impossible to define a feminine practice of writing [*écriture féminine*], and this is an impossibility that will remain, for this practice can never be theorized, enclosed, encoded – which doesn't mean that it doesn't exist. But it will always surpass the discourse that regulates the phallocentric system; it does and will take place in areas other than those subordinated to philosophico-theoretical domination.
>
> (Cixous [1975] 1981: 253)

Although *écriture féminine* is radically different from phallocentric writing because it inscribes the female body – 'Write yourself. Your body must be heard' – and female being in its texts, it is not the exclusive domain of women. It is a sort writing practice that 'surpasses' what Lacan calls the Symbolic and that we may associate – but not identify – with his Imaginary. Since repression is gender-blind, it represses males as much as it does females. Males, too, can escape 'philosophico-theoretical domination'. Cixous chooses to call the radically subversive writing that she has in mind 'feminine' or 'female' because the forces of repression are so clearly male. It is important to stress that Cixous does not think in terms of actual women in defining her 'feminine writing'. In typically poststructuralist fashion, her argument is not essentialist: it does not make claims for women's essential nature but points at structures in which both women and men are caught up and which both may resist and perhaps even transcend. I should perhaps add that not all French feminists saw Cixous's views in this light and that she has been accused of essentializing a stereotypically anti-rational women's nature with which some of her Parisian colleagues were decidedly unhappy.

The literary critic and psychoanalyst Julia Kristeva (b.1941) stays somewhat closer to Lacan with her concepts of the 'Symbolic' and the 'Semiotic' – which is a version of Lacan's Imaginary. For Kristeva, what has been repressed and consigned to the Semiotic finds its way into the not yet fully regulated language of children, into poetry, into the language of mental illness – into all uses of language that for whatever reason are not fully under the control of the speaker or writer. Symbolic and semiotic language are never to be found in their 'pure' states: all language is a mixture of the two.

> These two modalities are inseparable within the *signifying process* that constitutes language, and the dialectic between them determines the type of discourse (narrative, metalanguage, theory, poetry, etc.) involved; in other words, so-called 'natural' language allows for different modes of articulation of the semiotic and symbolic.
>
> (Kristeva [1974] 1984: 24)

Semiotic purity is possible only in 'nonverbal signifying systems', such as music. Whenever we use language, both our conscious (which participates in the 'Symbolic') and our unconscious (Kristeva's 'Semiotic') mark it with their presence. As in Lacanian psychoanalysis, the subject is irrevocably split.

The sort of writing that Cixous and Kristeva have in mind is fairly rare in the history of literature. We might think of James Joyce's *Finnegans Wake* (1939) or Virginia Woolf's *The Waves* (1931). The attitude that it presupposes, however, is much less rare nowadays. In *Surfacing* (1972), by the Canadian writer Margaret Atwood, we find a young woman caught in a rational, patriarchal, and often exploitative world exemplified by her lover, her father, and other male characters. During a trip to the wilderness, ostensibly in search for her missing father, she gradually strips herself of the perspective and the accoutrements of the rational modern world. Not accidentally, a dive deep into a pristine lake – into what hides under the surface – is the novel's turning-point. When she figuratively resurfaces at the end of the novel from a brief period of almost complete surrender to instincts, she will always take the experience and the resulting knowledge with her.

A final word on the poststructuralist uses of psychoanalysis. In recent years poststructuralist adaptations of psychoanalysis have proven useful in, for instance, criticism that is concerned with ecological issues. In his *Postmodern Wetlands: Culture, History, Ecology*

(1996), Rod Giblett examines Western descriptions of, and arguments about, swamps, wetlands, and other places that are neither land nor water, and suggests that '[t]he swamp, and the wetland more generally, is … a smothering place, or perhaps more precisely a (s)mothering place, where various desires and fears about the mother's body are played out' (Giblett 1996: 20). As 'the pre-Oedipal place par excellence' (20), wetlands have over the course of history been structurally maligned and have often even been definitively repressed, through filling or drainage. Giblett offers numerous readings of poems and passages taken from stories and novels to back up his claim. I will return to ecological criticism, of which Giblett's book is an example, in Chapter 10.

POSTMODERNISM

In the 1980s the writings of Derrida, Foucault, Lacan, Cixous, Kristeva, and other French theorists were often called 'postmodern', a term that has now lost much of its appeal, except in the field of contemporary fiction, where it still serves a useful purpose. 'Postmodernism' grouped together all those theorists who had abandoned or rejected structuralism and Marxism (although all of them remained committed, in one way or another, to ethics and social justice – 'Deconstruction is justice', Derrida would declare in 1990). The term had in the course of the 1970s been brought into wider circulation by the American literary critic Ihab Hassan, who not only identified a new 'postmodern' literature but diagnosed 'postmodern' tendencies in society at large. It became one of the buzz-words of the 1980s through the French philosopher Jean-François Lyotard's *La Condition postmoderne* (1979), translated into English as *The Postmodern Condition* (1984). Lyotard (1924–98), who had borrowed the term from Hassan, gave it a definite post-structuralist twist. The reign of what he called 'grand narratives' or 'metanarratives' was over, to be replaced by the far more modest and benign rule of limited, local narratives. Such grand, all-encompassing explanations and theories as religions, philosophical systems (including Marxism), psychoanalytic models (Freud, Lacan), ideologies (free-market capitalism), and socio-political projects (the Enlightenment narrative of never-ending progress and future social harmony) had been exposed as fictions, as the mere narratives that they are, and had run their various courses. Extremely simplified, Lyotard said postmodernism was an 'incredulity towards meta-narratives' (Lyotard 1984: xxiv). Recognizing that in the absence of metanarratives there is no way to reconcile diametrically conflicting and equally weighted 'local' narratives, he accepted that the post-modern condition inevitably involved incommensurability, and would produce unsolvable dilemmas. In other words, like Derrida's deconstruction, Lyotard's postmodernism led in the direction of undecidability.

For Lyotard, the dilemmas that the postmodern condition threw up were real enough. For another theorist who is usually seen as postmodern, Jean Baudrillard (1929–2007), they were both real and what he called 'hyperreal', which is to say that they were real to the parties involved and yet, simultaneously, unreal because reality itself had at some point become unreal, a simulation. Somewhere along the way, because of the ubiquitous commodification caused by free-market capitalism, we had become inauthentic, mere copies that simulated an originality and authenticity that we did not know was gone for ever (the 1999 film *The Matrix* comes to mind). A related diagnosis of the postmodern condition was offered by the American Marxist critic Fredric Jameson (b.1934), another impor-tant voice in what was a brief but intense discussion and equally out of sympathy with contemporary culture. Jameson suggested that the postmodern condition – which he, too, attributed to the ever more powerful march of capitalism (he defined postmodernism as 'the cultural logic of late capitalism') – had led to what he called a 'waning of affect' (Jameson 1984). Whereas before the advent of postmodernity we still had known authentic emotions, we now experienced mere 'intensities'.

More tenuously connected to postmodernism than the other French theorists who were associated with the term was the philo-sopher Gilles Deleuze (1925–95), who wrote part of his oeuvre in collaboration with the psychoanalyst Félix Guattari (1930–92). Deleuze's radical decentrings – some of his openly proclaimed aims are the subversion of Western philosophy and what his colleague Pierre Klossowski has called the 'liquidation of the principle of identity' (cited in Macey 1993: xv) – and his concept of the 'rhi-zome' clearly have elements in common with his poststructuralist colleagues. The 'rhizome' – a mode of lateral growth that 'has no beginning nor end' but 'is always middle, between things' (Deleuze and Guattari [1980] 1987: 21) – is contrasted with the rooted, vertical, arboresque that he sees as controlling Western thinking and social organization. Radically opposed to the hierarchical and to the rooted, the fixed, in whatever form, Deleuze advocates 'deterritorialization', 'flows', 'nomadic' thinking. He and Guattari enjoyed a brief vogue in Anglophone literary theory through their concept of 'minor' literatures, proposed in *Kafka: Towards a Minor Literature* (published in French in 1975; translated into English in 1986). A minor literature deterritorializes the major language in which it is written – because it is written from a marginalized position, 'in it language is affected with a high coefficient of deterritorialization' (Deleuze and Guattari [1975] 1986: 16). It is thus inescapably political and speaks for the marginalized minority as such, not simply for its individual author, and is even 'a revolutionary force for all literature' (19). But although Deleuze's ideas in particular have had considerable impact, there is no Deleuzean criticism. As my colleague (and loyal Deleuze expert) Rosi Braidotti has remarked, '[t]here are no Deleuzeans … there are only people who engage with Deleuze's thought, figurations and intellectual intensities – in order to construct alternative ways of thinking' (Braidotti 2006: 203).

Postmodernism as an intellectual enterprise, then, may almost be equated with the various poststructuralist positions that were first articulated in the 1960s and took American literary criticism, in particular, by storm in the 1970s and 1980s. It is only as a diagnosis of a supposed cultural malaise – usually seen as involving an extreme form of relativism and a mindless celebration of corporate capitalism – that it has no direct connections with poststructuralism. Indeed, such diagnoses tend to come from political conservatives who abhor poststructuralism – which they also see as radically relativist – or from Marxists such as Jameson (or his British colleague Terry Eagleton). As a mode of intellectual enquiry postmodernism may be seen as the common denominator of the various strands of poststructuralism, attributing great importance to a language that no longer functions as a window on the world, questioning – or even denying – the autonomous subject of humanism, and regarding Enlightenment rationality, which it sees as misleading and repressive, with the greatest suspicion.

POSTMODERN FICTION

The terms 'postmodern' and 'postmodernism', however, are still quite relevant when we talk about contemporary literature, in particular post-1960s fiction. In the American writer Donald Barthelme's novel *Snow White* (1967), a bizarre rewriting of the well-known fairy tale, we are suddenly confronted with a questionnaire that not only checks if we have understood that this is Snow White in disguise, but also wants to know whether we would like to see more or less emotion in the rest of the novel – as if that were a serious possibility.

Unexpected and unsettling twists abound in this sort of fiction. In the American Thomas Pynchon's *The Crying of Lot 49* (1966) the novel's main character, California housewife Oedipa Maas, tries to unravel the mystery of a powerful secret organization that may or may not have existed for the last three hundred years. Unfortunately, the novel stops right when she is on the point of finding out.

The British writer Peter Ackroyd's *Hawksmoor* (1985) presents chapters that alternately tell an eighteenth-century story featuring a satanic serial killer and a contemporary story featuring a policeman who happens to be hunting for a similar criminal. We find all sorts of tantalizing parallels between the stories, but nothing ultimately fits. In the American writer Paul Auster's *City of Glass* (1985) a writer, Quinn, receives a couple of telephone calls from a man who wants to hire the private detective Paul Auster. Giving in to a whim, he pretends to be Paul Auster, and accepts a strange assignment in the course of which he meets a writer called Paul Auster. The novel ends with Quinn alone in a room with the days getting shorter and shorter until he finally appears to have vanished into thin air. A novel by another American writer, Richard Powers's *Three Farmers on Their Way to a Dance*, also published in 1985, presents three storylines that increasingly would appear to hang together. At a certain point, however, one of these lines is inexplicably fractured. We are finally forced to conclude that Powers has taken everything from a picture by the well-known early twentieth-century photographer August Sander showing three young men who may or may not be farmers and who may or may not be on their way to a dance. Finally, the South African writer J.M. Coetzee's

Foe (1987) pretends to tell the real story of Robinson Crusoe. According to *Foe*, Crusoe and his servant Friday are joined after a number of years by a shipwrecked woman, Susan Barton. After they have finally been rescued, Crusoe dies during the voyage back home to England. Since Friday cannot speak because his tongue has been cut out, Susan is the only one who can inform the world about Crusoe's island and their years together. She succeeds in interesting the writer Daniel (De)Foe in the story and we know the rest: Defoe proceeds to write Susan out of the story and thus out of history.

Authors make appearances in their own fictions, violating the boundary between the real world and the fictional one and thus creating intractable ontological problems. Fictional characters leave the world of fiction to congratulate their creators (*Out* (1973) by Roland Sukenick). Characters may be lifted from various earlier fictions to populate a new fictional world (John Barth's aptly titled *LETTERS* (1979)). But fictional worlds may also break up: in 'The Babysitter' (1969) and other stories by Robert Coover, the reader is, without further explanation, offered rather different versions of one and the same story. Using a single starting-point, Coover develops various fictional possibilities. And we find a range of novels that demythologize and play around with highly conventionalized genres such as the Western and the detective novel (as in Pynchon's *The Crying of Lot 49*).

Central to this postmodern fiction is that it unsettles or even deconstructs traditional modes of fiction. Barthelme makes fun of traditional ways of presenting a story and transgresses the dividing line between high and popular culture. Pynchon refuses to give us the comfort of *closure*; in their own ways, Ackroyd and Auster do the same. In Ackroyd and Auster, identity is made highly problematic, while Powers' novel forces us to realize that we have all along been caught up in an illusion; it explicitly calls our attention to its own constructed nature. Through his rewriting of Daniel Defoe's *Robinson Crusoe* (1719), Coetzee creates the impression that one of the classics of English literature is built upon a misogynistic, discriminatory act and in so doing reminds us of the historical oppression of women. The fact that Crusoe's servant Friday, a black man, is literally unable to speak for himself similarly reminds us of historical injustice.

Although it would be stretching things to say that postmodern fiction is a sort of applied poststructuralism – poststructuralist ideas put into practice by writers – there would seem to be more than a little overlap between the interests of postmodern writers and those of poststructuralist theorists. To signal their suspicion of all-explanatory 'grand narratives' and the 'deep structures' of modernism that tell us there is an invisible reality – religious, philosophical, psychoanalytical – that is more 'real' and 'authentic' than the reality we see, postmodern writers create worlds that confusingly alternate 'flatness' and 'depth'. Although rarely simply caricatural, the characters of postmodern fiction are equally rarely the fully believable, seemingly authentic characters of modernist or realist fiction and usually oscillate between surface representation and humanist depth. Postmodern fiction presents us with two incompatible sets of reading instructions: we encounter textual elements that strongly suggest referentiality and create the illusion of reality as we know it, and elements that expressly counteract such an illusion and tell us that we are not dealing with authentic reality at all. In other words, we get textual elements that suggest depth and meaning and invite traditional interpretation, and, simultaneously, other elements that flaunt their distance from the world we know and undermine interpretational initiatives. The upshot is a dialogue between referentiality and non-referentiality, between realism and anti-realism, between historical verisimilitude and anti-history. In other words – and here we are on familiar territory – postmodern fiction deliberately works towards undecidability.

SUMMARY

In the course of the 1970s and the 1980s literary studies began to incorporate the thought of the poststructuralist historian Michel Foucault and the poststructuralist psychoanalyst Jacques Lacan. Foucault's work calls our attention to the role of language in the exercise and preservation of power. According to Foucault, the modern Western world is in the grip of so-called *discourses* that regulate our behaviour because we have internalized them and therefore for all practical purposes police ourselves. Foucauldian criticism focuses on the role of literary and other texts in the circulation and maintenance of social power. Lacan's psychoanalytic theories serve to explain why we would internalize discourses that effectively imprison us. Lacanian criticism has been especially illuminating with regard to the relationship that readers enter into with the texts they read. Under the influence of poststructuralism French feminism broke away from essentialist approaches to feminist issues, arguing that thinking in terms of fixed biological identities will only confirm a binary opposition that we should abandon for the sake of true equality.

The term 'postmodernism' refers, rather indiscriminately, to the various philosophies and views discussed in this chapter and Chapter 5, and to other positions that attribute great importance to language, seriously question the humanist notion of the autonomous subject, and are deeply suspicious of Enlightenment rationality. When applied to contemporary culture, postmodernism usually involves a negative appraisal of its superficiality and its subservience to corporate capitalism, which, in Lyotard's view, has even turned the sciences into instrumentalist tools.

SUGGESTIONS FOR FURTHER READING

The Foucault Reader, edited by David Rabinow (1984), is an excellent selection from Foucault's writings, with an emphasis on his later work. The interviews that are included serve as brief and lucid introductions to his thought. Another collection, *Power/Knowledge: Selected Interviews and Other Writings, 1972–1977* (1980), edited by Colin Gordon, also contains helpful characterizations of his work by Foucault himself (see 'Two Lectures' and 'Truth and Power'). Foucault's famous discussion of 'panopticism' was originally published in Part III of his *Discipline and Punish* ([1975] 1977). His important essay 'What Is an Author?' (1969) is reprinted in Lodge and Wood (2000).

A good, brief introduction to psychoanalytic criticism is Meredith Skura's 'Psychoanalytic Criticism' (1992). A comprehensive overview is offered by Elizabeth Wright in *Psychoanalytic Criticism: A Reappraisal* (2nd ed. 1998). Norman N. Holland's *Holland's Guide to Psychoanalytic Psychology and Literature-and-Psychology* (1991) is a somewhat older comprehensive guide to all types of psychoanalysis and their usefulness for literary criticism. Malcolm Bowie's *Lacan* (1991) is an excellent introduction to the complexities of Lacan, whose own writings are notoriously difficult. Readers who are not easily discouraged might try 'The Insistence of the Letter in the Unconscious' in Lodge and Wood (2000), Lacan's discussion of *Hamlet* ('Desire and the Interpretation of Desire in *Hamlet*', 1977), or his reading of Poe's 'The Purloined Letter' (in John P. Muller and William J. Richardson's *The Purloined Poe*, 1988). Bruce Fink provides a very helpful guide to the *Hamlet* discussion in his 'Reading Hamlet with Lacan' (1996). Lacanian criticism is usually not easily accessible, either. The essays collected by Robert Con Davis in *Lacan and Narration: The Psychoanalytic Difference in Narrative Theory* (1983) illustrate how Lacanian psychoanalysis may be brought to bear upon narrative theory. A good deal more accessible, and highly recommended, are Linda Ruth Williams's Lacanian readings in her *Critical Desire: Psychoanalysis and the Literary Subject* (1995). Continued interest in Lacan has led to two fairly recent introductions to his work – Sean Homer's *Jacques Lacan* (2005) and *How to Read Lacan* (2007) by the Slovenian philosopher Slavoj Žižek – and to *The Cambridge Companion to Lacan* (2003), edited by Jean-Michel Rabaté.

Literary Feminisms by Ruth Robbins (2000) gives a good and very readable account of French feminism in relation to Lacanian psychoanalysis, in particular. *Between Feminism and Psychoanalysis* (1989), edited by Teresa Brennan, collects fifteen essays on French feminism by major feminist critics. A more recent collection is *The French Feminism Reader* (2000), edited by Kelly Oliver.

For a very readable overview of the strategies of postmodern novels, see Brian McHale, *Postmodernist Fiction* (1987). For the more thematic aspects of postmodern writing see Linda Hutcheon's *A Poetics of Postmodernism: History, Theory, Fiction* (1988). Other studies of postmodern literature are *International Postmodernism: Theory and Literary Practice* (1997), edited by Hans Bertens and Douwe Fokkema, Mark Currie's *Postmodern Narrative Theory* (1998), and Ian Gregson's *Postmodern Literature* (2004). Fredric Jameson's 'Postmodernism, or the Cultural Logic of Late Capitalism' (1984) is an influential Marxist analysis of contemporary culture, including both postmodern literature and criticism. Hans Bertens's *The Idea of the Postmodern* (1995) discusses the rise of 'postmodern' and 'postmodernism' as critical concepts in literature, the arts, architecture, and the social sciences. Finally, Christopher Butler's *Postmodernism: A Very Short Introduction* (2002), Simon Malpas's *The Postmodern* (2005), and Tim Woods's *Beginning Postmodernism* (2nd ed. 2009) are excellent introductions to postmodern thought and postmodern cultural practice. For those who are intrigued by the complexities of Deleuze, Claire Colebrook's *Gilles Deleuze* (2002) and Peter Hallward's *Out of This World: Deleuze and the Philosophy of Creation* (2006) are good starting-points.

7

LITERATURE AND CULTURE

CULTURAL STUDIES, THE NEW HISTORICISM, AND CULTURAL MATERIALISM

CULTURAL STUDIES

In *Culture and Anarchy* Matthew Arnold, whose formative influence on English and American literary studies I discussed in the first chapter, sees as one of the sources of the 'anarchy' of his title a working class that 'assert[s] an Englishman's heaven-born privilege of doing as he likes' ([1869] 1971: 105). Unfortunately, this sense of personal freedom does not lead the working class towards 'the best that has been thought and said' but to activities and pastimes that in their brashness and thoughtless vulgarity are the antithesis of culture. As its title suggests, *Culture and Anarchy* sets up an opposition between culture – which for Arnold implies coherence and order – on the one hand, and chaos and lawlessness, on the other. The term 'culture' is explicitly reserved for what most literary academics would now consider to be a rather narrowly defined 'high' culture – the culture of a specific elite. Arnold never uses the term in the more anthropological or sociological senses in which we now often use it, referring to the way of life and the world view of, for instance, the working class with the term 'working-class culture'.

The opposition between a superior high culture, whose literary branch preserves the best that has been thought and said, and the debased anthropologically defined 'cultures' that always threaten its existence runs like a red thread through pre-1970s English and American criticism. It is, in fact, this opposition between high culture and the various – and socially dominant – ways of life or cultures that threaten it that gave English studies its extraordinary self-confidence. The idea that high culture is essentially different from other forms of culture and that it has an inherently oppositional role to play with regard to other cultural expressions explains the missionary zeal and the moral urgency that we so often encounter in classic English and American criticism. For Leavis, the guardians of Arnold's 'best' – first of all, the literary critics – had the moral duty to defend high culture and to offer the sort of cultural critique that would maintain its standards and weed out everything that was inferior.

However, although it had strong opinions about lower-class and/ or mass culture (which we should not conflate or confuse with each other), traditional criticism did little to examine and understand it. This changed in the late 1950s with the English critic Richard Hoggart's *The Uses of Literacy: Aspects of Working-Class Life with Special Reference to Publications and Entertainments* (1957), which offered a warm, autobiographical account of Yorkshire working-class culture of the 1930s and 1940s combined with a close reading of popular magazines of the period, and with Raymond Williams's *Culture and Society, 1780–1950* (1958), which traces the idea of culture as it developed in England from the late eighteenth century to (almost) the time of writing. Both Hoggart and Williams were literary academics, with Hoggart representing a leftist humanist perspective and Williams a Marxist one, and both emphasized the valuable and life-enhancing qualities of cultures, in particular working-class culture, that from the perspective of high culture had generally been condemned and ignored. Here is an example of Hoggart's firm but sympathetic attitude. Admitting that the more genuinely working-class magazines and the fiction that they print for their primarily female readers 'are in some ways crude', Hoggart goes on to stress that 'they still have a felt sense of the texture of life in the group they cater for' ([1957] 1958: 121). In fact, '[t]he strongest impression, after one has read a lot of these stories, is of their extraordinary fidelity to the detail of the readers' lives' (126). 'Most of the material is conventional', Hoggart tells us, 'that is, it mirrors the attitudes of the readers; but those attitudes are by no means as ridiculous as one might first be tempted to think' (122). Working-class culture is simple, often even 'childish', but it is genuine and affirmative, and it plays a valuable role in the lives of millions of people.

Still, although it does not hesitate to step across the barrier dividing literature from what we might call pulp fiction, in an important way Hoggart's book repeats the traditional juxtaposition of authenticity and inauthenticity that we have already seen in D.H. Lawrence and F.R. Leavis. While for Hoggart the older and more traditional working-class magazines convey authenticity (a 'felt sense of … life'), the newer ones tend to succumb to a sensationalism that is a sure sign of the postwar commodification of the genre at the expense of honesty and sincerity. A new, manipulative mass culture created by corporate interests and directed at the passive consumer is taking the place of an older popular culture that came from below and in which there was still a bond, a system of shared values.

In Williams we find similar echoes of the ideal of an organic and coherent culture. 'We need a common culture', he tells us in the concluding chapter of *Culture and Society*, 'because we shall not survive without it' (Williams [1958] 1961: 304). Paradoxically, he is fully aware that in any given society we will find more than one single culture – which in his use of the term signifies 'a whole way of life' that is ultimately characterized by its 'ideas of the nature of social relationship' (311). (In the case of, for instance, working-class culture such a 'social relationship' is determined by solidarity.) But the coexistence of alternative cultures does not rule out a common culture: 'In our culture as a whole, there is both a constant interaction between these ways of life and an area which can properly be described as common to or underlying both' (313). The further development of that common culture (about which Williams would later change his mind) is then described as organic growth monitored by its members: 'The idea of a common culture brings together … at once the idea of natural growth and that of its tending' (322).

What we see is that the basis for cultural critique has shifted from literature to culture. Hoggart uses an older, more authentic and organic working-class culture to expose the mercenary outlook of the new culture that is in the process of replacing it. Williams puts his hope in a common culture, based on working-class values such as democratic solidarity – 'the basic collective idea' that finds expression in, for instance, trade unions and cooperative ventures – as the place from which to critique the destructive developments unleashed by the free-market ideology of capitalism. Both radically expand the field of study for literary criticism, while they stay true to Leavis's notion that criticism – which now includes cultural criticism – should position itself in opposition to those socio-economic forces that threaten authentic life and its modes of expression.

Although in their ideal of authenticity and organic coherence Hoggart and Williams belong to what for many critics writing today is an older intellectual dispensation, with their work what we now call 'cultural studies' becomes a legitimate interest of Anglo-American literary academics, an interest vastly boosted when in the early 1970s French structuralist approaches to culture – such as Roland Barthes's *Mythologies* (1957), with its analyses of the most diverse cultural phenomena – became available in English. In the course of the 1970s and 1980s the question of culture, and in particular that of a culture that could offer resistance to, or even subvert, hegemonic capitalist culture – a place in which cultural critique could be lived or from where it could be offered – became ever more important. One reason for this was the ever-increasing dominance of everyday life by the corporate media, which soon became a major object of study for cultural studies. Another was the influence of first Althusser and then Foucault. Althusser's state apparatuses and Foucault's discursive practices suggested that cultural practices constituted a form of power with enormous influence. Power was no longer exclusively defined in terms of military, economic, or political power, but was discovered in activities that had always seemed innocuous or even diverting.

A third reason for the ascendance of culture (and cultural studies) was the insight, derived from French structuralism and post-structuralism, that all cultures, no matter how seemingly authentic, were constructions. And if cultures were constructed, they could be contested, and perhaps even changed. Anglo-American cultural studies, following those theorists, like Gramsci, who had argued that resistance to the dominant culture was a valid option, strongly focused on what it saw as oppositional culture. Such subversive cultures, critics told us, may even make use of whatever corporate mass culture comes up with, recycling it for its own purposes. Although the products of the culture industry – rap, musicals, action movies, computer games, and the like – inevitably function as vehicles for power, the way such products are received and used is often at odds with the message(s) they carry, so the subject position they offer is effectively refused. Some cultural studies critics have even argued that youth culture, especially, has liberating effects that are presumably wholly unintended. In any case, for a while cultural studies sought political subversion in practically every subculture, and tended to see hybridity – the coming together of elements taken from two or more cultures in one new (sub)culture – itself as oppositional, as a form of resistance to a homogeneous corporate culture.

The rise of culture had two other consequences. The first is intimately connected with the insight that cultures are constructions and could therefore be contested. If that is the case, and if you want to change things, then it is clearly worthwhile to try to bring whatever seems 'natural', fixed – or is claimed to be 'natural' by certain interests – into the realm of culture. If you can, for instance, show the nuclear family, or the matrimonial bond between husband and wife, to have its origin in culture rather than in 'nature', you can make a strong case for alternative family life or for same-sex marriage. So culture's territory was enormously enlarged at the expense of whatever had seemed unchangeably the case. The other consequence was an eager interest in the role that culture plays in the constitution of the subject, in the creation of individual (or group) identity. With the rise of theory, the problem of identity formation had become a hot topic, and culture obviously contributed to the process. Cultural studies sought to understand the ways in which, and the extent to which, culture in all its facets constitutes the subject.

Although cultural studies, in Simon During's words, 'does consistently drift back towards the interpretative and empathetic methods of traditional hermeneutic disciplines, including the literary criticism to which it owes so much' (During 2005: 8), its focus, then, is definitely not literature, but the vastly larger world of contemporary culture. But cultural studies would require a book in itself, so we return now to the more manageable world of literary theory.

THE NEW HISTORICISM AND CULTURAL MATERIALISM

The constructed character of culture and its annexation by literary studies are central in two other major modes within contemporary criticism: the new historicism, which was American in origin and has remained largely American; and cultural materialism, which was, and is, mainly British.

Before I discuss them separately, let me make clear what these critical modes have in common. First, both brought to the then still traditional study of Renaissance literature, in particular the work of Shakespeare, poststructuralist notions of the self, of discourse, and of power, with the new historicism leaning more towards Foucault in its focus on power, on the discourses that serve as vehicles for power, on the connections between them, on the construction of identity, and related issues; and with cultural materialism leaning more towards the Marxism of Raymond Williams (who had coined the term 'cultural materialism' in his *Marxism and Literature* of 1977) and its focus on ideology, on the role of institutions, and on the possibilities for subversion (or dissidence, as some cultural materialists prefer to call it).

The new historicism and cultural materialism reject both the autonomy and individual genius of the author and the autonomy of the literary work, and see literary texts as absolutely inseparable from their historical context. The role of the author is not denied, but at best he or she is only partially in command. The author's role is, to a large extent, determined by historical circumstances. As the prominent new historicist critic Stephen Greenblatt has put it: 'the work of art is the product of a negotiation between a creator or class of creators, equipped with a complex, communally shared repertoire of conventions, and the institutions and practices of society' (Greenblatt 1989: 12). The literary text, then, is always part and parcel of a much wider cultural, political, social, and economic dispensation. Far from being untouched by the historical moment of its creation, the literary text is directly involved in history. Instead of transcending its own time and place, as traditional Anglo-American criticism had argued (and was still arguing), the literary text is a time- and place-bound verbal construction that is always in one way or another political. Because it is inevitably involved with ideologically charged discourses, it cannot help but be a vehicle for power. As a consequence, and just like any other text, literature does not simply reflect relations of power, but actively participates in the consolidation and/or construction of discourses and ideologies, just as it functions as an instrument in the construction of identities, not only at the individual level – that of the subject – but on the level of the group or even that of the national state. Literature is not simply a product of history; it actively *makes* history. Because they do not see literature as a special category of transcendent, essentially ahistorical texts, new historicists and cultural materialists treat literary texts in the same way as they treat other texts. For their specific purposes – to trace and bring to light relations of power and processes of ideological and cultural construction – there is no longer a difference between literature and other texts, no matter whether these are religious, political, historical, or products of marginal subcultures that so far have been ignored. Finally, in their conviction that culture, including all beliefs and values, is a construction, the new historicists and cultural materialists are willing to grant that their own assumptions must also be constructed and may therefore be deconstructed. But that does not prevent them from taking up political positions that are motivated by a political vision. The prominent new historicist critic Catherine Gallagher (1989) has argued that new historicist and cultural materialist thought must be seen as a continuation of certain strands within the New Left of the late 1960s. As we will see, with regard to new historicist practice – as opposed to theory – not everybody accepts that claim at face value.

THE NEW HISTORICISM

If the new historicism and cultural materialism have so much in common, what could possibly distinguish them? One distinctive feature is the role that subversion, or dissent, is allowed to play in them. As Catherine Belsey has argued, the new historicism's view of culture 'allows no space for dissent. Instead, minor revolts simply offer occasions for extending social control; crime legitimates an extension of the police' (Belsey 2005: 29). But let us first look at the new historicism's own history.

Although the term had been used before, 'the new historicism' received its current meaning in 1982, when the prominent critic Stephen Greenblatt used it to describe recent work by himself and others on the Renaissance period. Most commentators situate its origin in 1980, though, when Greenblatt published his book *Renaissance Self-Fashioning: From More to Shakespeare* and when another prominent new historicist, Louis Montrose, argued for the presence of power in a genre usually not associated with its exercise, that of the pastoral. Following Foucault in his assumption that 'social relations are, intrinsically, relations of power', Montrose examined the role of Elizabethan pastorals in 'the symbolic mediation of social relationships' in his essay '"Eliza, Queene of Shepeardes", and the Pastoral of Power' (Montrose 1994: 88). *Renaissance Self-Fashioning* argues that 'in the sixteenth century there appears to be an increased self-consciousness about the fashioning of human identity as a manipulable, artful process' (Greenblatt 1980: 2). This should not be taken to mean, however, that it was possible for Renaissance individuals to 'fashion' themselves fully and authentically. Wyatt, for instance, 'cannot fashion himself in opposition to power and the conventions power deploys; on the contrary, those conventions are precisely what constitute Wyatt's self-fashioning' (214). *Renaissance Self-Fashioning* ultimately subscribes to the notion that the self is always a construction, that our identity is never given, but always the product of an interaction between the way we want to represent ourselves – through the stories we tell (or the incidents we suppress) and our actual presentations – and the power relations of which we are part. Inspired by Foucault's interest in large-scale historical ruptures, Greenblatt's study also introduced a major theme of the new historicism's earlier years: the way in which the workings of power and practices of regulation change with the advent of a new era: in this case the transition from the pre-modern to the early modern period, with its notion of the autonomy and freedom of the subject.

In short, there is good reason to accept John Brannigan's definition of the new historicism as 'a mode of critical interpretation which privileges power relations as the most important context for texts of all kinds' and his claim that '[a]s a critical practice it treats literary texts as a space where power relations are made visible' (Brannigan 1998: 6). In this Foucauldian context, power works through discourses and, like ideology, gives the subject the impression that complying with its dictates is the natural thing to do and thus a free, autonomous decision. The new historicists see literature as actively involved in the making of history through its participation in discursive practices. Louis Montrose's 1983 essay '"Shaping Fantasies": Figurations of Gender and Power in Elizabethan Culture' discusses a wide range of texts – including autobiography, travel writing, and a Shakespeare play – to examine how representations of Queen Elizabeth I – the 'shaping fantasies' of his title – contribute to the creation of the essentially political cult of the 'virgin queen'.

The new historicism is, in the tradition of Foucault, focused on thus far hidden and unsuspected sources of, and vehicles for, power and on the question of how power has worked to suppress or marginalize rival stories and discourses. It has a special interest in the disempowered, the marginalized, those whose voices we hardly ever, or never, hear. Its methods are anthropological rather than literary critical or historical. History, such as the socio-economic circumstances of a specific literary text's creation, is not read to illuminate literature; nor is literature read to shed a direct light on history. Rather, the historical period in question is seen as a cultural matrix – including economic relations – whose various discursive manifestations – the texts of all kinds that have come down to us – need detailed attention and need to be brought into contact with each other so that the power relations and the forces operating in that culture may be brought to light. This means that it does not much matter from which point we try to access it – the earlier new historicism of the 1980s is famous for opening its enquiries with seemingly anecdotal material that is later shown to have great relevance. Since under the regime of a specific hegemony (to use Gramsci's term) or dominant ideology everything is interrelated and since no specific body of texts has a privileged status, we can always start wherever we want in our explorations. In its focus on relations of power the new historicism follows the discursive forms that power takes – its figures of speech, its larger rhetorical manoeuvres – wherever they appear. Everything is culture, and culture can be read and picked apart like a literary text. In its rather loose methodology the new historicism is indebted to the American anthropologist Clifford Geertz, not only because of his insistence that all culture is 'manufactured' and for all practical purposes without origins – in line with the poststructuralist view of culture – but because of his method of 'thick description'; that is, analysis by way of minutely observed social and cultural practices that are recorded in great detail.

The pervasive influence of Foucault has elicited a good deal of criticism. Foucault's views of power and its effectiveness have been widely, and inconclusively, debated, but no matter how we finally judge those views there are passages in his work that suggest a deep pessimism regarding the possibility of resistance. In a seminal new historicist essay, 'Invisible Bullets' (1981), Stephen Greenblatt echoes Foucault's pessimistic strain and argues that Renaissance subversion inevitably played into the hands of power. In fact, power *needs* subversion and actively produces it: 'subversiveness is the very product of that power and furthers its ends' (Greenblatt 1981: 48). This pessimism is not necessarily shared by all new historicists and I should in all fairness say that Greenblatt himself has also defended himself against charges such as the cultural materialist Alan Sinfield's claim that the new historicism works with an 'entrapment' model of culture that leaves no room for effective action and change. Still, although he argues that '[a]gency is virtually inescapable' (Greenblatt 1990: 74), Greenblatt immediately goes on to sketch a very limited horizon for agency:

> new historicism, as I understand it, does not posit historical processes as unalterable and inexorable, but it does tend to discover limits or constraints upon individual intervention: actions that appear to be single are disclosed as multiple; the apparently isolated power of the individual genius turns out to be bound up with collective, social energy; a gesture of dissent may be an element in a larger legitimation process, while an attempt to stabilize the order of things may turn out to subvert it.
>
> (Greenblatt 1990: 74–75)

The new historicists are, of course, aware that the at-best-limited freedom of the subject within the culture's hegemonic discourse and its inevitable involvement with that discourse did not stop with the Renaissance period. As Louis Montrose has put it: 'I have a complex and substantial stake in sustaining and reproducing the

very institutions whose operations I wish to call into question'
(Montrose 1989: 30). However, as he suggests, although the 'possibility of political and institutional agency cannot be based upon
the illusion of an escape from ideology', an *awareness* of the omni-
presence and power of ideology, no matter how imperfect, may
give us some breathing space: 'A reflexive knowledge so partial and
unstable may, nevertheless, provide subjects with a means of
empowerment as agents' (30). '[C]onfrontations within or among
ideologies'(30) may make room for relatively independent thought
and action.

Let me conclude this section with a few observations. I have up
to this point created the impression that the new historicism is
concerned only with the Renaissance. Although it did indeed first
emerge within Renaissance studies, where it caused a true revolution, by the mid-1980s new historicist approaches had spread to the
study of other periods, and in the 1990s they were virtually everywhere. Second, in the later 1980s and early 1990s, the dividing
lines between the new historicism (and cultural materialism), on the
one hand, and feminism and the newly emerging field of postcolonial studies, on the other, began to fade. Greenblatt's *Marvellous
Possessions: The Wonder of the New World* (1991), for instance, operates in a field of enquiry that we would now call postcolonial. It
examines the role that 'wonder' plays in the response of European
explorers and travellers to the New World. He characteristically
sees that wonder as 'an agent of appropriation' (Greenblatt 1991: 24),
in the sense that the expressions of wonder that we find in those
(written) responses function as an instrument of power. Under
Greenblatt's scrutiny, 'European representational practice' turns out
to have played a vital role in the process of colonization that followed exploration and travel. Although its focus is on the Europeans
and not on the new worlds and new peoples that give rise to
European wonder – as is usually the case in the so-called postcolonial
studies that I will discuss in the next chapter – *Marvellous Possessions* is
as much postcolonial as it is new historicist.

The new directions we find in 1990s new historicism can be
interpreted as a sign of the times, as testimony to the sudden, and
pervasive, influence of the new field of postcolonial studies, but it is
also a response to serious critique. Feminist and other critics had
begun to object to the steamroller effect of the new historicism's

view of power – to how in new historicist criticism structures of
power flattened and homogenized all subjects that lived within
them so that differences in class, sex, and race practically disappeared from view. Responding to such criticisms, the new historicism had begun to take such differences into account in its
analyses of the way subjects are constructed. But the theorizing of
sex and race that has emerged from the – ultimately – poststructuralist insistence on difference will have to wait until the following chapters.

CULTURAL MATERIALISM

Cultural materialist criticism established itself permanently in the
field of literary studies in the mid-1980s, with the publication of
Jonathan Dollimore's *Radical Tragedy: Religion, Ideology and Power in
the Drama of Shakespeare and his Contemporaries* (1984), Catherine
Belsey's *The Subject of Tragedy: Identity and Difference in Renaissance
Drama* (1985), and two collections of essays: *Alternative Shakespeares*
(1985), edited by John Drakakis, and *Political Shakespeare: Essays in
Cultural Materialism* (1985), edited by Jonathan Dollimore and Alan
Sinfield.

For cultural materialism, too, the ideological constructions in
which authors live, and which they have internalized, inevitably
become part of their work, which is therefore always political and
always a vehicle for power. As Dollimore and Sinfield put it in their
introduction to *Political Shakespeare*, '[a] play by Shakespeare is
related to the context of its production – to the economic and
political system of Elizabethan and Jacobean England and to the
particular institutions of cultural production (the church, patronage,
theatre, education)' (Dollimore and Sinfield 1985: viii). Like the
new historicism, cultural materialism brings to light how ideology –
and thus the existing socio-economic (and religious) order – tries to
maintain itself or, as the case may be, adjust itself to new circumstances without losing its grip.

Cultural materialists agree that literary texts will at first sight seem
supportive of contemporary ideology, but they see that ideology as
less pervasive than their new historicist colleagues do. Although
Foucault is an obvious influence in their work – especially with
regard to their interest in the insane, the criminal, the exploited,

and all those who over the course of history have been margin-alized – cultural materialism follows Williams in his adaptation of Gramsci's view of hegemony. For Williams, as we have seen, the dominant culture is never more than one player in the cultural field, even if it is by far the most powerful. There are always resi-dual and emergent strains within a culture that offer alternatives to the hegemony. In other words, the dominant culture is always under pressure from alternative views and beliefs. So while cultural materialist analyses of literary texts bring to light how these texts function as instruments of a dominant socio-cultural order, they also demonstrate how the apparent coherence of that order is threatened from the inside, by inner contradictions and by tensions that it seeks to hide.

Alan Sinfield's discussion of Shakespeare's *Othello* in his *Faultlines: Cultural Materialism and the Politics of Dissident Reading* (1992) is a case in point. In the patriarchal culture that the play presents Desdemona is bound to obey her father, and the role of obedient daughter should in the normal course of things lead her to follow his wishes in her marital choice. However, in the early modern period we also find an increased emphasis on the idea that marriage should be personally fulfilling. This 'contradiction in the ideology of marriage' – one of Sinfield's 'faultlines' – allows Desdemona to disregard her father's wishes and to marry a man who is totally unsuitable from the perspective of the social group to which she belongs. As a result, the social order comes under immediate pres-sure. I should hasten to point out that Sinfield does not portray Desdemona in liberal humanist terms: she is not a free, autonomous agent in the dissident choice that she makes. It is the faultline in question that creates what Sinfield calls 'dissident potential'. Dissidence is not so much a matter of individual agency but is first of all produced by the inner contradictions that characterize any social order.

Since such faultlines are to be found in all cultures, it is only natural that they should turn up in literary texts – *especially* in lit-erary texts, in fact, because literature offers a place where contra-dictions and tensions can be addressed and worked through. Focusing on the cracks in the ideological façade that texts offer, cultural materialism reads even the most reactionary texts against the grain, offering readings of dissidence that allow us to hear the socially marginalized and expose the ideological machinery that is responsible for their marginalization and exclusion. Cultural materialists are also interested in the way in which the reception of literary texts – by, for instance, traditional Anglo-American criticism – has obscured the presence of ideological faultlines in those texts. Dollimore's *Radical Tragedy* argues (among many other things) that the traditional interpretations of the Jacobean tragedies that he discusses – including Marlowe's *Dr Faustus* and Tourneur's *The Revenger's Tragedy* – have ignored how the plays undermine humanist assumptions because they focus on what fits the humanist framework.

Cultural materialism sees dissident readings of texts from the past as political interventions in the present, as political challenges to the conservative, humanistically oriented positions and critical practices that are still very much in evidence among literary academics and among those who control educational institutions. Its critical practice, then, not only tries to offer alternative understandings of the past but equally, and overtly, tries to effect political change in the present from a broadly socialist and feminist point of view. (Belsey's discussion, in *The Subject of Tragedy*, of the various literary – and non-literary – representations of the sixteenth-century murderess-by-proxy Alice Arden immediately announces cultural materialism's investment in feminism.) As Dollimore and Sinfield polemically announce in their introduction to *Political Shakespeare*:

> Cultural materialism does not, like much established criticism, attempt to mystify its perspective as the natural, obvious or right interpretation of an allegedly given textual fact. On the contrary, it registers its commitment to the transformation of a social order which exploits people on grounds of race, gender and class.
>
> (Dollimore and Sinfield 1985: viii)

Because of its double focus on the past and on contemporary politics, cultural materialism is deeply interested in the ways in which literature from the past, say the works of Shakespeare, has been made to function in later periods and in our contemporary culture. As Dollimore and Sinfield point out, 'culture is made continuously and Shakespeare's text is reconstructed, reappraised, reassigned all the time through diverse institutions in specific contexts. What the plays signify, how they signify, depends on the cultural field in which they are situated' (viii). Cultural materialism could, for instance, ask: which Shakespeare plays, or parts of plays, feature on secondary-school reading lists? Which plays do we find within university curricula? Which sonnets are routinely anthologized? Which plays are still performed, and where, and within what context? How do we read the fairly recent film version of *Richard III* – starring Ian McKellen – which lifts the play out of its historical period and has its protagonist set up a monstrously fascist regime in 1930s Great Britain? In other words, how is 'Shakespeare' constructed, and from what ideological position?

In one of the essays collected in *Political Shakespeare* Sinfield concludes: '[i]n education Shakespeare has been made to speak mainly for the right ... that is the tendency which this book seeks to alter' (Dollimore and Sinfield 1985: 135). For cultural materialists, ideology takes on a tangible, material form in institutions like the university, the museum, the army, the school, the labour union, the church, and a range of less influential organizations. And ideology becomes material in the ways in which images and representations from the past are deployed in the service of its contemporary version – for instance, in the merchandising of the product called 'Shakespeare' (and other big sellers in the heritage industry) and in the use of 'Shakespeare' in commercials. In *Faultlines* Sinfield shows how a reference to Shakespeare's Globe Theatre, evoking the continuity of British tradition, is used by a manufacturer of defence equipment to promote itself and its wares. From the perspective of cultural materialism, contemporary culture is a battlefield where an omnipresent conservative ideology must constantly be challenged.

The acrimony of the debate that followed cultural materialism's emergence in the mid-1980s testifies to the effectiveness of its intervention, although it also demonstrates the strength and number of those literary academics who prefer a more traditional, and still broadly humanist, approach – especially to Shakespeare ('The Bard'), whose work was the focus of a protracted battle. Just like the new historicism, cultural materialism has in the years since its intervention in the field of Renaissance studies become an important critical practice in virtually every period; and just like the new historicism, in the early 1990s it expanded its original interests and incorporated issues of empire and sexuality (feminism had been on its agenda from the beginning). Jonathan Dollimore's *Sexual Dissidence: Augustine to Wilde, Freud to Foucault* (1991) and Alan Sinfield's *The Wilde Century: Effeminacy, Oscar Wilde and the Queer Moment* (1994) and *Cultural Politics – Queer Reading* ([1994] 2005) exemplify this development. But the so-called 'queer theory' that we see in the making in these texts – and in a wide range of other texts from around the same time – will have to wait until a later chapter. We will turn first to postcolonial theory – the issues of empire – that I have just mentioned and that in the 1990s became another direction in which cultural materialism developed.

SUMMARY

After the assimilation of poststructuralist theory, literary criticism increasingly begins to see literature as an integral part of a much wider cultural context. Initially in the field of Renaissance studies, but later in literary studies in general, critics start from the assumption that literary texts are inevitably situated within the sort of discourses that, according to Foucault, carry and maintain social power. The American new historicists and the British cultural materialists read literary texts for their role in the circulation of power, with the British critics having an additional interest in the usually conservative roles that cultural icons, such as Shakespeare, have been made to play in later times. In order to bring to light the political dimension of literary texts, new historicists and cultural materialists read them in conjunction with non-literary texts and with reference to the dominant discourse or discourses of a given period.

Cultural studies, which has its roots in British literary criticism and French structuralism and later takes on board poststructuralist perspectives, casts its net even wider, seeing the whole field of contemporary culture as its object of study. Like the new historicism and cultural materialism, it is interested in the workings of power, and in the way cultures and their products create subject positions for us in, for instance, our role as consumer. These positions, however, are not seen as absolutely compelling, and the subject is allowed a good

deal of agency, to the point of using and enjoying cultural com-
modities while still resisting their ideological appeal.

SUGGESTIONS FOR FURTHER READING

John Brannigan's *New Historicism and Cultural Materialism* (1998) is
an excellent introduction while Kiernan Ryan's *New Historicism and
Cultural Materialism: A Reader* (1996) presents important intellectual
sources and examples of critical practice. Brief but to the point is
Louis Montrose's 'New Historicisms' (1992). H. Aram Veeser's
collection *The New Historicism Reader* (1994) brings together a
number of important examples of the new historicism in action.
Excellent examples of new historicist readings are Stephen
Greenblatt's 'Invisible Bullets' (1981) and Louis Montrose's '"Eliza,
Queene of Shepeardes", and the Pastoral of Power' (1994).
Greenblatt, especially, is not easy, but both of these articles are
certainly rewarding. Christine Gallagher and Greenblatt's *Practicing
New Historicism* (2000) offers essays on a wide range of topics. *The
Greenblatt Reader* (2004), edited by Michael Payne, collects
Greenblatt's most important writings in a single volume, while
Jürgen Pieters's *Moments of Negotiation: The New Historicism of
Stephen Greenblatt* (2001) is a full-length study. Paul Hamilton's
Historicism (2nd ed. 2003) very usefully discusses the differences
between historicism and the new historicism.

Ryan presents an excerpt from Alan Sinfield's *Faultlines* (1992)
that wonderfully exemplifies cultural materialism's interest in dissidence. The second chapter of Sinfield's *Cultural Politics – Queer
Reading* ([1994] 2005) is a lively introduction to cultural materialism. Also very readable is the polemical introduction to Jonathan
Dollimore and Sinfield's *Political Shakespeare: Essays in Cultural
Materialism* (1985), a book that with its interest in 'Shakespeare' in
the twentieth century also illustrates cultural materialism's contemporary focus. Andrew J. Milner's *Re-imagining Cultural Studies:
The Promise of Cultural Materialism* (2002) and Sinfield's *Shakespeare,
Authority, Sexuality: Unfinished Business in Cultural Materialism* (2006)
illustrate that cultural materialism is not only unfinished but still
relevant. *Shakespeare and Contemporary Theory: New Historicism and
Cultural Materialism* (2012) by Neema Parvini revisits traditional

criticism, takes a new look at Althusser and Foucault, among others, and then discusses the latest developments in new historicism and cultural materialism.

Finally, Simon During's *Cultural Studies: A Critical Introduction* (2005) is a somewhat unorthodox but highly readable and very well-informed introduction to the subject, while Susan Hegeman's *The Cultural Return* (2012) is a wide-ranging and spirited defence of cultural history in general.

8

POSTCOLONIAL CRITICISM AND THEORY

INTRODUCTION

As we have seen in Chapter 4, in the 1920s and 1930s, with the so-called Harlem Renaissance and with the introduction of the concept of *négritude* – the idea that all black Africans and people of African origin somehow participated in a unified consciousness – 'race' began to be a factor of importance in literary studies. Refusing to be defined on the basis of race by the dominant white culture, African-American and French-speaking writers from Africa and the Caribbean began to define themselves and their culture in their own terms. After the Second World War, this project of cultural self-definition developed alongside the project of political self-determination that we find in the American Civil Rights movement and in the Asian, African and Caribbean demands for political independence and nationhood. This should not create the impression that cultural self-definition and political self-determination moved along two parallel lines that never met. On the contrary, the one cannot really be separated from the other. The African-American Black Arts movement saw itself as the cultural wing of the political Black Power movement of the 1960s, and we have seen how Frantz Fanon, a radical critic of colonialism, saw national cultures – including national literatures – as important instruments in the struggle for political independence. Cultural self-definition and political self-determination were two sides of the same coin.

The desire for cultural self-determination – that is, for cultural independence – is one of the driving forces behind the literatures that in the 1960s and 1970s sprang up in the former colonies. Wilson Harris (Guyana), Yambo Ouologuem (Mali), Chinua Achebe (Nigeria), Wole Soyinka, the winner of the 1986 Nobel Prize for literature (also from Nigeria), Derek Walcott, the 1992 Nobel laureate (Santa Lucia), and a wide range of other writers create novels and poems that respond to, and reflect, their immediate cultural environment. In their response to specific cultural contexts, these texts signal the emergence – and in some cases, where a literary tradition had already developed, the confirmation – of new national literatures. The desire to draw directly on one's own culture is defended vigorously in an essay called 'Colonialist Criticism' that Chinua Achebe first presented in 1974 (see Achebe 1995). Arguing that the 'universal' qualities that Western criticism expects from literature are not so much 'universal' as 'European' in a universal disguise, Achebe attacks the idea that literary art should transcend its time and place. Paradoxically, his own *Things Fall Apart* ([1958] 1976), which describes the effects of colonialism on an Igbo community in moving detail, has spoken to large audiences all over the world.

As its title indicates, *Things Fall Apart* is written in English, as are the large majority of literary works written in the former British colonies. That is not self-evident: English is usually the second language of these writers, in particular those from Africa. So they have made a conscious choice to write in English, and this has proved controversial. The Kenyan novelist Ngugi wa Thiong'o, for instance, argued in the 1970s that the continued use of the language of the colonizer – leading to what he called 'Afro-Saxon' literature – is a form of self-inflicted neocolonization. Consequently, he turned to Gikuyu, his native language, for the novels that have been translated as *The Devil on the Cross* (1980, translated 1982) and *Matigari* (1986, translated 1989). However, even if African writers use English, they often let the rhythms and idioms of their own language be heard because the defamiliarization that results from such a practice automatically draws our attention to the non-English linguistic and cultural context of their work – as in Ken

Saro-Wiwa's deftly titled novel *Sozaboy: A Novel in Rotten English* (1985). But how should we classify that work? We cannot very well claim that *Things Fall Apart*, although written in English and dealing with British colonialism, belongs to English literature, just as we cannot seriously claim that Derek Walcott's epic poem *Omeros* (1990) is English. In recognition of this new situation, in which writing in English from the former colonies – including India, Pakistan, Sri Lanka, and other Asian colonies – has proved itself as vital and as important as the literature written in England itself, we now usually speak of 'literatures in English' rather than 'English literature' if we want to refer to English-language writing from the United Kingdom and its former colonies.

COMMONWEALTH LITERARY STUDIES AND EUROCENTRISM

When in the later 1960s it first became clear that the former colonies were busy producing literatures of their own, the idea that 'English literature' was mutating into 'literatures in English', of which the literary production of England was only one – although still a very important – strand, was still unthinkable. Instead, English critics interested in the writings that came out of the former colonies developed the idea of a 'Commonwealth literature': the English-language literature of the dependencies and former colonies that, with Great Britain at its centre, formed the so-called Commonwealth of Nations, or British Commonwealth. With hindsight, we can see that the idea of a Commonwealth literature followed the hierarchy of the political Commonwealth in that it placed the literature of Great Britain at the centre of this otherwise rather loose configuration. Although Commonwealth literary studies rarely said so explicitly, English literature and English criticism set the norm.

In its early stages, the study of Commonwealth literature was traditionally humanistic. Its critical practice focuses on characters as free moral agents and on character development, and it is less interested in the historical and cultural context – with which it is often unfamiliar – within which they are placed by their creators. It concentrates on the meaning of texts, and assumes that its moral and aesthetic framework has universal validity because it draws on an unchanging, universal human condition. Because that is the case, it can without much further thought be applied to the work of writers ranging from Jamaica to Nigeria and from India to New Zealand. A writer like Chinua Achebe was not primarily seen as Nigerian, or even African, but as contributing to a humanistic English literary tradition. It was this idea that all Commonwealth writers were working within the English tradition that gave the otherwise hopelessly heterogeneous field of Commonwealth studies its unity.

At that time, admission to the ranks of English literature might still have counted as an official stamp of approval for writers from former colonies such as Australia and Canada. However, African, Asian, and Caribbean Commonwealth writers were on the whole not happy with the Western or *Eurocentric* perspective of Commonwealth criticism, not least because their experience of colonial rule had not invariably convinced them of British civilization's humanistic superiority. In the course of the 1970s their objections – voiced in Achebe's 'Colonialist Criticism' and other critiques – began to find a serious echo in the writings of a number of British literary academics who had themselves begun to question the supposedly universal validity of humanist values. These critics argued, first, that overseas writers must be seen within the specific context of the culture of which they were part and which informed their writing; and, second, that that culture was not inferior to, but only different from, the culture of the mother country. This new approach also exposed and contested the ideological underpinnings of the colonialist enterprise (in what was called 'colonial discourse analysis'), and in one important version argued that the relationship between the former colonial powers and their colonies could most rewardingly be analysed with the help of Marxist concepts (with the colonized as the oppressed class). Looked at from this perspective, not only the literatures of other Commonwealth nations but also English literature itself begins to appear in a new light – all of these 'literatures in English' become the site of a struggle over ideology. As I mentioned in the first chapter, English literature was in the course of the nineteenth century introduced in colonial India in order to 'civilize' the colonized elite. From this Marxist perspective, then, the work of Commonwealth writers was either involved in an ideological resistance against (neo)colonial forces or else ideologically complicit with them. (The work of the Trinidadian Nobel Prize-winner V.S. Naipaul has, for instance, been accused of such complicity.)

FROM COMMONWEALTH LITERARY STUDIES TO POSTCOLONIAL QUESTIONS

Over the last thirty years, the question of how we should read writers – such as the Commonwealth writers – who write in a European language but are geographically and often ethnically not European has become more and more pressing. We now find African writers writing in English, French, Afrikaans, and Portuguese, and Caribbean writers writing in English, French, Dutch, and Spanish. These writers may still live in their home country or they may have moved to the *metropolis* – that is, the centre of cultural power in a specific colonial relationship: London, and by extension all of England, for the Commonwealth nations; Paris (or France in general) for the French-speaking colonies. However, wherever they live, the question of how we should read them remains the same. There is now, moreover, a new category of writers that confronts us with the same question. All industrialized Western nations have in the postwar period absorbed substantial numbers of immigrants: people moving in from the former colonies, from labour reservoirs like Turkey and Morocco, and from war zones like Vietnam, Afghanistan, Somalia, and Iraq. The sons and daughters of these immigrants have by now begun to have an impact on the literatures of the places where they have grown up. In so doing they only rarely completely forsake their cultural heritage. Although German-born and educated, German writers of Turkish descent will usually work on the line where their own culture and the majority culture meet. They may, for instance, focus on the position of the Turkish minority and the various ways in which Islamic Turkish culture is forced to adjust to an alien cultural and religious environment. In a nation shaped by immigration like the United States such meetings of culture and the cultural displacements that usually follow from them are standard fare, from the encounters (and clashes) of Native American and English culture in James Fenimore Cooper's early nineteenth-century Leatherstocking novels to the uneasy negotiations between traditional Chinese and modern American culture that we find in

Maxine Hong Kingston's *The Woman Warrior* (1976). For Europe, however, such cultural encounters and the consequent displacements are new. Or perhaps it is more correct to say that the recognition of those encounters is new. After all, most European nations, no matter how small, have cultural and as often as not linguistic minorities within their borders.

As I have suggested above, Commonwealth literary studies saw little difference between English literature and the new literature from overseas. And the same holds true for the Marxist approach that developed in the course of the 1970s. From the perspective of Nigerian or Pakistani writers, Marxism, although fundamentally at odds with liberal humanism, is also alien to their own culture. The emphasis on class in Marxist Commonwealth studies was a valuable contribution, but in its focus on class Marxism, too, was not much interested in the specific cultural context from which a given literary text emerged. With hindsight, it is easy to see the extent to which Commonwealth literary studies was still marked by Eurocentric assumptions.

POSTCOLONIAL STUDIES

In the course of the 1980s Commonwealth literary studies and colonial discourse analysis became part of the then emerging (and now vast) field of literary, cultural, anthropological, political, economic, and historical enquiry into the consequences of (Western) colonization that we call 'postcolonial studies'. In the process, Commonwealth literary studies was radically transformed. Whereas it tacitly assumed common ground between the cultural products of the former colonies and the culture of the metropolis, postcolonial theory and criticism emphasizes the tension between the metropolis and the (former) colonies, between what, within the colonial framework, were the metropolitan, imperial centre and its colonial satellites. At the heart of postcolonial studies we find a trenchant critique of Eurocentrism and a strong focus on those who in one way or another have become the victims of Eurocentric thought (its utilitarian rationality), attitudes (racism), politics (military expansion), exploitation (economic or otherwise), and other unwarranted intrusions. In the field of literary studies it has led to new readings of virtually all canonical works (Shakespeare's *The*

Tempest and Joseph Conrad's *Heart of Darkness*, with their non-European dimensions, are obvious candidates for such new readings) and to a revision and expansion of the canon. This expansion is partly the result of the incorporation of non-European texts that fit the older canon's expectations (and might have been incorporated a good deal earlier), but it also results from a new appreciation of genuinely different aesthetic traditions.

Postcolonial theory and criticism radically questions the aggressively expansionist imperialism of the colonizing powers and in particular the system of values that supported imperialism and that it sees as still dominant within the Western world. It studies the process and the effects of cultural displacement that inevitably followed colonial conquest and rule and its consequences for personal and communal identities, and it studies the ways in which the displaced have offered resistance to colonization. In one of its most important versions, postcolonial theory sees such displacements, and the ambivalences and hybrid cultural forms to which they lead, as vantage points that allow us to expose the internal doubts and the instances of resistance that the West has suppressed in its steamrolling globalizing course and to deconstruct the seamless façade that the combination of imperialism and capitalism has traditionally striven to present. Homi Bhabha, one of the most prominent postcolonial theorists, has put it this way:

> Postcolonial perspectives emerge from the colonial testimony of Third World countries and the discourses of 'minorities' within the geopolitical divisions of east and west, north and south ... They formulate their critical revisions around issues of cultural difference, social authority, and political discrimination in order to reveal the antagonistic and ambivalent moments within the 'rationalizations' of modernity.
>
> (Bhabha 1992: 438)

Here, the postcolonial perspective, just like that of 'the marginal' in general, is a 'substantial intervention into those justifications of modernity – progress, homogeneity, cultural organicism, the deep nation, the long past – that rationalize the authoritarian, "normalizing" tendencies within cultures in the name of national interest' (Bhabha 1990: 4). For Bhabha, the postcolonial perspective has that disruptive potential because the effects of colonialism have in a curious way foreshadowed current poststructuralist views and concerns:

> the encounters and negotiations of differential meanings and values within 'colonial' textuality, its governmental discourses and cultural practices, have enacted, *avant la lettre*, many of the problematics of signification and judgment that have become current in contemporary theory – aporia, ambivalence, indeterminacy, the question of discursive closure, the threat to agency, the status of intentionality, the challenge to 'totalizing' concepts, to name but a few.
>
> (Bhabha 1992: 439)

Bhabha might have added 'otherness' – which he mentions later in the same essay – and which remains a vexing problem: how to deal with *real* otherness, with the absolute 'incommensurability of cultural values and priorities' (439) that has often characterized colonial encounters? Not all postcolonial theorists and critics would agree with Bhabha's suggestion that we can already discern post-structuralist themes and perspectives in colonial situations and that, in a sense, the experiences of the colonial subject and especially the migrant are emblematic for the way we experience ourselves – as 'living on the borderline of the "present"' (Bhabha 1994a: 1) – in the early twenty-first century. They would, however, surely agree with his claim that 'the language of rights and obligations' that operates in the various Western cultures 'must be questioned on the basis of the anomalous and discriminatory legal and cultural status assigned to migrant, diasporic, and refugee populations' (Bhabha 1992: 441).

Bhabha's reference to migrants and refugee populations might raise an important question. What exactly may postcolonial studies rightfully claim as its historical and geographical scope? Some critics have vigorously defended the inclusion of white settler colonies such as Australia, New Zealand, and Canada, arguing that their inhabitants, too, have suffered displacement and marginalization at the hands of imperialism and have been forced to develop cultural identities against the odds of imperial relations. Others have argued that white settler colonies cannot fruitfully be put in one and the same scholarly framework with, for instance, Kenya or India because the question of race does not feature in the relations between white overseas subjects and the metropolis. Those critics claim instead that in settler colonies the postcolonial approach is relevant only for the encounter between (white) settlers and indigenous populations (such as the New Zealand Maori).

And what about the historical range of postcolonial studies? Does colonization start in the wake of Columbus's first voyage to the Americas? Or should we see the late medieval Anglo-Norman conquest and consequent occupation of Ireland already within the framework of colonizing imperialism? There is no easy answer to such questions. However, all postcolonial theorists and critics would agree that they are engaged in a reassessment of the traditional relationship between the metropolis and its colonial subjects and in the radical deconstruction – along either poststructuralist or more traditional lines – of the imperialist perspective. They agree in their focus on colonial (and neocolonial) oppression, on resistance to colonization, on the respective identities of colonizer and colonized, on patterns of interaction between those subjectivities, on postcolonial migration to the metropolis, on cultural exchanges between colonizer and colonized, on hybridity, and on other, related themes. Central to these interests are issues of race, indigeneity, ethnicity, language, gender, identity, class, and, above all, power. Postcolonial theorists and critics would also agree on the relevance of their enterprise for the world of the early twenty-first century, from which colonies may have (largely) disappeared, but in which neocolonial relations abound – not only between Western nations and their former colonies but within those countries, between national majorities and ethnic minorities.

ORIENTALISM

With all due respect for the pioneering work done by postcolonial writers such as Edward Brathwaite, George Lamming, Wilson Harris, Chinua Achebe, and Wole Soyinka, postcolonial studies in its current form starts in 1978, with the publication of the Palestinian-American critic Edward Said's book *Orientalism*. Drawing primarily on Foucault, Said's study deeply influenced the agenda of the study of non-Western cultures and their literatures and pushed it in the direction of what we now call 'postcolonial theory'.

Orientalism is a devastating critique of how through the ages, but particularly in the nineteenth century – the heyday of imperialist expansion, which is the book's focus – Western texts have represented the East, and specifically the Islamic Middle East (for the sake of convenience I will simply refer to 'the Orient' or 'the East'). Using mostly British and French 'scholarly works ... works of literature, political tracts, journalistic texts, travel books, religious and philological studies' (Said [1978] 1991: 23), Said examines how these texts *construct* the Orient through imaginative representations (in, for instance, novels), through seemingly factual descriptions (in journalistic reports and travel writing), and through claims to knowledge about Oriental history and culture (histories, anthropological writings, academic studies). Together, all these texts constitute a Foucauldian discourse – a loose system of statements, claims, and the like that constitutes a discursive field within which knowledge concerning a particular subject matter is constructed: 'without examining Orientalism as a discourse one cannot possibly understand the enormously systematic discipline by which European culture was able to manage – *and even produce* – the Orient politically, sociologically, militarily, ideologically, scientifically and imaginatively during the post-Enlightenment period' (3). For Said, Orientalism has legitimized Western imperialism in the eyes of Western governments and their electorates and it has also insidiously worked to convince the East that Western culture represented universal civilization. Accepting Western culture could only benefit the East's inhabitants and would make them participants in the most advanced civilization the world had ever seen.

For Said, Western representations of the Orient, no matter how well intentioned, have always been part of this damaging discourse. Even those Orientalists who were clearly in sympathy with Oriental peoples and their cultures – and Said finds a substantial number of them – have unintentionally contributed to Western domination. So, instead of disinterested objectivity, we find representations tainted by Western subjectivity – not to mention outright, even if unconscious, fantasy – that have effectively paved the way for military domination, cultural displacement, and economic exploitation. Although we 'ought never to assume that the structure of Orientalism is nothing more than a structure of lies or myths', Said argues that 'Orientalism is more particularly valuable as a sign of European-Atlantic power over the Orient than it is as veridic discourse about the Orient' (Said [1978] 1991: 4). I should perhaps say at this point that in later publications, and in response to criticism, Said has presented a less homogeneous picture of Orientalism, while he has also acknowledged the importance of the response of native writers to the West's Orientalism. There is no doubt, however, that *Orientalism*, whatever its shortcomings may have been, revolutionized the way Western scholars and critics looked at representations of non-Western subjects and cultures.

Said's book also drew attention to the way in which the discourse of Orientalism serves to create the West just as it creates the East. West and East form a binary opposition in which the two poles define each other (see Chapter 5). The inferiority that Orientalism implicitly attributes to the East, in spite of its acknowledged achievements, simultaneously serves to construct the West's superiority. As Said puts it, 'European culture gained in strength and identity by setting itself off against the Orient as a sort of surrogate and even underground self' (3). The sensuality, irrationality, primitiveness, and despotism of the East constructs the West as rational, democratic, and progressive. The West always functions as the 'centre' and the East is a marginal 'other' that simply through its existence confirms the West's centrality and superiority.

Not surprisingly, perhaps, the opposition that the West's discourse about the East sets up makes use of another basic opposition – that between the masculine and the feminine. Naturally, the West functions as the masculine pole – enlightened, rational, entrepreneurial, disciplined – while the East is its feminine opposition: irrational, passive, undisciplined, and sensual. Once we have been alerted to this opposition we have no trouble finding it exemplified. Here is a passage from *A Short Walk in the Hindu Kush* (1958), a classic of travel writing by the English writer Eric Newby:

> there was a sudden outburst of screams and moans from the other side of the road, becoming more and more insistent and finally mounting to such a crescendo that I went to investigate.
>
> Gathered round a well or shaft full of the most loathsome sewage was a crowd of gendarmes in their ugly sky-blue uniforms and several women in a state of happy hysteria, one screaming more loudly than the rest.

'What is it?'

'*Bābā*,' said one of the policemen, pointing to the seething mess at our feet and measuring the length of quite a small baby. He began to keen; presumably he was the father. I waited a little, no one did anything.

This was the moment I had managed to avoid all my life; the rescue of the comrade under fire, the death-leaper from Hammersmith Bridge saved by Newby, the tussle with the lunatic with the cut-throat razor.

Feeling absurd and sick with anticipation I plunged head first into the muck. It was only four feet deep and quite warm but unbelievable, a real eastern sewer. The first time I got hold of something cold and clammy that was part of an American packing case. The second time I found nothing and came up sputtering and sick to find the mother beating a serene little boy of five who had watched the whole performance from the house next door into which he had strayed. The crowd was already dispersing; the policeman gave me tea and let me change in the station house but the taste and smell remained.

(Newby [1958] 1974: 62–63)

Admittedly, the irony of Newby's highly entertaining book is also, and consistently, directed at the author himself – and at his companion – but in emergencies it is their character that makes the difference. We see this even in a more recent and, with regard to the representation of the East, far more sophisticated travel book – *The Places in Between* (2004) by the redoubtable Rory Stewart – who in the winter of 2002 walked through the wilds of central Afghanistan from Herat to Kabul. (One might add that this author exemplifies empire in his personal history: born in Hong Kong and raised in Malaysia and Scotland.) Stewart is a highly sympathetic outsider who even speaks the local language, but in his fascinating narrative he is a beacon of reason in an unpredictable, dangerous, and often medieval world.

Race, ethnicity, and the dominant position of the metropolis were already well established on the literary-critical agenda when *Orientalism* appeared, as was the study of Commonwealth writing and that of English literature dealing with colonial relations (E.M. Forster's *A Passage to India* (1924), for instance). Said, however, was the first to draw on the new French theory and on the recently discovered Gramsci in dealing with what are now called postcolonial themes. *Orientalism* offered a challenging theoretical framework and a new perspective on the interpretation of European writing about the East (and other non-European cultures) and, perhaps even more importantly, on writing produced under colonial rule. Whereas in the study of Commonwealth writing novels from, say, India, Pakistan, or Kenya were seen to have heterogeneous, discrete backgrounds, each with its own particulars, now all such novels could be read within one unifying theoretical framework. Said's book also highlighted the role of Europe's cultural institutions (the universities, literature, newspapers, museums, to mention only a few) in its military, economic, and cultural domination of non-European nations and peoples, and asked questions that we still ask concerning literature's role in past and present racial, ethnic, and cultural encounters. As a matter of fact, our questions have only proliferated since 1978. Can we, for instance, really see all Western writings about Said's Orient – and, by implication, the non-West in general – as more or less indistinguishable from each other as far as their representations of the non-Western world are concerned? Mary-Louise Pratt's *Imperial Eyes* (1992) argues convincingly that travel writing by women about the non-West is rather different from travel writing by men. Said himself would be the first to admit that such differences are real enough, and postcolonial criticism is still busy mapping them.

COLONIZED AND COLONIZER

Orientalism does not address the question of what happens in the cultural interaction between colonizer and colonized. However, this topic is central to the work of Homi Bhabha. In earlier writings on colonialism, such an interaction was often denied. Aimé Césaire, for instance, claimed in *Discourse on Colonialism* (1955) that between colonizer and colonized there is '[n]o human contact, but relations of domination and submission which turn the colonizing man into a classroom monitor, an army sergeant, a prison guard, a slave driver, and the indigenous man into an instrument of production' (Césaire [1955] 1997: 81). British and French official accounts of colonial life generally presented a wholly different, and benign, view of colonialism, but saw just as little interaction between colonizer and colonized. The colonizer remained his civilized and disciplined European self even in the most trying circumstances. The West has always been convinced that its presence overseas greatly affected the 'natives' (telling itself that the smartest and most sensitive of them immediately started scrambling to adopt Western ways and values), but has never been comfortable with the idea that its sons and daughters might in turn be affected by the cultures they encountered. It is mostly in literature that we find alternative perspectives. In Joseph Conrad's *Heart of Darkness* (1899) the colonial experience has the effect of turning the ivory collector Kurtz into a megalomaniacal barbarian; and in E.M. Forster's *A Passage to India* (1924) two British women suffer experiences in India that permanently unsettle them.

For Bhabha, who is a major theorist of the subjectivities of colonizer and colonized, their encounter always affects both. Said's *Orientalism* analyses the process by which Orientalist discourse sets up a binary opposition between Europe and the Orient, between colonizer and colonized, but Bhabha sets out to deconstruct that opposition, at least on the level of the subjects involved. Colonialism, with the displacements and terrible uncertainties that it brings, is such a radically unsettling 'affective experience of marginality' (Bhabha 1992: 438) that the colonized subject's plight can be seen as prefiguring poststructuralist decentring. But the colonial experience also affects the colonizer. More specifically, for Bhabha, the colonizer cannot escape a complex and paradoxical relationship with the colonized. Drawing on Lacan's views of the way identity is constructed, Bhabha offers us analyses in which the identity of the colonizer – in Bhabha's work the British colonizer of India – cannot very well be separated from that of the colonized. Instead of being self-sufficient with regard to his identity ('his' because colonialism is an almost exclusively male enterprise), the colonizer at least partly constructs it through interaction with the colonized. The colonizer's identity has no 'origin' in himself and is not a fixed entity, but is differential, a product of relations. The identity of the colonizer as colonizer can become a 'reality' only after the colonial contact that truly confirms it.

Bhabha sees signs of the colonizer's partial dependency on none-too-friendly 'others' – and the resulting inherent uncertainty – in a range of phenomena. Racial stereotyping, for instance, first of all repeats this process of identity-creation in that it construes not only those who are stereotyped but the stereotyper himself – in opposition to the stereotyped. It functions to construe or confirm the stereotyper's identity. However, the repetitiveness of acts of stereotyping points to a continuing uncertainty in the stereotyper: apparently the stereotyper has to convince himself over and over again of the truthfulness of the stereotype – and thus, by extension, of his own identity. The self-confidence of the colonizer is further undermined by what Bhabha calls *mimicry* – the always slightly alien and distorted way in which the colonized, either out of choice or under duress, will repeat the colonizer's ways and discourse. This is exemplified in Wole Soyinka's plays *The Road* (1965) and *Death and the King's Horseman* (1975), and in V.S. Naipaul's significantly titled novel *The Mimic Men* (1967). In mimicry the colonizer sees himself in a mirror that slightly but effectively distorts his image – that subtly and unsettlingly 'others' his own identity. And mimicry may play a part in 'sly civility', a seemingly submissive attitude that still succeeds in conveying the colonized's sense of independence, if not superiority. More than sixty years after the end of Dutch colonial rule over the Dutch East Indies (now Indonesia) the Dutch language still has the expression 'Oost-Indisch doof' – deaf in the East Indies way – which means that an addressee has heard and understood a question or an order perfectly well, but simply refuses to acknowledge it, thus forcing the speaker, who is fully aware of that refusal, to repeat him- or herself – a procedure that over time becomes highly embarrassing.

The colonizer's discourse, his most effective weapon in the cultural encounter, is also less stable and less secure than he thinks. One reason is that stereotyping is a basic element of colonial discourse. Because it is one of its mainstays, colonial discourse cannot possibly be as authoritative as it would like to be (and as it presents itself). Apart from this, the colonizer's language is always subject to the effects of Derridean *différance* and is therefore never fully under his control. Colonial power is thus always under the threat of destabilization. Its lack of complete control is, as we have just seen, partly due to reasons that have nothing to do with either colonizer or colonized. But colonial power's lack of complete control is also the result of acts of conscious resistance on the part of the colonized. In the physical encounter between colonizer and colonized the latter may, for instance, refuse to meet his oppressor's gaze and in so doing reject 'the narcissistic demand that [he] should be addressed directly, that the Other should authorize the self, recognize its priority, fulfill its outlines' (Bhabha 1994a: 98).

Perhaps the most influential of Bhabha's contributions to postcolonial theory is his notion of *hybridity*. In his rather inhospitable prose, 'hybridity is a problematic of colonial representation and individuation that reverses the effects of the colonialist disavowal, so that other "denied" knowledges enter upon the dominant discourse and estrange the basis of its authority' (115). While Said's *Orientalism* keeps the spheres of colonizer and colonized rather firmly apart, Bhabha, with his interest in their interaction, sees important movements going both ways. Shifting his focus from 'the noisy command of colonial authority' and 'the silent repression of native traditions', to 'the colonial hybrid', Bhabha argues that the cultural interaction of colonizer and colonized leads to a fusion of cultural forms that from one perspective, because it signals its 'productivity', confirms the power of the colonial presence, but that as a form of mimicry simultaneously 'unsettles the mimetic or narcissistic demands of colonial power' (112). Hybridity 'intervenes in the exercise of authority not merely to indicate the impossibility of its identity but to represent the unpredictability of its presence' (114). Like most of Bhabha's notions, hybridization and hybridity – which seem to present an in-between position, halfway between two cultures of equal weight and power – thus get positive connotations. In fact, Bhabha's application of poststructuralist theorizing to colonial and postcolonial relations has more generally positive overtones. Some critics have objected that this is armchair theorizing which in its 'reconciliatory' approach (Simon During) takes the sharp edges off the colonial encounter and cannot have much relevance in the analysis of the everyday practice of colonial rule. For them, poststructuralist theory leads Bhabha to see the identity and position of the colonizer as far too precarious and to see those of the colonized in a far more positive light than is warranted. The gun you are carrying as a fledgling colonizer may not fundamentally strengthen your identity, but it may give it enough of a boost to disregard all signs of mimicry that you are likely to encounter. Other critics have objected to what they see as Bhabha's tendency to romanticize the in-between position, the 'double consciousness' – Bhabha's term – of the colonized and of migrants who, because they are by definition between cultures, are granted an awareness of relativity and an insight into their own and others' positions that may not come as naturally or be experienced as positively as Bhabha would seem to think. In Chinua Achebe's *Things Fall Apart* such a double consciousness is seen as divisive and destructive. As one of the wise elders in the novel says

> The white man is very clever. He came quietly and peaceably with his religion. We were amused at his foolishness and allowed him to stay. Now he has won our brothers, and our clan can no longer act like one. He has put a knife on the things that held us together and we have fallen apart.
>
> (Achebe [1958] 1967: 160)

In the historical and partly autobiographical novel *Bumi Manusia* (1980; *This Earth of Mankind*) by the Indonesian author Pramoedya Ananta Tur, a young boy belonging to the Javan aristocracy is delighted to be admitted to a Dutch school only to discover that what he gains in knowledge is outweighed by the loss of his original identity, and that he will never gain real access to the colonizer's world. In Kiran Desai's *The Inheritance of Loss* (2006), too, 'in-betweenness' is not a viable option and its main character returns in disillusionment to the Indian subcontinent (where he is subsequently robbed of all his American savings). A 'double consciousness' may surely bring the broadened perspective that Bhabha associates with it, but it might equally be a painful rather than an enlightening condition. And, of course, it may be both.

A final criticism concerns the level of abstraction at which Bhabha's work often operates. Marxist and feminist critics have argued that there can be no such thing as a generalized encounter between colonizer and colonized. To them, a theory that addresses the colonial situation without paying serious attention to the differences between men and women and to socio-economic circumstances cannot do justice to the heterogeneity of the colonial encounter. For Marxist critics, especially, Bhabha's exclusive interest in the psychoanalytic dimension of that encounter – the subjectivities involved – while disregarding its economic framework is a serious deficiency. However, Bhabha's focus on interaction and his notion of hybridity have sharpened our awareness of what actually happens (or may happen) in the colonial or postcolonial situation. Whereas Said prompts us to question Western representations of the East, Bhabha asks us to submit the actual encounter between West and East – in his case India – to the closest (psychoanalytic) scrutiny.

THE SUBALTERN

Postcolonial Marxists such as Aijaz Ahmad have perhaps unfairly suggested that Bhabha and other 'Westernized' non-Europeans are hardly in the best position to speak for the colonized and neocolonized masses. The third postcolonial theorist I will consider here, Gayatri Chakravorty Spivak, has no trouble admitting that her position as an academic working in the West separates her from the masses of India, her country of origin. At the same time, however, she has drawn our attention to that large majority of the colonized that has left no mark upon history because it could not, or was not allowed to, make itself heard. Many millions have come and gone under the colonial dispensation without leaving a trace: men and even more so women. Since colonized women almost by definition went unheard within their own patriarchal culture, they were doubly unheard under a colonial regime. Spivak can be said to be the first postcolonial theorist with a feminist agenda. That agenda includes the complicity of female writers with imperialism. 'It should not be possible to read nineteenth-century British fiction without remembering that imperialism, understood as England's social mission, was a crucial part of the cultural representation of England to the English,' Spivak tells us in her 1985 essay 'Three Women's Texts and a Critique of Imperialism' (Spivak [1985] 1995b: 269). Noting that '[t]he role of literature in the production of cultural representation should not be ignored' (269), she goes on to analyse, in terms of cultural representation, Charlotte Brontë's *Jane Eyre* (1847) and the way in which it chooses to present the 'Creole' Bertha Mason – the mad wife of Jane's future husband Rochester. For Spivak, too, the so-called 'metropolitan' subject defines itself either explicitly or implicitly through its encounter, real or imagined, with the non-European 'other'. Spivak's insistence on the importance of feminist perspectives is part of a larger role that she has played over the last three decades: that of the theoretical conscience of postcolonial studies. Freely drawing on Marxism, feminism, and deconstruction, her work has as much addressed theoretical shortcomings in postcolonial theorizing and what she sees as simplifying approaches of 'otherness' as it has focused on postcolonial issues itself.

Spivak represents the voice of difference among the major post-colonial theorists. In spite of their poststructuralist sources of inspiration, Said and Bhabha do not focus upon the question of difference. As I have pointed out, feminist scholars have argued that female representations of the Orient are different from male ones. Bhabha, too, makes no difference between men and women in his theorizing of the interaction between colonizer and colonized. Said and Bhabha also largely ignore cultural difference. Setting up his opposition between Europe and the Orient, Said is not much interested in the differences between the various European cultures – Protestant or Catholic, liberal or authoritarian – he puts on the rack in *Orientalism*, while Bhabha, with his focus on subjectivity, writes as if the interaction of colonizer and colonized can be completely separated from the cultures involved. Spivak, however, is attentive to difference, to heterogeneity, even within feminism itself: she has taken Western feminism to task for operating within a horizon determined by white, middle-class, and heterosexual preoccupations.

As we might expect from a theorist who is as sensitive to difference as Spivak is, social class – which also plays little role in Said or Bhabha – is one of her major analytic categories. Of all postcolonial theorists, Spivak has most consistently focused on what in postcolonial studies has come to be called the *subaltern*: the category of those in the lowest social positions (in the military terms that are always appropriate to the colonial situation, the lowest ranks). Spivak employs the term (which derives from Gramsci) to describe the lowest and least powerful layers of colonial and postcolonial (or, as many would say, neocolonial) society: the homeless, the unemployed, the subsistence farmers, the day labourers. She is aware, however, that categorizations by way of class, too, tend to make difference invisible: 'one must nevertheless insist that the colonized subaltern *subject* is irretrievably heterogeneous' (Spivak [1988] 1995a: 26). One result of this attentiveness to difference is Spivak's focus on the female subaltern, a very large – and of course differentiated – category among the colonized that, she argues, has traditionally been doubly marginalized: 'If, in the context of colonial production, the subaltern has no history and cannot speak, the subaltern as female is even more deeply in shadow' (28).

This focus does not mean that she speaks for – or has the intention of speaking for – the female subaltern. Rather, she is motivated by the desire to save the female subaltern from misrepresentation. In a famous essay from 1988, 'Can the Subaltern Speak? Speculations on Widow Sacrifice' (expanded in her *Critique of Postcolonial Reason* (1999)), Spivak, in the wider context of a critique of what she sees as appropriations of the colonial subject, examines the nineteenth-century controversy between the colonized Indians and their British colonizers over what she calls 'widow sacrifice': the burning of widows on the funeral pyres of their deceased husbands. Spivak concludes that neither party allowed women – the victims of this practice – to speak. The British texts construct a position for the woman in which she is made to represent Western individualism and, by implication, a superior Western civilization that emphasizes modern freedom, while the Indian ones present her as choosing duty and tradition. Although both parties claim that they have them on their side, the women themselves remain unheard. It is this concern with misrepresentation that led Spivak to intervene in the project of the so-called Subaltern Studies group, a number of Indian historians who try to write history outside the frameworks of both colonialism and Indian elite politics. For Spivak, the naïve traditional faith in reconstructing history of the Subaltern Studies group – 'real historical experience', as one of them put it – no matter how well intentioned, could lead only to further damage. It is because we must take the subaltern seriously that we cannot speak for her. In later publications Spivak took a far more positive view of at least the contemporary subaltern's position, first arguing that 'the "subaltern" must be rethought' because '[s]/he is no longer cut off from lines of access to the centre' (Spivak 2000: 319) and later that 'the subaltern cultures need to be known in such a way that we can suture their re-activated cultural axiomatics into the principles of Enlightenment' (Spivak 2004: 538), a project that is apparently possible.

Spivak combines an emphasis on class as a differentiating factor with a deconstructionist approach to texts and to identity. In one way the decentred subject of deconstruction serves her purpose well: it radically undermines all essentialist pretensions on the part of colonizer and neocolonizer and it equally undermines the post-colonial fundamentalism – and some of the absolutist leanings of theory – for which she has little patience. In her analyses of, and attacks on, forms of renascent essentialism she again acts as post-colonial theory's theoretical conscience. On the other hand, deco-lonized nations and cultures, just like the political movements of the decolonized, arguably need some sort of identity that does not immediately deconstruct itself. A political platform that takes itself apart in public cannot be very effective. In her earlier work, Spivak's solution to this dilemma is what she calls a '*strategic* use of positivist essentialism' that is not afraid to put forward a clear poli-tical agenda but remains fully aware of its constructed under-pinnings. But here, too, she has moved towards what one might, with some trepidation, call a more traditional position, telling us that 'after I gave up my apologetic formula for Subaltern Studies (which the collective did not need anyway): strategic use of essen-tialism', she 'found instead a different one emerging from my own subaltern study: learning to learn from below' (Spivak 2000: 326).

POSTCOLONIAL STUDIES IN THE TWENTY-FIRST CENTURY

As this call for a political strategy illustrates, postcolonial studies soon ranged far and wide beyond its original literary provenance. It now discusses contemporary events and developments in post-colonial cultural studies and postcolonial media studies; it has pushed its historical interest back to the medieval period (the Crusades and their encounters with the Muslim world) and even to antiquity; it studies religions and concepts of the sacred; it has taken on board the ecological effects of colonialism (following up on Alfred W. Crosby's *Ecological Imperialism: The Biological Expansion of Europe, 900–1900* (1986)); it examines how the body has been a site of oppression (and of resistance); it has discovered and opened a fruitful dialogue with Latin American studies; it studies postcolonial films, dance, and sports – there seems no end to its interests, which also extends to the original colonizing nations. As Ato Quayson recently remarked, with reference to 'diasporic writing', 'we find that Britain, Germany, France, and the Netherlands may be productively understood as themselves being postcolonialized by people from their erstwhile margins' (Quayson 2012b: 366). This should not surprise us, of course. After all, three-quarters of the globe has at one time or another been colonized, and colonization affects the whole life-world of the colonized while simultaneously it is a contributing factor in the constitution of the colonizer's subjectivity.

Although in the field in which postcolonial studies originated, that of literary studies, Said, Bhabha, and Spivak remain important, in recent years postcolonial studies in its current, much more encompassing incarnation can be said to have moved away considerably from its poststructuralist inspiration, even if in some areas it remains very much aware of poststructuralist concerns (as, for instance, in studies of the postcolonial body). This broadening of the field has led to criticisms of postcolonial studies' earlier, primarily literary bias. So we find the cultural critic Simon Featherstone pointing out that one of the standard readers in the field – Ashcroft, Griffiths, and Tiffin's *Postcolonial Studies Reader* – does not present such important postcolonial politicians as Gandhi, Mao, Kwame Nkrumah, Julius Nyerere, Kenneth Kaunda, Amilcar Cabral, Ho Chi Minh, 'or any other of the first generation of postcolonial leaders and theorists' (Featherstone 2005: 19). In *Postcolonial Studies and Beyond*, edited by Ania Loomba *et al.*, we find a similar – although very politely phrased – critique: 'A keynote' of the volume, the editors tell us, 'is the reassertion of a certain historical urgency that may have been leached from postcolonial studies during its period of theoretical refinement and institutional consolidation' (Loomba *et al.* 2005: 5). For many of the contributors to *Postcolonial Studies and Beyond*, some of the central assumptions of postcolonial studies will have to be rethought. Its 'refinement' and 'consolidation' have harmed its political relevance and its focus on texts and subjectivities will not enable postcolonial critics to arrive at an understanding of the processes of globalization that have followed in the wake of decolonization and that arguably constitute one of the most important developments of the last thirty years. Other critics, focusing on indigenous peoples and their plight, point out that these as often as not defend homogeneous identities, myths of origin, a bond with land regarded as sacred, and other values that they see as essential to their survival but that cannot very well be reconciled with poststructuralist assumptions (see, for instance, Stam and Shohat 2012).

Some critics claim that colonialism was more ambivalent than postcolonial studies has been willing to admit and call for a balanced approach to its history and legacy. In a recent exchange on the current state of postcolonial studies Simon During argues that

> colonialism involved expropriation after expropriation, oppression after oppression, atrocity after atrocity. Nonetheless, even among those very aware of this, it has long been recognized that there is also a strong case for arguing that empire brought benefits to its subject peoples too. Marx himself came early to this cause.
>
> (During 2012: 333)

Others, like Benita Parry – another participant in this exchange – reject this position as 'accommodationist' (Parry 2012: 352) and defend what During calls an 'anticolonialist' line, with a strong focus on political economy. Especially Parry and Robert Young (the latter in *Postcolonialism: An Historical Introduction* (2001) and other books) have worked to ask attention for 'a politics grounded in the material, social and existential', as Parry put it in a 2002 article (Parry 2002: 77). (Young, by the way, should also be mentioned for his positive valuation of such 'traditional' issues as religion, nationalism, and pan-Africanism.)

There is, then, no shortage of views on colonialism or on the colonial subject, whose subjectivity and agency – or lack of it – are still hotly disputed. But I should not hide that outside the somewhat closed world of Western theory there is also serious doubt about the importance of all this. As Simon Gikandi – an expert on African and Caribbean literature – and other critics have observed in recent years, postcolonial theory has had a lukewarm or even hostile reception in much of the postcolonial world.

But let me return to postcolonial writing. In her overview of postcolonial literature in English, C.L. Innes tells us that '[c]ritics have sometimes described postcolonial literatures as very roughly falling into several phases: literature of resistance; literature of national consolidation; literature of disillusion and/or neocolonialism; post-postcolonial literature; and diaspora literature' (Innes 2007: 17). It is indeed easy enough to find, for instance, novels that exemplify these phases, even in the career of one single novelist. Achebe's *Things Fall Apart* fits well into the resistance phase, while his *Anthills of the Savannah* (1987), like Ngugi's *Petals of Blood* (1977), with its emphasis on Nigeria's internal tensions and its corruption, exemplifies post-independence disillusionment. Wole Soyinka's memoir *Aké* (1981), which celebrates Yoruba culture, might be seen as representing the literature of national consolidation. We also find texts that with great and almost mocking self-confidence deal with colonization and its aftermath. Here are the first two stanzas of the Jamaican poet Louise Bennett's 'Colonization in Reverse', published four years after Jamaica's independence in 1962:

Wat a joyful news, Miss Mattie,
I feel like heart gwine burs'
Jamaica people colonizing
England in Reverse
By de hundred, by de t'ousan
From country and from town,
By de ship-load, by de plane-load
Jamaica is Englan boun.

(Bennett [1966] 1983: 107–08)

Not surprisingly, it is especially diaspora literature in which hybridity is a recurrent motif. V.S. Naipaul's *The Enigma of Arrival* (1987), Kiran Desai's *The Inheritance of Loss* (2006), Hari Kunzru's significantly titled *Transmission* (2004), and a host of other novels in English, French, German, and Dutch have postcolonial or diasporic identity as a central theme. Under the influence of important theorists like Bhabha, the postcolonial in general was often 'associated', in Elleke Boehmer's terms, 'with metropolitan, diasporic, migrant and minority spaces for which the nation as a horizon of expectation had retreated' (Boehmer 2005: 247). But the most recent generation of postcolonial writers has moved beyond hybridity.

They 'work', to quote Boehmer again, 'to build local "structures of feeling" positioned at several removes from the dominant North, drawn from their life worlds' (250), to the point that contemporary African novelists 'turn increasingly towards local audiences and narrative traditions, and away from the implied European reader' (251). In what seems indeed a post-postcolonial development, the former colonizer, the metropolis, no longer dominates the cultural horizon.

SUMMARY

Postcolonial studies critically analyses the relationship between colonizer and colonized from the earliest days of exploration and colonization. Drawing on Foucault's notion of 'discourses', on Gramsci's 'hegemony', on deconstruction, and, as the case may be, on Marxism, it focuses on the role of texts, literary and otherwise, in the colonial enterprise. It examines how these texts construct the colonizer's (usually masculine) superiority and the colonized's (usually effeminate) inferiority and in so doing have legitimated colonization. It is especially attentive to postcolonial attitudes – attitudes of resistance – on the part of the colonized and seeks to understand the nature of the encounter between colonizer and colonized. With regard to literature, it argues that 'English literature' and 'American literature' have in the postwar period been replaced by 'literatures in English', a term that captures the multicultural and multi-ethnic nature of current writing in English. It is especially, although by no means exclusively, interested in postcolonial rewritings of English classics – Marina Warner's *Indigo, or Mapping the Waters* (1992), Coetzee's *Foe* (1987) – that contest the implicit ideology of the original, and in texts that in other ways critically analyse the colonial relationship. Given the fact that most of Western Europe's nations – and, arguably, the United States – have been involved in imperialist projects that culturally, and often physically, displaced 'native' populations, postcolonial studies covers a large period of Western history and a vast geographical area. More recently, it has paid close attention to how for new generations of writers in postcolonial nations the colonial horizon would seem to be disappearing from sight.

SUGGESTIONS FOR FURTHER READING

The importance of postcolonial criticism within contemporary literary studies is reflected in the number of good introductions that have appeared in the last ten years. Elleke Boehmer's *Colonial and Postcolonial Literature: Migrant Metaphors* (2nd ed. 2005) provides a very readable historical overview of literary writing from both the colonial and the postcolonial periods that in one way or another is concerned with imperialism. Other useful guides include Gareth Griffiths, *African Literatures in English, East and West* (2000), Nicholas Harrison, *Postcolonial Criticism: History, Theory, and the Work of Fiction* (2003), Alison Donnell, *Twentieth-Century Caribbean Literature: Critical Moments in Anglophone Literary History* (2006), and S. Patke Rajeev, *Postcolonial Poetry in English* (2006). *Postcolonial Criticism* (1997), edited by Bart Moore-Gilbert, Gareth Stanton, and Willy Maley, has a very useful and relatively brief introduction and presents essays and excerpts from a broad range of postcolonial critiques plus numerous suggestions for further reading. Moore-Gilbert's *Postcolonial Theory* (1997) is an excellent introduction to postcolonial studies' major theorists and to the tensions between theory and criticism. Ania Loomba's *Colonialism/Postcolonialism* (2nd ed. 2005) complements these studies because of the attention she pays to questions of gender and sexuality. The historian Robert Young's *Postcolonialism: An Historical Introduction* (2001) is a Marxist-oriented activist intervention in the discussion, as is Benita Parry's *Postcolonial Studies: A Materialist Critique* (2004), which, like Young's book, critiques the poststructuralist orientation of much of the work in postcolonial studies. *The Routledge Companion to Postcolonial Studies* (2007), edited by John McLeod, offers essays on colonialism's major theatres of operation, on various postcolonial 'locations', and on postcolonial approaches. *The Cambridge Companion to Postcolonial Literary Studies* (2004), edited by Neil Lazarus, is a collection of excellent essays, although not all of them are equally concerned with literature, while his *The Postcolonial Unconscious* (2011), with its discussions of Jameson, Fanon, and Said, pursues the political in the postcolonial. For those interested in what happens outside the sphere of Anglo-American criticism, there is Charles Forsdick and David Murphy's *Francophone Postcolonial Studies: A Critical Introduction* (2003). With *The Cambridge Introduction to*

Postcolonial Literatures in English (2007) by C.L. Innes, we return to postcolonial literature (including Irish and Australian literature), the last word about which has, at least for now, been provided by the massive *Cambridge History of Postcolonial Literature* (2012a), edited by Ato Quayson.

The Postcolonial Studies Reader (2nd ed. 2005), edited by Bill Ashcroft, Gareth Griffiths, and Helen Tiffin, is one of the standard readers in the field and contains a wealth of material on the major issues. *Key Concepts in Post-Colonial Studies* (1998), compiled by the same editors, offers brief and lucid discussions of not just the key concepts but an impressive list of minor terms, and so does a more recent book, Gina Wisker's *Key Concepts in Postcolonial Literature* (2006). Finally, Edward Said's *Orientalism* (1978) still offers one of the best opportunities to see an important form of postcolonial analysis in action.

9

SEXUALITY, LITERATURE, AND CULTURE

In the previous chapters we have repeatedly seen how exclusion and marginalization are basic to the organization of Western culture, and presumably to the organization of all cultures. Differences that are in themselves neutral become the starting-point for oppositions in which one of the poles of the opposition is privileged at the expense of the other. The centres and margins that are thus created together constitute a structure that underlies the culture that seems 'natural' to us and governs our 'natural', commonsensical assumptions.

Until fairly recently critical interest was primarily focused on the three areas of difference – gender, race, and class – that seemed to be most central in the way Western culture has organized itself over the ages. (Other areas of difference are age – with the opposition young/old – and place – with the opposition urban/rural.) Gender, race, and class were shown to have provided abundant sources for cultural self-definition through a wide range of binary oppositions. Feminism and feminist-inspired cultural studies, for instance, demonstrated how gender pervades Western culture – with its standard privileging of 'masculinity' – and even invades categories such as 'race' that are at first sight totally unrelated to the gender issue. A great many colonial texts contrast the masculine white colonizer to equally male colonial subjects that are presented in feminine terms. Gender and race have traditionally gone together in organizing the West's response to non-Western peoples and in establishing Western subjectivity.

Since the 1980s a fourth area of difference – sexuality – has gained prominence as an important principle of social and cultural organization. The exclusions and marginalizations that we see with regard to sexuality – think, for instance, of the stigmatization of homosexuals – are seen by a number of influential theorists as equally pertinent to the way Western culture is organized as other structural exclusions. In fact, some theorists even see sexuality as the *central* principle of social organization. Before I get around to that, however, I will first sketch some of the developments that led up to this relatively new theoretical angle, which, although it emerged within literary studies, was strongly interdisciplinary from the beginning and in the course of the 1990s shifted in the direction of cultural studies.

LESBIAN AND GAY CRITICISM

Sexuality and literature first became an issue within the feminist movement. In its early stages, feminism spoke, or at least seemed to speak, on behalf of all women. A common female front against what looked strongly like a common oppression seemed only natural. In the course of the 1970s, however, various groups within the feminist movement began to express their dissatisfaction with a collective feminism that they increasingly saw as shaped by the interests of the dominant group within the movement: white, middle-class, college-educated, heterosexual women. As a result, the groups that did not or could not identify with this mainstream image gradually broke away to formulate their own feminisms. These breakaway communities included groups of black feminists, Chicana feminists, and, most important for this chapter, lesbian feminists. For a good many lesbian feminists, the subversiveness of mainstream feminism did not extend to sexuality. While mainstream feminists questioned traditional views of gender, they failed to question similarly traditional views of same-sex relations. As a result, lesbian feminism turned away from mainstream feminism to pursue its own, separate path.

Lesbian feminism in turn led to lesbian literary criticism. In 1975 Jane Rule published her pioneering *Lesbian Images*, and with Lillian

Faderman's comprehensive *Surpassing the Love of Men: Romantic Friendship and Love between Women from the Renaissance to the Present* (1981) lesbian criticism definitively established itself. However, the vanguard of critics that tried to lay out the ground rules for a specific lesbian criticism found that a focus on lesbianism in literature runs into serious practical problems. In the words of one critic:

> What is a lesbian text? Is it one describing lesbian relationships? Is it one written by a lesbian author? Is it one in which hidden kinds of pleasure are offered to an implied lesbian reader? Are texts lesbian if neither author nor content are *explicitly* lesbian? How much of a text has to be about lesbianism to be regarded as 'lesbian'?
>
> (Humm 1995: 162)

And what, for that matter, is a lesbian, exactly? The answer might seem fairly straightforward, but it is easy enough to ask questions that complicate the picture. For instance, are sexual acts a necessary condition? Should we consider a woman who has felt a strong and life-long attraction to other women but has never acted upon it as a lesbian? If not, we will disqualify a good many women who in their own time never had an opportunity to follow their sexual preference, but who, if they were alive today, might well live openly with a female lover. This problem leads us to two important issues. The first is the issue of sexual identity. With my rather off-hand introduction of 'a woman who has felt a strong and life-long attraction to other women' I have taken sides in the controversial issue of what constitutes a lesbian identity. The phrase 'life-long attraction' strongly implies that this woman's erotic orientation is simply programmed into her, just as a heterosexual or a gay orientation is programmed into the rest of us. But is that really the case? For many radical lesbians of the early 1970s, lesbianism was a matter of choice – a political anti-patriarchal choice. Or is lesbianism a matter of socialization – of the individual experiences that some of us go through and that turn us into lesbians? The same questions may be raised with regard to homosexuality. I will come back to the problem of lesbian and gay identities below, but it should already be clear that there is room for a considerable variety of opinions.

The other issue that is raised by my introduction of the woman who does not act upon her lesbian inclinations is that of visibility – or, rather, invisibility. Gender and race are visible and recognizable categories. There are exceptions, of course: men who choose to dress like women; and every racial minority has members who can 'pass', that is successfully pose as members of the majority. But on the whole gender and race are obvious. Sexual orientation, however, is not visible. What is more, since it is only really visible at those moments when it is actively acted upon, it can be kept hidden even from one's immediate social environment. So how do we establish which writers have been gay or lesbian when it was impossible for them to reveal their sexual identity in their writings? How can we reconstruct a gay or lesbian literary tradition? I will look here at the answers given by lesbian criticism, not because it is in any way superior to gay criticism, but because it has a longer independent history. As Julie Rivkin and Michael Ryan have observed, '[m]ore so than Gay Studies, Lesbian Studies has demonstrated a tendency towards separatism, perhaps because as women, lesbians suffer a double oppression' (Rivkin and Ryan 1998: 677). Clearly, though, there are many parallels between lesbian and gay criticism.

LESBIAN WRITING

Lesbian criticism, then, faces a number of very specific and rather intractable problems. One way around them is to opt for lesbian *readings*; that is, for interpretations that leave unresolved the question whether a given author, or character, or situation, really *is* lesbian, but instead create the possibility for lesbian recognitions and moments of identification. This does not mean that lesbian criticism can make no firm claims and is never more than a reading strategy that could be easily dismissed by people who take a dim view of everything that is not solidly anchored in textual 'evidence'. There is a fast-growing body of texts – most of them dating from the last thirty years – that clearly announce themselves as lesbian. But a lesbian reading strategy is a complementary and necessary instrument. Especially in the case of texts published before the twentieth century, when lesbianism was largely unmentionable, lesbian readings of close friendships between single women have led to often revealing new appreciations of the plays, novels, and poems in question. (The same goes for gay criticism: a well-known example is Alan Sinfield's reading of the poems in which the Victorian poet Alfred Tennyson nostalgically remembers his very intimate friendship with a long-dead friend. See Sinfield (1986).) Such new lesbian interpretations have led to the identification of texts that together can be said to create a sort of lesbian literary tradition – or at least a tradition of texts that would seem to invite a lesbian reading. Simultaneously, lesbian criticism has drawn our attention to the way that lesbians have traditionally been portrayed in mainstream texts. As might be expected, lesbians (and homosexuals) have usually been pictured as 'other' and have served to define and confirm the heterosexuality of the centre.

But on what grounds can critics defend a lesbian reading of a text that is in no way explicitly lesbian and that until twenty years ago was never considered within a lesbian framework? Lesbian and gay critics generally agree that lesbian and gay writers work from a special awareness of the constructedness of language and culture and of the fact that the constructions that they see in operation can be contested. After all, lesbian and gay writers have until very recently been forced either to hide their sexual orientation altogether from their audience or to present it so indirectly that only the initiates were in a position to recognize it. *À la Récherche du temps perdu*, Marcel Proust's early twentieth-century great novel cycle, offers a famous example. The girl Albertine, with whom Proust's novelistic alter ego falls in love, was in the reality of Proust's life a boy. Lesbian and homosexual writers saw themselves forced to disguise same-sex relationships as heterosexual ones. Because of such suppressions even the most realistic mode of writing must always have been more than slightly unreal and false for lesbian and gay writers. Naturally, then, we find lesbian writers gravitating away from realism and towards other modes of writing. For Terry Castle, writing in 1993, lesbian fiction should never be read as straightforward realism: 'Even as it gestures back at a supposedly familiar world of human experience, it almost invariably stylizes and estranges it – by presenting it parodistically, euphemistically, or in some other rhetorically heightened, distorted, fragmented or phantasmagoric way' (Castle 1993: 90). Moreover, we may expect to find gender ambiguities, role playing that involves gender, and other coded references – such as certain recurrent symbols – to the fact that not everything is what it would seem to be to the unsuspecting reader.

More generally, the lesbian (and gay) writer's constant awareness of the gap between their own reality and that of the repressive heterosexual majority, coupled with the necessity – which often still applies – to keep that private reality secret, leads to an all-pervasive sense of irony and theatricality. Here we are moving towards that 'blurring of boundaries between self and other, subject and object, lover and beloved' that by the early 1990s for many lesbian critics had come to constitute 'the lesbian moment' in literary texts (Zimmerman 1992: 11). We are, in fact, moving towards what we now call 'queer theory', in which such exemplary lesbian moments – and their gay equivalents – are accorded a significance that far exceeds specific lesbian or gay conditions.

THE PRODUCTION OF SEXUALITY

Queer theory – which has turned a term that traditionally disparages homosexuality into a proud banner – comes in more than one form. However, all modes of queer theory, to which the remainder of this chapter will be devoted, are indebted to Michel Foucault's multi-volume *History of Sexuality* (1976–84) and his argument that especially 'deviant' – that is, non-heterosexual – forms of sexuality play a prominent role in the organization of Western culture. Although 'perversion' is actively marginalized, it is discursively central: the effort to police 'perversion' through a discourse on sexuality that continuously puts it in a negative light paradoxically keeps it in the centre of attention. For Foucault, Western culture has turned sexuality into a discourse that enables it to monitor us constantly and to exercise power: if we do not internalize its sexual rules and police ourselves, then it can step in and force us to conform.

In the first volume of his *History of Sexuality* (1976, translated 1978) Foucault argues that homosexuality and homosexuals date from the 1870s (a claim that would seem to be supported by the fact that the term 'homosexual' was coined in 1869). It is easy to misunderstand this. Foucault does not mean to say that sexual acts that we would now call homosexual acts were unknown before the 1870s. What he is saying is that in the later nineteenth century sexual acts between men were no longer seen as incidental to their lives – that is, as acts that anyone might engage in under certain circumstances – but as expressions of their *identity*. For the first time, Foucault tells us, homosexual acts were seen as part of the essential *nature* of the men involved, as the result of an inclination that was always there. Whereas before that turning-point a man who had sex with another man – a so-called 'sodomite' – was seen in terms of 'a temporary aberration', the homosexual 'was now a species'. The homosexual had come into existence: 'Nothing that went into his total composition was unaffected by his sexuality' (Foucault [1976] 1978: 43). What we have here is a crucial shift from behaviour to identity. Although this new homosexual identity naturally predisposed its owners to homosexual activity, men could now be classified as homosexual even if they had never been involved in homosexual acts.

For Foucault, homosexuality and homosexuals were *produced* by a nineteenth-century discourse that claimed new knowledge with regard to sexuality. This 'production' of homosexuality (and of other 'perversions' that were similarly tied to new identities) led to its codification (and condemnation) in legal, medical, psychological, and religious discourses. It led to the fixation of identities (homosexual, heterosexual) and the surveillance of the border between them. In other words, this production of homosexuality is intimately connected with power. Just like other sexual identities, homosexuality is 'a result and an instrument of power's designs' (Foucault [1976] 1978: 43). We should not make the mistake of thinking that what Foucault has in mind is only how homosexuality allowed the various authorities – legal, medical, religious – to tighten the screws of social and cultural repression and to legitimate themselves further, although they certainly availed themselves of the opportunity. As I have noted, 'power' often has a virtually autonomous status in Foucault's work (see Chapter 6). It works *through* us and imprisons us, even if occasionally it may also work to our advantage. In Foucault's view, the production of homosexuality by the human sciences has led to a very general surveillance under whose regime we even regulate and police our own sexuality. As Jonathan Dollimore summarizes Foucault's argument: 'Perversion is the product and vehicle of power, a construction which enables it to gain a purchase within the realm of the psychosexual: authority legitimates itself by fastening upon discursively constructed, sexually perverse identities of its own making' (Dollimore 1991: 106).

QUEER THEORY

Queer theory's point of departure is that there is no 'natural' sexuality – a status traditionally accorded to heterosexuality – and that there is no stable relationship between biological sex (male or female, to mention the most frequent categories), gender, and sexual desire. Casting its net wider than gay or lesbian criticism, it has a strong interest in everything that contributes to the destabilization of accepted sexual categories, even categories such as 'gay' and 'lesbian'. Its topics therefore include forms of sexual self-expression such as cross-dressing that cut across existing gender lines, sexual fantasies that are never put into practice, but also phenomena such as hermaphroditism or the desire to become female (if you are male) that similarly call into question the basis for what seem 'natural' categorizations. Queer theory, then, insists on the constructed nature of all classifications in terms of (biological) sex, sexuality, and gender. More recently, it has even expanded its not inconsiderable territory, in what others may well see as an unwarranted act of usurpation, to take in all potentially unstable and fractured identities. We find Donald E. Hall arguing that

> it is broadly useful to think of the adjective 'queer' in this way: it is to abrade the classifications, to sit athwart conventional categories or traverse several ... In this way, we are all queer, if we will simply admit it. We are all athwart if we expose and repudiate some of the comforting lies told about us and that we tell ourselves.
>
> (Hall 2003: 13)

It does not surprise us that on the basis of such a view of 'queer', Hall can claim that '[i]n its emphasis on the disruptive, the constructed, the tactical, and performative, queer analysis reveals some of the ways in which many late-modern individuals experience the fractured and contingent nature of human existence in the twenty-first century' (5). This reminds us of the emblematic status accorded to the migrant in much postcolonial theorizing, and although it should not be wholly dismissed, it tends to blunt queer theory's radicalism (although Hall himself is radical enough). But let me return to queer theory proper, the queer theory that focuses on sex, sexuality, and gender. And let me return to the issue of power, which is at the heart of queer theory.

For British queer theorists like Dollimore and Sinfield, the power that is at work in the field of sexuality can be contested. Queer theory questions traditional constructions of sexuality and sees non-heterosexual forms of sexuality as sites where hegemonic power can be undermined. In Sinfield's words, subcultures – in which he expressly includes sexual subcultures – 'may be power bases – points at which alternative or oppositional ideologies may achieve plausibility' (Sinfield [1994] 2005: vii). British queer theory, whose political context is 'a general left-wing orientation' (73), takes the assumptions and the interests of cultural materialism into the contemporary debate on sexuality. For Sinfield, sexuality is a faultline (see Chapter 7), a point at which the hegemonic surface may crack and reveal the warring forces underneath: 'Sexuality is an unstable construct in our societies, and hence produces endless textual work. Such an awkward issue has continually to be revisited, disavowed, rediscovered, affirmed' (56). Sexual dissidence – the title of Dollimore's 1991 book – is therefore always at least potentially a political act. As queer theorists, Sinfield and his British colleagues apply the methods of cultural materialism. They read literary texts against the grain – 'cultural materialists read for incoherence' (38) – in the manner of Pierre Macherey (see Chapter 4) because faultline stories 'hinge upon a fundamental, unresolved ideological complication that finds its way, willy-nilly, into texts' (4). They examine the constructions that a culture has put upon sexually ambivalent texts in order to expose its ideological repressiveness (see Sinfield's *Cultural Politics – Queer Reading*, from which I am quoting here, for a discussion of the reception of Tennessee Williams's plays). At the institutional level they question 'literature' itself – in particular the ideologically motivated marginalizations and exclusions that have played a crucial role in the creation of the idea of 'literature'. This is not to say that we should turn our backs to the literary tradition. We should, however, approach it from a faultline perspective. As Sinfield tells us: 'successful [texts] are usually risky; they flirt, at least, with the danger that prevailing values might not be satisfactory, or might not prevail' (56).

The queer theory that develops out of cultural materialism draws on Foucault and has strong affinities with British cultural studies. In the United States, however, queer theory has followed a different path. I will focus here on the queer theory that develops out of lesbian feminism and draws on Derrida, and more specifically on the work of two prominent and highly influential theorists: Eve Kosofsky Sedgwick and Judith Butler.

Lesbian criticism had split off from feminist criticism because lesbian critics felt that mainstream feminism did not do justice to the lesbian presence in literature. Striking out on their own, they assumed that there was such a thing as a lesbian identity – a core identity that all lesbians shared – that expressed itself in certain ways in literary texts. As we would say now, they saw lesbianism in essentialistic terms: as an unchanging condition that is an inalienable part of one's personality. However, in the course of the 1990s a number of influential lesbian critics began to reject that essentialism and to suggest that sexual identities – not just lesbianism or homosexuality – were social constructions that needed to be deconstructed, just as gender and race had been deconstructed to expose the binary oppositions at work within them. Like gender categories, traditional sexual categories were now assumed to be 'regulatory fictions' – instruments of a repressive discourse about sexuality. The obvious privileging of the heterosexual orientation of the majority at the expense of all other sexual orientations was the work of a centre that defined itself through that which it excluded. In other words, sexuality was added to the axes that for the theorists we have discussed have traditionally organized Western society.

For Eve Kosofsky Sedgwick, the power structure working within the hetero/homo axis is even central to the organization of Western culture. In her *Between Men* (1985) she argues that in a society dominated by men women are basically instruments with the help of which men establish or confirm intermale relations. In a patriarchy the *real* relations exist between men so that women function primarily within male–male relationships – as 'symbolic property' that can even be exchanged. The structure of such a male-dominated society is therefore *homosocial* – a term that should not be confused with homosexual, especially as homosocial societies usually see homosexuality in strongly negative terms. 'Homosocial' indicates the true nature of *social* relationships, not of sexual ones. Still, sexual classification in fixed categories is central to a homosocially structured society. Sedgwick redefines, in Donald E. Hall's words, 'heterosexuality as a fear of male homosexuality that motivates men to route their desire for another through women'

(Hall 2003: 198). For Sedgwick, the homosocial nature of the Victorian society on which she focuses, with its intimate connections between male sexual and non-sexual relationships, inevitably informs its writing: its literature, too, reveals that the underlying relationships of the Victorian period were relationships between men. Like the British queer theorists I have just mentioned, Sedgwick reads against the grain to bring to light what might be called a socio-sexual structure that is not immediately apparent.

In a later book, Sedgwick proposes an equally wide-ranging thesis. *Epistemology of the Closet* (1990) begins with a classic Derridean deconstruction of the heterosexuality/homosexuality opposition (which in Western culture usually takes the form of contrasting naturalness, health, fertility, and other terms that stand for 'life' with artificiality, sickness, sterility, and death):

> The analytic move [this book] makes is to demonstrate that categories presented in a culture as symmetrical binary oppositions – heterosexual/homosexual, in this case – actually subsist in a more unsettled and dynamic tacit relation according to which, first, term B is not symmetrical with but subordinated to term A; but, second, the ontologically valorized term A actually depends for its meaning on the simultaneous subsumption and exclusion of term B; hence, third, the question of priority between the supposed central and the supposed marginal category of each dyad is irresolvably unstable, an instability caused by the fact that term B is constituted as at once internal and external to term A.
>
> (Sedgwick 1990: 9–10)

Not just morally but theoretically, then, the privileging of heterosexuality turns out to be indefensible.

Sedgwick goes on to subject contemporary views of homosexuality to a similar analysis, finding that those views are still 'organized around a radical incoherence' of which 'the current impasse within gay theory between "constructivist" and "essentialist" understandings of homosexuality' (91) is only one manifestation. We find ourselves, Sedgwick argues, in 'a crisis of homo/heterosexual definition' (11) that has been with us ever since the identification and categorization of homosexuality as such and that has strongly affected virtually every sphere of life. To the point, in fact, that homo/heterosexual definition has been a presiding master term of the past century, one that has the same, primary importance for all modern Western identity and social organization (and not merely for homo-sexual identity and culture) as do the more traditionally visible cruxes of gender, class, and race.

(Sedgwick 1990:11)

This is a far-reaching claim. In *Epistemology of the Closet* Sedgwick tries to back it up with detailed analyses of a number of late nineteenth-century and early twentieth-century literary texts. However, since most of these texts invite homosexual readings anyway because of what we know of their authors (Oscar Wilde, Marcel Proust, and others), their support for Sedgwick's overarching claim is less convincing than one might hope. This does not neces-sarily invalidate her claim and the homo/heterosexual axis is clearly entangled with the other oppositions in the quote. Fierce homo-phobia often goes together with racism, hatred of everybody 'foreign', and even an often barely disguised contempt for women. (The homophobia of the German Nazis is a case in point.) It would, in fact, seem to be central to a loud and self-congratulatory sort of masculinity that with its feminine gendering of homosexuality seeks to affirm its own virility. Even if the repressions and struggles for power unleashed by the homo/heterosexual axis have not had all the cultural implications that Sedgwick claims in the passage quoted above, a critical awareness of that axis clearly adds substantially to our understanding of the culture we inhabit and the literature we read.

In the same year that *Epistemology of the Closet* appeared, Judith Butler published her own attack on the centrality and 'naturalness' accorded to heterosexuality. Her *Gender Trouble: Feminism and the Subversion of Identity* (1990) still stands as the most influential book within the field of queer theory. Butler denies the pretensions to 'naturalness' of heterosexuality even more radically than Sedgwick does. For her, heterosexuality is not only a 'melancholic' structure but, in a sense, second best. Sigmund Freud had argued that we end up with a melancholic ego because as infants we are forced to give up our sexual desire for our parents as a result of the incest taboo. For Butler, there is an even more fundamental taboo – the taboo that rules out homosexuality. Butler argues that our sexual identities are founded on the fact that we are absolutely forbidden to realize a primary homosexual desire. Heterosexual identity, then, is not only 'melancholic' because it is the result of a deep sense of loss; it is also built upon the repression of homosexual desire. Heterosexuality, in other words, is unthinkable without homosexuality. (I will leave aside here why some of us later in life return to a homosexual orientation.) As Sarah Salih puts it, in her discussion of Butler's work, a heterosexual identity

> is 'acquired' through the repudiation of homosexual attachments, and the abjected same-sex of desire is installed in the ego as a melancholic identification, so that I can only be a woman to the extent that I have desired a woman, and I can only be a man to the extent that I have desired a man.
>
> (Salih 2002: 132)

Heterosexuality, then, is not the 'natural' state of affairs that it usually claims to be. (Nor is homosexuality, which no longer is the primary desire that we once experienced.) But if heterosexuality is not 'natural' behaviour, then how should we see it? Like all forms of sexuality, heterosexuality is *performative*. In fact, what I consider to be my identity is performative. My 'I', as Butler puts it in an article published the following year, is 'the effect of a certain repetition, one which produces the semblance of a continuity or coherence' (Butler 1991: 18). My sexual orientation is likewise the effect of repetition, of the fact that I repeatedly *perform* certain sexual acts. In other words, a string of identical or similar performances takes the place of sexual identity (and of identity as such). As Butler herself tells us in *Gender Trouble*: 'There is no gender identity behind the expressions of gender; that identity is performatively constituted by the very "expressions" that are said to be its results' (Butler 1990: 25). Gender 'is always a doing, though not a doing by a subject who might be said to pre-exist the deed' (25). As these quotations make clear, Butler also reverses our commonsense assumptions about our 'I': instead of an 'I' that exists prior to our actions – sexual or otherwise – we have an 'I' that is the result of repetition. It is the continuous repetition of a certain set of acts – which of course will differ from person to person – that creates what might be called an identity effect: the illusion that we are coherent, even if that illusion is under constant pressure:

In my view, the self only becomes a self on the condition that it has suffered a separation ... a loss which is suspended and provisionally resolved through a melancholic incorporation of some 'Other'. That 'Other' installed in the self thus establishes the permanent incapacity of the 'self' to achieve self-identity; it is as if it were always already disrupted by the Other; the disruption of the Other at the heart of the self is the very condition of the self's possibility.

(Butler 1990: 27)

In any case, 'performativity' does not imply choice. There is no pre-discursive, ungendered subject prior to gender identification: 'the "I" neither precedes nor follows the process of this gendering but emerges only within and as the matrix of gender relations themselves' (Butler quoted in Culler 2011: 104). So heterosexuality is a 'repetition that can only produce the *effect* of its own originality; in other words, compulsory heterosexual identities, those ... phantasms of "man" and "woman", are theatrically produced effects that posture as grounds, origins, the normative measure of the real' (Butler 1990: 21). Heterosexual activity can only try to pass itself off as the authentic form of sexuality by suggesting that other forms of sexuality, such as lesbianism and homosexuality, are *in*authentic: by setting up a binary opposition in which it turns itself into the centre by relegating other sexualities to the margins. It needs non-heterosexual identities and activities to authenticate and validate itself. Heterosexuality and other forms of sexuality are deeply implicated in each other and they are all equally inauthentic.

If what I take to be my 'self' is the effect of repetition of acts that do not originate within me, then what are the possibilities for agency, for effecting change? In *Gender Trouble* Butler speaks of 'the performative possibilities for proliferating gender configurations outside the restricting frames of masculine domination' (141). We cannot help performing gender – which is 'a regulated process of repetition' – and repeating our gendered identity, but those repetitions will not always be completely identical and it is the slight variations from one performance to the next that create the necessary space for change, for 'something we might still call agency', as she terms it in *Excitable Speech* (Butler 1997a: 38). Such an agency may manifest itself in 'the repetition of an originary subordination for another purpose, one whose future is partially open' (38). With her deconstruction of the difference between gender and sexuality Butler comes close to drawing the physical sexual drive itself into the realm of culture. In *Gender Trouble* she argues that the body – which for her is never neutral but inevitably gendered – 'has no ontological status apart from the various acts which constitute its reality' (Butler 1990: 136). But perhaps it is more correct to say that, for Butler, sex – the biologically given physical drive – and sexuality cannot really be effectively distinguished.

I should point out that not everybody would be happy with such a state of affairs. As the prominent theorist Donna Haraway, whom we will meet later (and who has an advanced degree in biology), put it:

> to lose authoritative accounts of sex, which set up productive tensions with gender, seems to be to lose too much; it seems to be to lose not just analytic power within a particular Western tradition but also the body itself as anything but a blank page for social inscription.
>
> (Haraway 1988: 591)

DRAG AND CROSS-DRESSING

Because of its political potential, queer theory has come to focus on the actual practice of sexuality. Here, too, it is interested in boundaries and, in particular, on the (for queer theorists) significant circumstance that seemingly clearly visible boundaries turn out to be blurred upon closer inspection. Not surprisingly, queer theory has taken a special interest in cross-dressing, and in particular cross-dressing by males (in which Butler has also repeatedly shown an interest). Cross-dressing is perfect for destabilizing generally accepted views of gender and sexuality: a man in a long evening dress or a pleated skirt will in most places draw a good deal of attention. Men in drag are so interesting to queer theorists because they simultaneously position themselves on the 'wrong' end of two axes: on the gender axis they identify with the feminine pole, in spite of their maleness; and on the axis of sexual orientation (with its hetero/homo opposition) they often take up the homosexual position. In so doing they first of all blur the boundary between gender and sexuality (which the feminists had fought so hard to establish with the argument that while sexuality is a biological given, gender is nothing but a social construct). Clearly the act of cross-dressing – the appropriation of gender characteristics normally associated with the other sex – has significance beyond gender and is simultaneously a *sexual* act. In drag, gender and sexuality have become inseparable. From the perspective of queer theory, cross-dressers effectively illustrate the constructed character of gender and sexuality, while they also draw attention to the enormous difference between sexuality and acts of mere procreation. Human sexuality clearly involves much more than procreation. Drag exposes femininity as a role, as a performance. Cross-dressing undermines the claim to naturalness of standard heterosexual identities and emphasizes a theatrical, performance-like dimension of gender and sexual orientation that our discourses seek to suppress. For queer theory, drag and other unusual intersections of gender and sexuality are sites where the constructedness of sexuality becomes visible. Because of their parodic character, drag and other 'deviant' sexualities thus come to function as the heavy artillery in the war against the fixed categorizations of the 'phallogocentric' centre. They are important instruments in the development of what Judith Halberstam has called 'new sexual vocabularies that acknowledge sexualities and genders as styles rather than life-styles, as fictions rather than facts of life, and as potentialities rather than as fixed identities' (Halberstam [1994] 1998: 759).

Queer theory's contribution to literary and cultural studies lies in its efforts to denaturalize and destabilize all sexual categories (with the ultimate purpose of dislodging heterosexuality from its central position and of showing up its supposed 'naturalness' for what it is). It then uses sites of instability – those sites where the constructedness of sexual behaviours comes to the surface – as vantage points for political action. Some of its theorists see in queer strategies not just a way to deconstruct sexualities and genders but, since the homo/heterosexual axis has so profoundly shaped the world in which we live, an apparatus for a much more comprehensive interrogation of that world.

SUMMARY

In the course of the 1980s lesbian and gay studies made sexuality – not to be confused with gender – next to race, gender, and class, a fourth major category of analysis in literary and cultural studies. They confront us with the various meanings that our culture attaches to the range of sexual identities and sexual activities that we know; or, to put it in somewhat different terms, with the structures that our culture has set up to deal with those identities and activities. They also confront us with the way these structures function as conduits of power and instruments of oppression.

For the queer theory that under the influence of Foucault develops out of lesbian and gay criticism – and, in the United Kingdom, out of cultural materialism – the homo/heterosexual opposition is absolutely central to the structuration of Western culture. Queer's major project, then, is the deconstruction of that axis through a radical critique of liberal humanist views of sexuality. Dismantling the homo/heterosexual opposition will radically affect the self-definition and ideological organization of Western culture and allow us to escape from its sexual prison house. As one prominent queer theorist has put it, 'queer' stands for 'the open mesh of possibilities' that presents itself 'when the constituent elements of anyone's gender, of anyone's sexuality aren't made (or *can't be made*) to signify monolithically' (Sedgwick 1994: 8). Some queer theorists use cross-dressing and other non-standard forms of sexuality to force a breach in the wall of traditional classifications of sexual identity. Others seek to undo those classifications on purely theoretical grounds, but all of them are engaged in revealing the extent to which Western and other cultures have organized themselves around the repression and even denial of homosexuality and other sexualities that do not conform to the heterosexual norm.

SUGGESTIONS FOR FURTHER READING

Annamarie Jagose's *Queer Theory* (1996) still is a good overview, while Alan Sinfield's *Cultural Politics – Queer Reading* (2nd ed. 2005) offers lively accounts of both the major themes of cultural materialism and the more leftist-oriented queer theory that we find in the United Kingdom. Very readable introductions to queer theory are Nikki Sullivan's *A Critical Introduction to Queer Theory* (2003) and Donald E. Hall's *Queer Theories* (2003). Iain Morland and Annabelle Willox's *Queer Theory* (2005) presents essays by a number of prominent queer theorists. David Gerstner's *Routledge International*

Encyclopedia of Queer Culture (2006) has an impressive range and contains a wealth of information, as does *The Routledge Queer Studies Reader* (2012), edited by Hall and Jagose. E.L. McCallum and Mikko Tuhkanen's *Queer Times, Queer Becomings* (2011) collects recent work by leading queer critics.

Eve Kosofsky Sedgwick's *Between Men* (1985) and *Epistemology of the Closet* (1990) are classics, but unfortunately not very easy. The opening chapters, however, should be accessible. Judith Butler's books – *Gender Trouble: Feminism and the Subversion of Identity* (1990) and *Bodies that Matter* (1993) – also tend to be difficult, but her article 'Imitation and Gender Insubordination' (1991) is a very accessible exception. *Novel Gazing: Queer Readings in Fiction* (1997) is a massive, wide-ranging, but on the whole rather theoretical collection of essays edited by Sedgwick. Marjorie Garber's *Vested Interests: Cross Dressing and Cultural Anxiety* (1992) is a good introduction to the complex fusion of sexuality and gender – and its unsettling cultural effects – that we find in some forms of sexual behaviour. *Black Queer Studies: A Critical Anthology* (2005), edited by E. Patrick Johnson and Mae G. Henderson, collects essays at the interface of black studies and queer studies while Philip Holden and Richard J. Ruppel's *Imperial Desire: Dissident Sexualities and Colonial Literature* (2003) operates at the interface of queer studies and postcolonial studies. In *After Sex: On Writing since Queer Theory* (2011), edited by Janet Halley and Andrew Parker, important contributors to the debate consider the current state of queer studies.

More traditional and accessible forms of gay and lesbian criticism are to be found in Mark Lilly's *Gay Men's Literature in the Twentieth Century* (1993) and Gregory Woods' excellent and thorough *A History of Gay Literature: The Male Tradition* (1998). Terry Castle's *The Apparitional Lesbian: Female Homosexuality and Modern Culture* (1993) is a good example of a more traditional, but sophisticated, lesbian criticism (see, for instance, her interpretation of Sylvia Townsend Warner's *Summer Will Show* (1936)). Castle's *The Literature of Lesbianism* (2003) is an enormously comprehensive historical anthology.

10

POSTHUMANISM, ECOCRITICISM, AND ANIMAL STUDIES

Terms such as 'posthuman' and 'posthumanism' are at first sight pure hyperbole. Posthumanism is undoubtedly the more plausible of the two – if humanism means individual autonomy and agency, then clearly those theorists and philosophers who deny that we possess such qualities do not subscribe to humanism, although the 'post' in 'posthumanism' still remains rather puzzling. But 'posthuman' is harder to swallow. How could we possibly be 'post' being human? We are not, and the theorists who use these terms are fully aware of that, although some would claim that being human is not what it was until, say, twenty or thirty years ago. 'Posthumanism' is shorthand for a fundamental questioning of the premises of humanism without abandoning humanism wholesale. As the prominent American posthumanist theorist Cary Wolfe put it recently in *What Is Posthumanism?* (2009), 'the point is not to reject humanism *tout court* – indeed, there are many values and aspirations to admire in humanism – but rather to show how those aspirations are undercut by the philosophical and ethical frameworks used to conceptualize them' (Wolfe 2010: xvi). If this reminds us of deconstructionist practices, we are right on track. Wolfe explicitly works within a Derridean framework and so does the British posthumanist Neil Badmington, who, like Wolfe, seeks to modify humanism from within, if only because thinking 'outside' humanism is impossible:

> If the version of posthumanism I am trying to develop here repeats
> humanism, it does so *in a certain way* and with a view to the decon-
> struction of anthropocentric thought. If the pure outside is a myth, it is
> nonetheless possible to 'lodg[e] oneself within traditional conceptuality
> in order to destroy it' (Derrida 1978: 111), to reveal the internal instabil-
> ities, the fatal contradictions, that expose how humanism is forever
> rewriting itself as posthumanism.
>
> (Badmington 2003: 14)

So how is posthumanism different from humanism while 'repeating' at least some of its positions? Although there are different
strands within posthuman thought, they are closely connected,
pursuing the same end along different lines, and one might say, in
Christopher Peterson's words, that they all embrace 'a conception
of the human that refuses to define itself in violent opposition to
the nonhuman' (Peterson 2011: 127). This description clarifies what
posthumanists see as the central flaw in humanism – its so-called
exceptionalism, its assertion of mankind's uniqueness and superiority vis-à-vis the world of nature, from which it deliberately sets
itself apart.

POSTHUMANISM

One of the seminal texts of posthumanism is Donna Haraway's
polemical 1985 essay 'A Cyborg Manifesto: Science, Technology,
and Socialist-Feminism in the Late Twentieth Century' (in spite of
her later claim, in *When Species Meet* (2008), that she is 'not a
posthumanist'). In a cyborg – a combination of *cyb*ernetic and
*org*anism – cybernetic and organic parts work together to create a
being that is neither fully human nor completely machine-like but
ends up somewhere in between. That is not how cyborgs are
usually portrayed. In William Gibson's famous so-called 'cyber-
punk' novels of the 1980s – *Neuromancer* (1984), *Count Zero* (1986),
and *Mona Lisa Overdrive* (1988) – the emphasis is strongly on the
human qualities of the numerous cyborgs. In fact, having a human
consciousness is enough to qualify as fully human, even with a body
that is largely prosthetic. Mind and non-biological, often electronic,
matter are even kept firmly apart when the cyborg in question is in

fact a machine. In the science-fiction writer (and scientist) Isaac Asimov's story 'All the Troubles in the World' (1958) the mega-computer Multivac, which practically runs the whole world, has become so deadly tired that it thinks up a plan to have itself killed (for which, rather ironically, it needs human help). And in the novelist Richard Powers's *Galatea 2.2* (1995) a computer that has acquired consciousness through brilliant programming does indeed effectively kill itself once it has fully understood the horrors that humans are capable of perpetrating. In both cases the machines have minds so human that deep unhappiness leads to the autonomous decision to commit suicide. But if such autonomy is absent, as in *Star Trek*'s mostly human 'borgs', whose minds are fully controlled by an outside force, the cyborgs are presented as robotic, as machines. Representations of the cyborg tend to emphasize its human side – not just its cognitive powers but its consciousness of itself and its very human emotions.

However, in 'A Cyborg Manifesto' Haraway argues that the figure of the cyborg – and in either a literal or a figurative sense 'we are all ... hybrids of machine and organism' (Haraway [1985] 1990: 191) – explicitly compromises the boundary between natural organism and machine, just as it undermines the human/animal, male/female, and physical/non-physical distinctions. It questions the central position that humanism has traditionally accorded the human. We do not stand apart from the world, watching it from a superior distance, but are fully entangled with it and, 'like any other component or subsystem, must be localized in a system architecture whose basic modes of operation are probabilistic' (Haraway cited in Gane 2006: 138). Because of this inevitable entanglement, what we need, Haraway tells us in a later essay on feminist epistemology, is not 'the knowledges ruled by phallogocentrism (nostalgia for the presence of the one true Word) and disembodied vision' (Haraway 1988: 589), but less patriarchal, authoritarian, and anthropocentric '[s]ituated knowledges ... that require the object of knowledge be pictured as an actor and agent, not as a screen or ground or a resource' (592). We can come by such knowledges only through non-judgemental modesty, never through a master–slave relationship with the object of enquiry. In later publications Haraway introduces the figure of the 'modest witness' who meets the object of research with full respect and empathy in relationships of response, even (or perhaps especially) if that object – Haraway trained as a biologist – is a laboratory animal used in cancer research (such as the genetically modified 'OncoMouse', the world's first patented animal, in her *Modest_Witness@Second_Millennium. FemaleMan©_Meets_OncoMouse* (1997)).

When Species Meet focuses on so-called 'companion animals', a category first represented by Haraway's own dog, but stretched to include other non-human 'companions', such as the laboratory animals of her earlier work and even symbiotic bacteria. It is, in the words of one reviewer, 'a book about how to think about connections among species – about the importance of moving past myths of exceptionalism to recognize the ties that bind humans to other species as well as to other humans' (Mullin 2008: 374). Although Haraway sees the book as 'my effort to be in alliance and in tension with posthumanist projects' (quoted in Gane 2006: 140), the alliance clearly dominates. Like the cyborg, the companion species relates the human to the non-human, and through its feed-back-loop interactions with humans tends to blur the distinction between them: 'I am who I become with companion species, who and which make a mess out of the categories in the making of kin and kind' (Haraway 2008: 19). In less Derridean phraseology (the book pays close attention to Derrida's influential essay 'The Animal that Therefore I Am' of 2002): 'We are in a knot of species coshaping one another in layers of reciprocating complexity' (42). This is a plea not for seeing those other species as equal to our own, but for an acceptance of our situatedness within that knot and an acceptance of our reciprocal relations with the other species involved. If we accept that reciprocity as a defining feature of what it means to be human, then we have, in a sense, been posthuman ever since we became human – that is, long before humanism came along and separated us from the non-human. 'We have never been human', as the first section of *When Species Meet* tells us, because animals have always contributed to human practices, because the human has always been shaped in interrelationships with the non-human.

The point that we have never been human could also be made by posthumanist philosophy, which positions itself in the post-structuralist tradition and tries to arrive at a posthumanist theory of the subject on the basis of the work of Derrida and other theorists, such as the Italian philosopher Giorgio Agamben (see, for instance, *The Open: Man and Animal* of 2004). Indeed, Cary Wolfe, whose above-mentioned *What Is Posthumanism?* is a major recent contribution to the debate, argues that posthumanism 'comes both before and after humanism' (Wolfe 2010: 121): '"posthumanism" as I use the term ... returns us to our messy, material and embodied contingency – including (but not limited to) our evolutionary inheritance and symbiotic entanglements as *animals*, as fellow creatures' (Wolfe quoted in Cole *et al.* 2011: 101).

But let me return to the more targeted sort of questioning of anthropocentrism that we find in Haraway – who, although obviously deeply familiar with high theory, is also somewhat sceptical of 'always already absent referents, deferred signifieds, split subjects, and the endless play of signifiers' (Haraway 1988: 576) – and in the new field of animal studies, in which human–animal relations, the anthropomorphizing of animals, animal 'alterity', and the ethics involved are all central, posthumanistically inflected areas of enquiry. (Although animal studies is not inherently posthuman, its focus on, and interest in, animals often challenges the premises of humanism.) For our purposes, that more targeted questioning, with its interest in how posthuman themes are articulated in literary texts, is more pertinent than a purely philosophical enquiry.

A second important line of posthuman criticism I would like to discuss here focuses on the interface where we meet the world of digital information – the world where, more generally, humans work with intelligent machines – which over the last twenty years has been intensively explored by N. Katherine Hayles. In an article published in 2006, 'Unfinished Work: From Cyborg to Cognisphere', Hayles argues that Haraway's cyborg still operated within a humanist sphere, as an autonomous subject:

> Problems with the cyborg as a metaphor include the implication that the liberal humanist subject, however problematized by its hybridization with cybernetic mechanism, continues as a singular entity operating with localized agency. In other words, the cyborg is not *networked* enough to encompass the emergent possibilities associated with the internet and the world-wide web and other phenomena of the contemporary digital era.
>
> (Hayles 2006: 159)

Hayles's view of the posthuman is closer to the one she attributes to 'the American tradition in cybernetics' (Hayles 1997: 242), a view that 'privileges informational pattern over material instantiation', that downplays the importance of human consciousness and equally downplays the uniqueness and integrity of the human body, which it is perfectly willing to improve upon with prostheses or through biological interventions (such as gene therapy), and that, finally and most importantly, 'configures human being so that it can be seamlessly articulated with intelligent machines' (242).

Much of Hayles's work has addressed the ways in which we inevitably enter into processes of interaction when we are involved with 'intelligent machines' and how through such interactions our own intelligence is in a sense co-produced by the machines we work with, thus crossing the border into posthuman territory.

In her analysis of Richard Powers' *Galatea 2.2*, in which researchers work to build an artificial intelligence that is complex enough to pass a master's examination in English – involving not just ordinary but literary language – Hayles, deconstructing the absolute difference between human and machine, emphasizes how the computer (called Helen) interacts with her tutor: 'As he is training her, the experience of working with her is also training him, denaturalizing his experience of language so that he becomes increasingly conscious of its tangled, recursive nature' (Hayles 1997: 249). Even more invasive is the active involvement of the machine when we read electronic hypertexts. Because such texts

> are written and read in distributed cognitive environments, the reader is necessarily constructed as a cyborg, spliced into an integrated circuit with one or more intelligent machines. To be positioned as a cyborg is inevitably in some sense to become a cyborg, so electronic hypertexts, regardless of their content, tend toward cyborg subjectivity.
>
> (Hayles 2000)

In the heart of the computer, where everything is coded into strings of ones and zeros, the different ontological levels of character, writer, and reader disappear and 'the subjectivity we attribute to characters, authors, and ourselves as readers' begins to mingle with 'the non-anthropomorphic actions of the computer program' (Hayles 2000).

In numerous articles and in books such as *How We Became Posthuman: Virtual Bodies in Cybernetics, Literature, and Informatics* (1999), *My Mother Was a Computer: Digital Subjects and Literary Texts* (2005), and *Electronic Literature: New Horizon for the Literary* (2008) Hayles analyses novels – William Gibson's *Neuromancer*, Neal Stephenson's *Snowcrash* and *Cryptonomicon*, David Mitchell's *Cloud Atlas*, to mention a few – short stories, and electronic fiction (Michael Joyce's *Afternoon* and *Twelve Blue*, Shelley Jackson's *Patchwork Girl*), but also non-fiction and computer simulations, and asks how human subjectivity, language, and computer technology's 'regime of computation' intersect and interact. *How We Became Posthuman* is especially interested in the question of how information has traditionally come to be seen as completely separate from its 'material instantiation', its carrier, and as more essential (as in the classic separation of mind – the seat of cognition and information – and body). Recognizing that in contemporary discussions about 'cybernetic subjects' information is similarly privileged at the expense of its 'material instantiation', Hayles tries to undo the separation of information and its material embodiment, its 'materiality'. Since some 10 per cent of even a simple text file is code, invisible to both writer and reader, who usually are not even aware of it, '[l]anguage alone is no longer the distinctive characteristic of technologically developed societies; rather, it is language plus code' (Hayles 2005: 16). It is the presence of that code, leading to an 'interaction' of the 'embodied' text's 'physical characteristics with its signifying strategies' (103), that is characteristic of contemporary communication.

For Hayles, then, the posthuman is a relatively recent development, bound up with our use of an intelligent technology that has become an active component of our own intelligence, eroding the special status of the subject in humanist thinking: 'As you gaze at the flickering signifiers rolling down the computer screens … you have already become posthuman' (Hayles 1999: xiv). The 'distributed cognition' of Hayles's techno-posthumanism undercuts humanist agency because 'there is no a priori way to identify a self-will that can be clearly distinguished from an other-will' (Hayles 1997: 242). Posthumans are not necessarily unfree, but they cannot know the extent to which their freedom is compromised.

REPRESENTATION AND THE WORLD OF NATURE

In *The Two Towers*, the second part of Peter Jackson's film version of J.R.R. Tolkien's epic narrative *The Lord of the Rings* (and the second book of the trilogy), we meet the Ents. These are ancient, treelike creatures, gigantic of stature and with slow, rumbling voices that call to mind gusts of wind in autumn trees. Although they have lived in Tolkien's Middle Earth since time immemorial, they have no interest in the business of men – or elves, dwarves, and other non-human races – and keep to themselves in remote forests, feeling more kinship with great trees than with anything else alive. No wonder, then, that they refuse to take sides in the war that breaks out between the forces of evil and those who try to save Middle Earth from death and destruction. But their feeling that this is not their war changes completely when they see the bleak wasteland that the wizard Saruman, who has joined the evil side, has created in his preparations for war. As far as the eye can see, woods have been felled and burned and all that remains are charred stumps in a grey and black desert. Enraged by this wanton destruction of the natural world, the Ents attack, scattering Saruman's Orc forces before them and using their incredible strength to wreck the dam that Saruman has had built in order to harness and utilize a river's natural power. The river's pent-up waters, freed from their yoke, flood Saruman's plain, extinguishing the hellish fires that burn above and under ground, destroying foul armies, and returning the potential for life to a place taken over by death.

The message is clear: there is a close link between the natural and the good, just as there is a close link between unnatural environments and evil. The lands of Sauron, who in Middle Earth is the Evil One himself, are a barren volcanic wasteland, whereas the Shire, where the peaceful (if somewhat simple-minded) Hobbits live, is a pastoral idyll of rolling hills and fertile valleys.

Such an intimate connection between landscape and moral framework is nothing new. In fact, the term 'pastoral' traditionally refers to a literary genre in which, since classical times, a particular landscape and a certain harmonious moral order have been associated with each other and have been juxtaposed with a more urban and corrupted order. Literary academics have for a long time been aware of that connection, not just in the pastoral, but in every imaginable genre and every imaginable form. Sometimes the connection is rather obvious, as in *The Lord of the Rings*; sometimes it is quite subtle, as in the novels of Jane Austen, where upon closer inspection moral authority always turns out to be linked to an attitude of respect and even reverence for nature, whereas a lack of that respect is unfailingly indicative of moral fallibility or worse (see Bate 2000). Nature would seem to be a self-evident source of metaphors for our own moral concerns.

The role of nature is not limited to that of moral barometer. Nature may appear in aesthetic terms, admired for its majesty, its – less awesome – beauty, or even for a wholly unintimidating gentleness. It may be praised for its authenticity, and its pristine quality may be favourably contrasted with the domesticated landscapes that we humans have created. In more religious terms, its state of grace may be held up in contrast to our own fallen state. It may be used to convey a feeling of nostalgia, as in the eighteenth-century English poet William Cowper's 'The Poplar-Field':

The poplars are felled; farewell to the shade,
And the whispering sound of the cool colonnade!

(Cowper 1980: 403)

In its wilder states nature may function as a place of temptation and trial (as in Nathaniel Hawthorne's short story 'Young Goodman Brown'), but it may also serve as a place of freedom (as in the Leatherstocking tales of James Fenimore Cooper and countless other American writers) and even as a place of healing and redemption (as in the work of D.H. Lawrence and many nature writers). But nature may be also presented as wholly enigmatic, something upon which we project our own fears and desires. In Herman Melville's *Moby-Dick* the white whale that will in the end destroy the monomaniacal Captain Ahab and his crew (except for Ishmael, the novel's narrator) remains an inscrutable force of nature, presumably goaded into action only by Ahab's apparent resolve to kill it or die in the attempt.

The imaginative uses of nature are practically inexhaustible because nature is everywhere. After all, even today's weather is nature, as is the cat that comes up to me in the morning expecting another day of culinary delights. Or *is* it? Does a thoroughly domesticated animal still qualify as 'nature'? Is it still possible to speak of nature, in the sense of something truly itself, wholly authentic, completely untouched by human intervention? Or are even the places that are untouched now ever so subtly affected by a process of global warming caused by our carbon-dioxide emissions? Would today's weather be different if we had never learned that coal can burn and had never invented the combustion engine?

DOMINION

While an interest in the ways that nature features in the products of our imaginations has for a long time featured in literary criticism, the questions I just asked are fairly new. This is not to say that there never was an interest in the way we intervened in natural processes or affected our natural environment. We have just seen how William Cowper lamented the felling of a 'colonnade' of poplars. But almost invariably such laments centred on *our* feelings, looked exclusively at things from our human point of view. In another poem we find Cowper very straightforwardly expressing that human-centred view of the natural world:

> I am monarch of all I survey,
> My right there is none to dispute;
> From the centre all round to the sea,
> I am Lord of the fowl and the brute.

(Cowper 1995: 25)

We may, to be fair to him, not ascribe this view to Cowper himself. I have quoted here from his 'Verses Supposed to be Written by Alexander Selkirk' (1782), which purportedly gives us the sentiments of the sailor whose sojourn on an uninhabited island had much earlier provided Daniel Defoe with the material for his novel *Robinson Crusoe* (1719), whose eponymous hero quickly turns the island on which he finds himself into a version of early eighteenth-century rural – and therefore thoroughly cultivated – England.

It does, however, not really matter what Cowper thought of the supremely self-confident and assertive outlook that he attributes to Selkirk in these lines. What is important is that such a position was widely shared in Europe and its colonies. Had not God Himself ordained that we, human beings, would have a special place in His creation, and would 'have dominion over the fish of the sea, and over the fowl of the air, and over the cattle, and over all the earth, and over every creeping thing that creepeth upon the earth' (Genesis 1:26)? In Western culture our relationship with the natural world has, for a very long time, remained virtually unquestioned because our dominion over that world was anchored in God's word. The exact meaning of 'dominion' in this particular context was indeed debated by theologians – after all, dominion may give rise to all sorts of practices, ranging from responsible stewardship to exploitation – but the hierarchy it implies, with us as masters and the natural world in a position of servitude, seemed clear enough. It is only in more recent times that we find a critical awareness of the exploitation to which unchecked dominion may lead. In *Walden* (Thoreau [1854] 2007: 1959) we find the American nature writer Henry David Thoreau complaining that 'the landscape is deformed' by 'avarice and selfishness' and that the farmer 'knows Nature but as a robber'. And contemporaries of Thoreau were outraged by the mass slaughter of bison on the American Great Plains, resulting in the near-extinction of the species by 1890. Clearly, 'dominion' was not supposed to include the reduction, within one single century, of herds totalling tens of millions to a few hundred animals. In the United Kingdom, the consequences of the Industrial Revolution for a landscape that had remained essentially unchanged for centuries provoked similar protests. But the relationship of dominion, so central to Western culture's views of humans and the natural world, still remained largely unchallenged. There were, of course, those who did not accept this order because they no longer could subscribe to the Christian view that underpinned it. But their alternative did not fundamentally change things. While for the large majority of the population man and nature were bound together, even if on unequal terms, in one organic whole overseen by a divine being, for those who embraced the scientific discoveries of the seventeenth and eighteenth centuries and regarded the universe as nothing but a vast machine, governed by eternal natural laws, there was no reason to look at nature with anything but indifference. The Scientific Revolution involuntarily facilitated a utilitarian, calculating view of the natural world that not much later would become the driving force behind its exploitation by the Industrial Revolution.

It is only in the last fifty years that the seemingly 'natural' hier-archical relationship between human beings and the natural world has started to be thoroughly questioned, not least because we reached the point, unimaginable until then, that with our nuclear arsenals we could practically – if not completely – wipe out both ourselves and all other living things. Total destruction clearly stret-ches the idea of dominion beyond acceptable limits. Moreover, even if we succeeded in keeping our ballistic missiles under lock and key, we still seemed on the point of creating damage to the natural world that was truly irreversible. In 1962, in her book *Silent Spring*, Rachel Carson told a startled public that with the way things were going, with an uncontrolled use of agricultural pesti-cides, there would soon be no birds left to brighten our springs. *Silent Spring* and other urgent warnings that we were taking irre-sponsible risks with our natural environment led to a broad envir-onmental awareness, which, in turn, led to a strong, even if heterogeneous, ecological movement, which, in turn, in the early 1990s inspired the branches of literary and cultural studies that are now called ecocriticism.

ECOCRITICISM AND ANIMAL STUDIES

Ecocriticism and its close ally animal studies do a great many widely different things. First, they examine representations of nature in literary – and non-literary – texts, and in other modes of cultural production. In so doing, they pay particular attention to the ques-tion of how nature is constructed in those texts and cultural arte-facts. The animal world may be presented as apparently benign, loyal, and even courageous in Disney movies and in television series such as *Lassie* and *Flipper* – in which a friendly neighbourhood collie and dolphin, respectively, clearly match us in intelligence and are more human than most of us – or as dangerous, unpredictable, and definitely non-human in films such as *Jaws* and *Jurassic Park*. A novel such as Richard Adams's *Watership Down* (1972), which tells the story of a desperate trek by a rebellious group of rabbits who flee their warren because one of them foresees its destruction at the hands of what we humans call 'development', tries to follow a middle road. It resists the almost complete anthropomorphization that we find in Disney's representations of animals and emphasizes the 'otherness' of its rabbit characters, while they still recognizably resemble us.

Ecocriticism examines representations of landscapes and of nature in its original state: the landscape of pastoral, for instance, and the wilderness, which, as I have already suggested, is often represented as a place with a special significance, a place of healing and redemption, or evil and danger where the individual's moral resolve is severely tested. But it may also examine representations of nature in government reports, developers' plans, ecological studies, philosophical treatises, wildlife documentaries (with zoos most people's main source of information about wild animals), and other texts and films in which nature plays a role. It may look at the uses of 'nature' in theme parks, at the way 'nature' is given a presence inside and outside shopping malls, at roof gardens, at fashions – as they come and go – in the florist business, at the landscaping of golf courses, at the role of 'nature' in suburbia. Ecocriticism's analyses of these representations bring to light the various discourses regarding our natural environment that we have produced since we became consciously aware of it. And, of course, ecocritics pay special attention to the hierarchies that operate in these discourses and that establish value systems within them.

The most obvious hierarchy privileges us at the expense of the natural world, but there are many others at work in our representations of nature. To give a familiar example, a major discourse found in nature writing will extol the virtues of the wilderness and of the wild animals that inhabit it – often in terms of a robust masculinity – while it will look condescendingly at domesticated animals, with pity and sometimes even with angry impatience, because they have sold out to the oppressor and are practically made out to be complicit in their own state of degradation. Where traditional criticism was mostly content with simply noting such hierarchies, ecocriticism actively seeks to dismantle them, especially the human/nature hierarchy, and sides with posthumanism in its deconstruction of the human/nature dichotomy, an opposition that for ecocritics involves both the human/animal and the culture/nature oppositions.

In its focus on discourses and discursive constructs, ecocriticism also looks at such concepts as 'nature' and 'wilderness' themselves. It traces their development as constructs – the eighteenth century was particularly productive with regard to the construction of 'wilderness' – and follows their history to chart how their meaning has changed over time. Ecocriticism, then, functions within the radically questioning intellectual climate of contemporary literary and cultural studies. But it does so with a difference because of its specifically 'green' agenda. 'Ecocriticism began', Jonathan Bate tells us, 'in consciousness-raising' (Bate 2000: 8), in alerting us to the way in which our activities posed an ever-greater threat to our natural environment and in making us think about what it means to live *with* rather than simply on the earth. Its analyses of the discourses that govern our representations of nature focus, therefore, on the various ways in which these discourses have contributed, and still contribute, to our environmental problems.

Absolutely central (although certainly not unique) to the way it deals with issues of representation and all the other issues that fall within its scope is its refusal to adopt a human-centred perspective. (It realizes that that refusal is in itself anthropocentric, in the sense that it is a unilateral decision that has not been taken after intense rounds of consultation with the representatives of nature, but that cannot be helped.) Ecocriticism takes an 'earth-centred approach to literary studies', as Cheryll Glotfelty put it in the introduction to her and Harold Fromm's seminal *Ecocriticism Reader* (Glotfelty and Fromm 1996: xix). The interests of a natural world that is seriously under threat come first or are at least taken very seriously into account. As Richard Kerridge put it two years later: 'Most of all, ecocriticism seeks to evaluate texts and ideas in terms of their coherence and usefulness as responses to environmental crisis' (Kerridge and Sammells 1998: 5). According to Lawrence Buell, one of ecocriticism's founding fathers, the ideal text would have the following features:

1. The nonhuman environment is present not merely as a framing device, but as a presence that begins to suggest that human history is implicated in natural history.
2. The human interest is not understood to be the only legitimate interest.
3. Human accountability to the environment is part of the text's ethical orientation.
4. Some sense of the environment as a process rather than as a constant or a given is at least implicit in the text.

(Buell 1995: 7–8)

POSTHUMANISM, ECOCRITICISM, AND ANIMAL STUDIES **227**

If a text fails to live up to these ecocritical standards it is the eco-critic's business to point out in which ways it fails to do so, and more especially *why* it fails – which discourses, as often as not hidden in seemingly natural hierarchies, are responsible for its ultimately anti-environmental message.

Ecocriticism's moral and political agenda and the rejection of anthropocentrism are practically the only things the various strands of ecocriticism have in common. Within ecocritical studies we find the same variation of positions that we find in the ecological movement from which it took its original inspiration. Within that movement we find proponents of 'deep ecology', who find authenticity and purity only in the virgin wilderness, who attribute intrinsic value to all life, and who believe that the interests of non-human life on this planet can be protected only by a reduction of its human population. For deep ecologists, nature takes precedence over human beings. As Rupert Birkin, in D.H. Lawrence's *Women in Love*, puts it rather radically, 'Let mankind pass away – time it did' (Lawrence [1922] 1960: 65).

For eco-feminists, the historically unequal relationship – a relationship of domination – between human beings and nature mirrors that between men and women and has, not accidentally, the same origins: our Judaeo-Christian heritage, which historically has privileged men; and the Enlightenment, which, building upon a long history of inequality, constructed men as responsible and rational and women as their more 'natural' – but less rational and therefore inferior – opposite. This has led some of eco-feminists to identify rationality itself as primarily responsible for our environmental crisis and to adopt a wilfully anti-rational, mystical approach to the natural world.

Marxist ecologists, in their turn, see the degraded state of our environment as the direct result of the unrestricted activities of international capital. The exploitation of the environment that is responsible for the environmental crisis follows the pattern of the capitalistic exploitation of labour and it is that exploitation that should have our attention in the first instance. (For deep ecologists, who would point to the environmental disasters in the former Soviet Union, this would leave the unequal relationship between humans and nature intact and could never offer a solution.) Marxist ecologists would also argue that the principle of the 'free' market contributes to environmental problems because the market will always try to meet demand, even if supply can be realized only at great cost to the environment.

Social ecologists will again have a different take on things and will be interested in the social cost of environmental problems. Not surprisingly, that cost – a waste disposal site around the corner, a new runway ending near our back yard – is usually borne by the socially and politically powerless, and social ecologists target the power relations they see at work in the process of decision-making that leads to socio-environmental problems. Although still relatively marginal to the business of ecocriticism, the writings related to the enormous environmental problems created by the Western world's pollution and its staggering production of waste – and the discourses of pollution and waste themselves – have in recent years drawn ever-increasing ecocritical attention. Since especially members of ethnic minorities in the Western world and, with the outsourcing of much dirty and dangerous work, the inhabitants of Third World countries are confronted with socio-environmental problems, critics have recently realized that social ecology has a productive interface with postcolonial studies. (See, for an example of that interface, Graham Huggan's '"Greening" Postcolonialism: Ecocritical Perspectives' (2004). Huggan's article, by the way, opens with the question 'What do a polemical report on dams, a (pseudo-) philosophical treatise on animal welfare, and a novel about elephants have in common?' The answer is that '[t]hey are all legitimate objects of the practice of ecocriticism' (Huggan 2004: 701), which gives a fair idea of ecocriticism's range.)

The animal welfare mentioned in the previous paragraph is a major focus of animal studies, one of whose aims is, in the words of Greg Garrard, 'to undermine the moral and legal distinction between humans and animals' (Garrard 2004: 149). Animal studies critics do not necessarily claim the same rights for animals that we humans (at least ideally) enjoy – although some of them do, arguing that intrinsically all sentient species are equal – but they are certainly willing to grant animals, at least those that are sentient, far more rights than they currently have. How can we justify exploiting other sentient species the way we do? Both the Christian and the humanist tradition have pointed at our mental superiority, which supposedly puts us in a class all by ourselves and creates what seems to be a solid distinction between us and all other species (an idea called 'speciesism' by the philosopher Peter Singer). Animal studies has particularly tried to show how the supposed inferiority of animals has traditionally been used to construct our own superiority and uniqueness.

ECOCRITICAL REALISM

I have just suggested that ecocriticism operates within the matrix of contemporary criticism, but with a difference. Ecocritics range in their beliefs from a deep ecological faith in the perfect – and stable – self-organization of nature to a view of nature as ever changing, as process rather than state. And in their sense of how we should tackle ecological abuses and problems they range from radically anti-modern solutions (away from the modern, technological, and utilitarian state and back to self-supporting communes, or, as the case may be, to so-called 'bioregions') to enlisting the help of advanced technology itself. There is no love lost between 'deep' ecocritics and the so-called 'environmentalists' (Greg Garrard's term) who would not be averse to using technology in order to undo the damage that earlier and other technologies have done.

But both parties, and ecocritics in general, agree on a fundamental principle that has often been under attack in contemporary literary and cultural studies: that we can roughly know the world as it is. There would, after all, be no reason to have ecological concerns if we did not really know for sure that our human activities caused real damage to the natural environment. Although ecocritics disagree on the extent to which we can know things and are, on the whole, not naïve in epistemological matters, they agree that we can know enough to be sure that we are on a destructive – and ultimately self-destructive – course. An environmental disaster – say, the meltdown in the nuclear power plant at Chernobyl in 1986 – is not a social construction, even if all reports on what happened will inevitably be constructions that will show the respective agendas of their creators. As a result of their epistemological realism – not shared, I should say, by those deep ecologists and eco-feminists who see science as complicit with the forces of exploitation – the relations of ecocritics with the world of science differ rather strongly from, for instance, those of the poststructuralist critics who tend to see science first of all as a cluster of repressive discourses.

For many ecocritics, and certainly for the environmentalists, science is a source of truths with regard to the natural world. They are willing to accept scientific data and are prepared to take seriously solutions suggested by the scientific community – provided, of course, that these are 'earth-' rather than human-centred.

SUMMARY

Generally speaking, posthumanism views humanism's belief in the uniqueness and superiority of humans vis-à-vis the natural world as a source of injustice and oppression. Even if posthumanists do not necessarily share that view, they work to undo the unique status of humans, deconstructing the human/animal opposition and/or the human/machine opposition. In both cases the boundary turns out to be blurred, invalidating the moral and legal consequences traditionally attached to the human/animal distinction in particular.

Ecocriticism and animal studies focus on the many and widely different ways in which the natural world – wild and domestic animals, landscapes, the wilderness – and our relations with that world are represented in our culture. Initially focusing on texts – first nature writing and Romantic poetry, then all texts that in one way or another deal with nature – it has gradually expanded its interests to all cultural products and even the way 'nature' is utilized in the creation of golf courses or in urban settings. The object is to analyse the discourses that govern these representations and uses of nature and to show how their often hidden assumptions have contributed, and still contribute, to our environmental problems. Ecocriticism and animal studies see as the most damaging of these assumptions the widespread belief that the human species has a right to use, and even exploit, nature because of its place in either a divinely sanctioned or a 'natural' hierarchy. Like posthumanists, ecocritics and critics working in animal studies have a strong interest in the dismantling of human/animal and human/nature binaries. They differ from many other contemporary critics, however, in their rejection of the more radical forms of constructionism. While they would generally accept that our knowledge of our natural environment, and of the damage we do to it, is always compromised (up to a point), most of them would also claim that that does not exclude knowledge of things as they are and that the knowledge we think we have is reliable enough. Ecocritics especially, on the whole, are not hostile to the world of science and are willing to accept its empirical data, its analyses, and its authority in matters where laymen tend to be helpless (for instance, the long-term effects of global warming).

SUGGESTIONS FOR FURTHER READING

Ecocriticisms late arrival is illustrated by the fact that the first introduction to the field, Greg Garrard's *Ecocriticism*, dates from 2004. Garrard's book, now in its second edition (2012), is highly readable and gives an excellent idea of the various strands within the ecocritical enterprise while also discussing animal studies. *The Future of Environmental Criticism: Environmental Crisis and Literary Imagination* (2005), by Lawrence Buell, one of the founding fathers of ecocriticism, follows a more conventional organization, is highly sophisticated and packed with erudite detail, but, because of its thoroughness, is somewhat less readable. Buell's earlier and very influential ecocritical studies, *The Environmental Imagination: Thoreau, Nature Writing, and the Formation of American Culture* (1995) and *Writing for an Endangered World: Literature, Culture, and Environment in the US and beyond* (2001), must also be mentioned.

Eco-feminism began with Louise Westling's *The Green Breast of the New World: Landscape, Gender, and American Fiction* (1996) and is a going concern, witness the essays collected in Douglas A. Vakoch's *Feminist Ecocriticism: Environment, Women, and Literature* (2012). The anthology that put ecocriticism firmly on the map is Cheryll Glotfelty and Harold Fromm's *The Ecocriticism Reader: Landmarks in Literary Ecology* (1996). Other useful anthologies are Richard Kerridge and Neil Sammells' *Writing the Environment* (1998), Greta Gaard and Patrick D. Murphy's *Ecofeminist Literary Criticism* (1998), Laurence Coupe's *The Green Studies Reader: From Romanticism to Ecocriticism* (2000), Karla Armbruster and Kathleen R. Wallace's *Beyond Nature Writing: Expanding the Boundaries of Ecocriticism* (2001), and Michael P. Branch and Scott Slovic's *The ISLE Reader: Ecocriticism: 1993–2003* (2003). An outstanding British contribution to ecocriticism is Jonathan Bate's *The Song of the Earth* (2000), which examines texts by Jane Austen, Thomas Hardy,

Jean-Jacques Rousseau, Mary Shelley, Elizabeth Bishop, and many others. Ecocriticism's expansion beyond its original base in literary studies is illustrated by Deborah A. Carmichael's *The Landscape of Hollywood Westerns: Ecocriticism in an American Film Genre* (2006), and its productive joining of forces with postcolonial studies by Graham Huggan and Helen Tiffin's *Postcolonial Ecocriticism: Literature, Animals, Environment* (2010). Todd A. Borlik's *Ecocriticism and Early Modern English Literature: Green Pastures* (2012) shows us that ecocriticism may even throw new light on sixteenth- and seventeenth-century literature.

Animal studies is a fast-emerging field. Much of the work that is being done, however, like Margo DeMello's sizeable *Animals and Society: An Introduction to Human–Animal Studies* (2012), or Paul Waldan's *Animal Studies: An Introduction* (2013), is only marginally concerned with literature. Exceptions, at least partially, are Cary Wolfe's *Animal Rites: American Culture, the Discourse of Species, and Posthumanist Theory* (2003), Kari Weil's *Thinking Animals: Why Animal Studies Now?* (2012) – both of which link animal studies and posthumanism – and some of the essays collected in Aaron Gross and Anne Vallely's *Animals and the Human Imagination: A Companion to Animal Studies* (2012). However, *Animals Stories: Narrating across Species Lines* (2011), by Susan McHugh, places literature – 'girl–horse stories', literary representations of farm animals – at the centre of attention, while Shefali Rajamannar connects animal studies and postcolonial literature in *Reading the Animal in the Literature of the British Raj* (2012).

Like animal studies, posthumanism has gained ground rapidly in recent years. An early anthology is Neil Badmington's *Posthumanism* (2000), while the same author's *Alien Chic: Posthumanism and the Other within* (2004) is an early but brief introduction. *What Is Posthumanism?* (2009) by Cary Wolfe is a densely argued theorization of the posthuman. More accessible are Stefan Herbrechter's *Posthumanism: A Critical Analysis* (2013) and Mads Rosendahl Thomsen's historical overview in *The New Human in Literature: Posthuman Visions of Changes in Body, Mind and Society After 1900* (2013). Rosi Braidotti's excellent *The Posthuman* (2013) critically examines various approaches to the posthuman and makes a case for a 'posthuman subjectivity'.

11

CONCLUSION

In the introduction to their *Theory after 'Theory'* (2011), a collection
of essays on the current state of literary theory by critics working in
a wide range of areas, Jane Elliott and Derek Attridge review the
main characteristics and aims of the last thirty-five years of what
they simply call 'Theory'; that is, the Anglo-American literary and
cultural theorizing that takes its intellectual inspiration from poststructuralism. To the 'recurring gestures' of Theory – I'll drop the
quotation marks – belong the 'foregrounding of culture over
nature' (as in the blurring of the line between gender and sexuality)
and 'the conviction that epistemological closure is necessarily a form
of domination' – in other words, that claims to knowledge always
involve the exertion of power (Elliott and Attridge 2011: 2). Seeing
resistance to closure – and to nature as ontologically given,
uncontestable, 'fact' – as an act of political resistance, Theory
embraced 'temporal disruption, epistemological uncertainty and
logical paradox' (3), and invested much effort in 'the attempt to
locate a form of thought or experience that might escape current
systems without immediately becoming a system itself' (6), an
outcome that would, after all, merely substitute one form of domination for another. And it rejected the 'ideals of Liberal selfhood'
that characterize humanism because, apart from their supposedly
shaky intellectual foundation, those ideals were 'usually seen to

require the production of Others who were necessarily designated incapable of achieving these ideals of rationality and self-definition' (6). Liberal humanism, seemingly on the barricades to defend individual freedom and personal growth, stood accused of defining itself vis-à-vis those who had no access to such alluring prospects or were even denied such access.

To put this in other terms, while it sought to undermine everything that common sense and tradition had told us, Theory did not suggest new certainties, new truths. On the contrary, in its struggle against systematization, unity, permanence, knowledge, sameness, purity, and other instantiations of repression, Theory found and privileged indeterminacy, fluidity, fragmentation, hybridity, alterity, and similar intellectual weapons. Its default position was one of deep suspicion, as in these observations on the rights of the individual by the Italian philosopher Giorgio Agamben, who has figured regularly in the debate over the past fifteen years:

> It is almost as if, starting from a certain point, decisive political events were double-sided: the spaces, the liberties, and the rights won by individuals in their conflicts with central powers always simultaneously prepared a tacit but increasing inscription of individuals' lives within the state order, thus offering a new and more dreadful foundation for the very sovereign power from which they wanted to liberate themselves.
>
> (Agamben 1998: 121)

This very sketchy summary of Theory's fundamental assumptions is doubtlessly unfair, but it may suggest why on both sides of the Atlantic, and even among those academics who welcomed the insights that it brought, Theory often met with fierce resistance. It was accused of monopolizing the moral high ground and of knee-jerk condemnations of practically all of Western literature. As the English critic Valentine Cunningham (who in no way denies Theory's enormous contribution to the current state of literary studies) memorably puts it:

> The text is a criminal occasion; it criminalizes; it abets and affirms the reader's own criminality. Of necessity Theory accuses the text of crime, arraigns it before the dock of righteous criticism, affirms its guilt. The

text arises as a result of oppression; it's in the pay of malign institutions, wicked state apparatuses, false consciousness; it's the agent of oppressions, repressions, subjugations. It needs careful policing and, naturally, psychoanalytic treatment.

(Cunningham 2002: 61)

Another regularly voiced objection is that Theory leaves an all-important question unresolved. In most of its guises, Theory has a strong anti-humanistic emphasis, telling us that what we think of as our 'self' is merely a construction and emphasizing how we are manoeuvred into subject positions that are ready and waiting to ensnare us. We would seem to have very little say, or perhaps none at all, in what we are and what we do. But how are we to reconcile that with Theory's political, emancipatory thrust? And so we usually find the tacit assumption that becoming conscious of one's lack of autonomy will, in itself, lead to agency and enable political intervention – although the exact margins of our freedom are not spelled out. Perhaps we should not let this worry us: the problem of free will is one of the thorniest conundrums in philosophy and has, in over two thousand years of philosophical debate, not yet been resolved. (For an excellent and very lucid discussion, see Robert Kane's *A Contemporary Introduction to Free Will* (2005).)

Since the 1990s, the radical privileging of culture over nature and the suspicion of epistemological closure that for more than twenty years dominated Theory have themselves increasingly come under scrutiny and have lost some ground – witness the rise of ecocriticism, with its interest in incontrovertibly real environmental problems. But reports of Theory's demise are strongly exaggerated. The debate on the posthuman is in full swing and theorists have recently returned, after a long absence, to the field of aesthetics, to the specific aesthetic qualities of literature. Long seen as indissolubly bound up with such notions as the creativity of the autonomous subject, the universality of aesthetic principles, the coherence of the individual work of art, all of them rejected by theorists as fundamentally ideological, aesthetics is now increasingly brought within Theory's sphere of interest, as is illustrated by Derek Attridge's description of his own *The Singularity of Literature* (2004), which 'draws on a vocabulary of alterity, singularity and inventiveness to offer a theory of the artwork as an event that introduces the pre-viously unthought and unfelt into a culture' (Elliott and Attridge 2011: 12). Another, earlier, revival of aesthetic theory is Isobel Armstrong's *The Radical Aesthetic* (2000), which examines what was often seen as the collusion between aesthetics and power, and, drawing on the philosopher Emmanuel Levinas and others, pro-poses a radically democratic aesthetic in which cognition and 'affect' will not be kept apart. Such a democratic aesthetic rejects what she calls the 'master/slave model' of reading in which the reader seeks to dominate the text. Armstrong suggests a reversal of roles in which readers unconditionally open themselves to whatever the text has to offer and risk the 'terrors of closeness' (Armstrong 2000: 102). More recently, theorists thinking about aesthetics have been inspired by the writings on the aesthetic and politics of the French philosopher Jacques Rancière, who suggests that genuine art, through innovative artistic practices, deliberately obscures the distinction between art and 'the other' of art, as when the French novelist Honoré de Balzac uses the epic mode to represent the trivial.

Two of the terms just mentioned, 'event' and 'affect', have in recent years gained prominence. An 'affect', borrowed in this par-ticular context from the seventeenth-century Dutch philosopher Spinoza by way of Deleuze and Guattari, may be defined as 'a force of existing (*vis existendi*) that is neither the realized thing (an idea), nor the accomplishment of a thing (an act, *potentia agendi*)' (Povinelli 2011: 105). For Deleuze, this force of existing creates a space with political potential where new configurations may arise. In Deleuze's tracks, theorists have started to explore 'affects' such as love, hope, and pleasure – terms that at one point seemed to have disappeared from the critical vocabulary for ever. Attridge's 'event' is borrowed from the French philosopher Alain Badiou, for whom an 'event' is something that does not make sense according to the rules of the 'situation' and is only possible after a prior 'interven-tion' that has broken up those rules. 'Evental' ruptures, which may permanently change the 'situation', may take place in several domains, art among them, but it takes 'fidelity' to the event on the part of its witnesses to effect change. For Badiou, such 'fidelity' is thus an ethical obligation (although it is not so clear on what basis we can evaluate events). (That not all theorists see eye to eye is neatly illustrated by Rancière's dismissal of the 'absolute disconnection or unrelation' of event and situation and 'the quasi-miraculous force of the evental statement' (Hallward 2003: 209).)

As the current debates on posthumanism, aesthetics, and ethics make clear, literary theorizing still looks towards what is often called Continental philosophy, even if the more recent imports from Europe are not exactly newcomers. (Badiou was born in 1937, Rancière in 1940, Agamben in 1942, and Slavoj Žižek, a Slovenian philosopher known for his analyses of films and popular culture in terms of Lacanian psychoanalytic theory, in 1949.) But there are also new games in town. The new millennium has seen a renewed philosophical interest in the notion that we can come to know, at least partly, a reality that is independent of our linguistic practices and conceptual resources, and theorists are tentatively exploring the potential of such 'speculative realism' for theoretical projects, while seeking to maintain the critical and emancipatory function that for Continental philosophy is philosophy's true mission (and that it sees as lacking in the empirical–scientific habit of thought that is the dominant mode in Anglo-American philosophy). There is also a renewed interest in what Theory dismissed as 'liberal humanism'. In a spirited contribution to the *Theory after 'Theory'* collection that I mentioned earlier, Amanda Anderson defends the 'liberal aesthetic' – with particular reference to the American critic Lionel Trilling's *The Liberal Imagination* (1950) – and, more importantly, liberalism itself:

> The liberal tradition is characterized by devotion to the examined life in its many dimensions, including the rigorous scrutiny of principles, assumptions and belief systems; the questioning of authority and tradition; the dedication to argument, debate and deliberative processes of legitimation and justification; and the commitment to openness and transparency ... Acknowledging the philosophical complexities and existential predicaments attending liberal thought allows us to begin to conceptualize, and to disclose, a richer tradition of liberal aesthetics.
>
> (Anderson 2011: 251)

Implicit in Anderson's appraisal of liberalism is the suggestion that a modest liberalism, aware of its limitations, is – at least in actual critical practice – much closer to Theory than either party had thought possible.

A final, more traditional, development that deserves to be mentioned is the emergence of 'world literature', vigorously promoted by David Damrosch's *What Is World Literature?* (2003) and since then picked up by other critics. In what amounts to a reconfiguration of the field of comparative literature studies, Damrosch proposes that we read works of world literature – 'all literary works that circulate beyond their culture of origin, either in translation or in their original language' (Damrosch 2003: 4) – with an awareness of their original cultural context, but also of the new life they have acquired after moving into a new context. As Damrosch argues, a 'culture's norms and needs profoundly shape the selection of works that enter into it as world literature, influencing the ways they are translated, marketed and read' (26). Works of world literature will be 'multiply refracted in the process of transculturation' (24) and it is the critic's business to pay close attention to that process. Damrosch and other critics who champion world literature steer clear of the anti-humanist premises of recent literary theory, but their refusal to read a text only in its original cultural context and their giving equal weight to the text's transformations in new contexts – historical, geographical, linguistic – make them, too, attentive to 'hybridity, creolization, and métissage' (84). In fact, the power of such a text 'comes from our doubled experience of both registers together' (164).

There is no telling which way literary theory will go. It is possible that in the first decade and a half of the new millennium we have witnessed a parting of the ways between those theorists who continue to be inspired by the poststructuralist and related perspectives that have their source in Continental philosophy and those who pursue a line that is closer to philosophical realism and to a liberal humanist perspective. In Jeffrey Williams and Heather Steffen's recent *The Critical Pulse: Thirty-Six Credos by Contemporary Critics* (2012), which presents the views of thirty-six well-known critics, both camps are well represented – as are some cross-overs. But that should put nobody off. Ever since, long ago, the idea was abandoned that a literary text can have only one single meaning, major texts have been examined from countless different perspectives and submitted to countless critical strategies. The resulting interpretations may reinforce, complement, or contradict one another, but they always give us a fuller sense of the potential of those texts. We should not be afraid of critical pluralism or eclecticism. Contemporary critical practice could do worse than echo the nineteenth-century American poet Walt Whitman in one of his more exuberant moods:

Do I contradict myself?
Very well then I contradict myself,
(I am large, I contain multitudes.)

(Whitman [1855] 2007: 2253)

SUGGESTIONS FOR FURTHER READING

Theory after 'Theory' (Elliott and Attridge 2011) and *The Critical Pulse* (Williams and Steffen 2012) give a good idea of the diversity of contemporary criticism. The recently discovered Jacques Rancière discusses the politics of aesthetics (and has a sceptical look at Badiou and Lyotard) in his *Aesthetics and Its Discontents* (2009). Derek Attridge proposes the reading of literature as a model for ethics in *J.M. Coetzee and the Ethics of Reading* (2004), while Christopher Butler's *Pleasure and the Arts: Enjoying Literature, Painting and Music* (2005) and Melissa Gregg and Gregory Seigworth's *The Affect Theory Reader* (2010) – in admittedly rather different ways – bring our emotional responses back into the debate. Good introductions to 'world literature' are Mads Rosendahl Thomsen's *Mapping World Literature* (2008) and Theo D'haen's *The Routledge Concise History of World Literature* (2012).

BIBLIOGRAPHY

Achebe, C. (1976) *Things Fall Apart*, London: Heinemann [1958].
—— (1995) 'Colonialist Criticism', in Ashcroft *et al.* (1995) [1974].
Ackroyd, P. (1985) *Hawksmoor*, London: Hamish Hamilton.
Agamben, G. (1998) *Homo Sacer: Sovereign Power and Bare Life*, trans. D. Heller-Roazen, Stanford, CA: Stanford University Press.
—— (2004) *The Open: Man and Animal*, Stanford, CA: Stanford University Press.
Ahmad, A. (1992) *In Theory: Classes, Nations, Literatures*, London: Verso.
Althusser, L. (1966) 'Réponse à André Daspré', *La Nouvelle Critique* 175: 141–146.
—— (1971) *Lenin and Philosophy and Other Essays*, trans. B. Brewster, London: New Left Books.
Anderson, A. (2011) 'The Liberal Aesthetic', in Elliott and Attridge (2011).
Armbruster, K. and K.R. Wallace (eds) (2001) *Beyond Nature Writing: Expanding the Boundaries of Ecocriticism*, Charlottesville: University Press of Virginia.
Armstrong, I. (2000) *The Radical Aesthetic*, Oxford: Oxford University Press.
Arnold, M. (1970) *Matthew Arnold: Selected Prose*, ed. P.J. Keating, Harmondsworth: Penguin.
—— (1971) *Culture and Anarchy*, ed. J. Dover Wilson, Cambridge: Cambridge University Press [1869].
Ashcroft, B., G. Griffiths, and H. Tiffin (1989) *The Empire Writes back: Theory and Practice in Post-Colonial Literatures*, London and New York: Routledge.
—— (eds) (1995) *The Postcolonial Studies Reader*, London and New York: Routledge.

—— (1998) *Key Concepts in Post-Colonial Studies*, London and New York: Routledge.

—— (eds) (2005) *The Postcolonial Studies Reader*, 2nd ed., London and New York: Routledge.

Attridge, D. (2004) *The Singularity of Literature*, London and New York: Routledge.

—— (2004) *J.M. Coetzee and the Ethics of Reading*, Chicago: University of Chicago Press.

Ayers, D. (2008) *Literary Theory: A Reintroduction*, Oxford and Malden, MA: Blackwell.

Badmington, N. (ed.) (2000) *Posthumanism*, Basingstoke and New York: Palgrave Macmillan.

—— (2003) 'Theorizing Posthumanism', *Cultural Critique* 53: 10–27.

—— (2004) *Alien Chic: Posthumanism and the Other within*, London and New York: Routledge.

Baker, H.A. Jr (1972) *Long Black Song: Essays in Black-American Literature and Culture*, Charlottesville: University Press of Virginia.

—— (1984) *Blues, Ideology, and Afro-American Literature: A Vernacular Theory*, Chicago: University of Chicago Press.

Bakhtin, M. (1981) *The Dialogic Imagination: Four Essays*, ed. M. Holquist, trans. C. Emerson and M. Holquist, Austin: University of Texas Press.

Bal, M. (1997) *Narratology: Introduction to the Theory of Narrative*, 2nd ed., Toronto: University of Toronto Press.

Baldick, C. (1983) *The Social Mission of English Criticism, 1848–1932*, Oxford: Clarendon Press.

—— (1996) *Criticism and Literary Theory 1890 to the Present*, London and New York: Longman.

Barr, M.S. (1987) *Alien to Femininity: Speculative Fiction and Feminist Theory*, New York: Greenwood.

Barry, P. (2009) *Beginning Theory: An Introduction to Literary and Cultural Theory*, 3rd ed., Manchester: Manchester University Press.

Barthelme, D. (1984) *Snow White*, New York: Atheneum [1967].

Barthes, R. (1972) *Mythologies*, London: Jonathan Cape [1957].

—— (1977) *Image–Music–Text*, London: Fontana.

—— (1986) *The Rustle of Language*, New York: Farrar, Straus and Giroux.

—— (1990) *S/Z*, trans. R. Miller, Oxford and Malden, MA: Blackwell [1973].

—— (2000) 'The Death of the Author', in Lodge and Wood (2000) [1968].

Bate, J. (2000) *The Song of the Earth*, London: Picador.

Belsey, C. (1980) *Critical Practice*, London: Methuen.

—— (1985) *The Subject of Tragedy: Identity and Difference in Renaissance Drama*, London: Methuen/Routledge.

—— (2002) *Poststructuralism: A Very Short Introduction*, Oxford: Oxford University Press.

—— (2005) *Culture and the Real: Theorizing Cultural Criticism*, London and New York: Routledge.

Bennett, L. (1983) *Selected Poems*, ed. M. Morris, Kingston, Jamaica: Sangster's.

Bennett, T. (2003) *Formalism and Marxism*, London and New York: Routledge [1979].

Bertens, H. (1995) *The Idea of the Postmodern: A History*, London and New York: Routledge.

Bertens, H. and D.W. Fokkema (eds) (1997) *International Postmodernism: Theory and Literary Practice*, Amsterdam and Philadelphia, PA: Benjamins.

Bhabha, H.K. (ed.) (1990) *Nation and Narration*, London and New York: Routledge.

—— (1992) 'Postcolonial Criticism', in Greenblatt and Gunn (1992).

—— (1994a) *The Location of Culture*, London and New York: Routledge.

—— (1994b) 'Signs Taken for Wonders', in Bhabha (1994a) [1985].

Bobo, J. (ed.) (2001) *Black Feminist Cultural Criticism*, Malden, MA, and Oxford: Blackwell.

Boehmer, E. (2005) *Colonial and Postcolonial Literature: Migrant Metaphors*, 2nd ed., Oxford: Oxford University Press.

Booth, W. (1961) *The Rhetoric of Fiction*, Chicago: University of Chicago Press.

Borlik, T.A. (2012) *Ecocriticism and Early Modern English Literature: Green Pastures*, London and New York: Routledge.

Bowie, M. (1991) *Lacan*, London: Fontana; Cambridge, MA: Harvard University Press.

Braidotti, R. (2006) 'Posthuman, All too Human: Towards a New Process Ontology', *Theory, Culture, & Society* 23, 7–8: 197–209.

—— (2013) *The Posthuman*, Cambridge: Polity Press.

Branch, M.P. and S. Slovic (eds) (2003) *The ISLE Reader: Ecocriticism: 1993– 2003*, Athens, GA: University of Georgia Press.

Brannigan, J. (1998) *New Historicism and Cultural Materialism*, Basingstoke and London: Macmillan; New York: St Martin's Press.

Brathwaite, E. (1974) *Contradictory Omens: Cultural Diversity and Integration in the Caribbean*, Mona: Sacavou Publications.

—— (1984) *History of the Voice: The Development of Nation Language in Anglophone Caribbean Poetry*, London: New Beacon Books.

Bremond, C. (1966) 'La logique des possibles narratifs', *Communications* 8: 60–76.

Brennan, T. (ed.) (1989) *Between Feminism and Psychoanalysis*, London and New York: Routledge.

Brooks, C. (1968) *The Well-Wrought Urn: Studies in the Structure of Poetry*, London: Methuen [1947].

—— (1972) 'The Language of Paradox', in Lodge (1972) [1942].

Brooks, C. and R.P. Warren (1943) *Understanding Fiction*, New York: F.S. Crofts.

—— (1976) *Understanding Poetry*, 4th ed., New York: Holt [1939].

Buell, L. (1995) *The Environmental Imagination: Thoreau, Nature Writing, and the Formation of American Culture*, Princeton, NJ: Princeton University Press.

—— (2001) *Writing for an Endangered World: Literature, Culture, and Environment in the US and beyond*, Cambridge, MA: Belknap Press.

—— (2005) *The Future of Environmental Criticism: Environmental Crisis and Literary Imagination*, Oxford and Malden, MA: Blackwell.

Butler, C. (2002) *Postmodernism: A Very Short Introduction*, Oxford: Oxford University Press.

—— (2005) *Pleasure and the Arts: Enjoying Literature, Painting and Music*, Oxford: Oxford University Press.

Butler, J. (1990) *Gender Trouble: Feminism and the Subversion of Identity*, New York and London: Routledge.

—— (1991) 'Imitation and Gender Insubordination', in Fuss (1991).

—— (1993) *Bodies that Matter: On the Discursive Limits of 'Sex'*, New York and London: Routledge.

—— (1997a) *Excitable Speech: A Politics of the Performative*, New York and London: Routledge.

—— (1997b) *The Psychic Life of Power: Theories in Subjection*, Palo Alto, CA: Stanford University Press.

Byatt, A.S. (1990) *Possession*, London: Chatto and Windus.

Carby, H. (1987) *Reconstructing Womanhood: The Emergence of the Afro-American Woman Novelist*, New York: Oxford University Press.

Carmichael, D.A. (ed.) (2006) *The Landscape of Hollywood Westerns: Ecocriticism in an American Film Genre*, Salt Lake City: University of Utah Press.

Castle, T. (1993) *The Apparitional Lesbian: Female Homosexuality and Modern Culture*, New York: Columbia University Press.

—— (ed.) (2003) *The Literature of Lesbianism: A Historical Anthology from Ariosto to Stonewall*, New York: Columbia University Press.

Césaire, A. (1997) 'From *Discourse on Colonialism*', in Moore-Gilbert, Stanton, and Maley (1997) [1955].

Christian, B. (1985) *Black Feminist Criticism: Perspectives on Black Women Writers*, New York: Pergamon.

—— (2007) *New Black Feminist Criticism, 1985–2000*, ed. G. Bowles, M.G. Fabi, and A. Keizer, Urbana and Chicago: University of Illinois Press.

Cixous, H. (1981) 'The Laugh of the Medusa', in E. Marks and I. de Courvitron (eds), *New French Feminism: An Anthology*, Hemel Hempstead: Harvester Wheatsheaf [1975].

—— (2000) 'Sorties', in Lodge and Wood (2000) [1975].

Cohn, D. (1978) *Transparent Minds: Narrating Modes for Presenting Consciousness in Fiction*, Princeton, NJ: Princeton University Press.

Cole, L. *et al.* (2011) 'Speciesism, Identity Politics, and Ecocriticism: A Conversation with Humanists and Posthumanists', *Eighteenth Century: Theory and Interpretation* 52, 1: 87–106.

Colebrook, C. (2002) *Gilles Deleuze*, London and New York: Routledge.

Collier, P. and H. Geyer-Ryan (eds) (1990) *Literary Theory Today*, Cambridge: Polity.

Collins, P. Hill (2000) *Black Feminist Thought: Knowledge, Consciousness and the Politics of Empowerment*, 2nd ed., New York and London: Routledge.

Coupe, L. (ed.) (2000) *The Green Studies Reader: From Romanticism to Ecocriticism*, London and New York: Routledge.

Cowper, W. (1980) *The Poems of William Cowper*, vol. 1: *1748–1782*, ed. J.D. Baird and C. Ryskamp, Oxford: Clarendon Press.

—— (1995) *The Poems of William Cowper*, vol. 2: *1782–1785*, ed. J.D. Baird and C. Ryskamp, Oxford: Clarendon Press.

Crosby, A.W. (1986) *Ecological Imperialism: The Biological Expansion of Europe, 900–1900*, Cambridge: Cambridge University Press.

Culler, J. (1975) *Structuralist Poetics: Structuralism, Linguistics and the Study of Literature*, Ithaca, NY: Cornell University Press.

—— (1982) *On Deconstruction: Theory and Criticism after Structuralism*, Ithaca, NY: Cornell University Press.

—— (ed.) (2006) *Structuralism*, New York and London: Routledge.

—— (2011) *Literary Theory: A Very Short Introduction*, Oxford: Oxford University Press.

Cunningham, V. (2002) *Reading after Theory*, Oxford and Malden, MA: Blackwell.

Currie, M. (1998) *Postmodern Narrative Theory*, Basingstoke: Palgrave.

Damrosch, D. (2003) *What Is World Literature?*, Princeton, NJ: Princeton University Press.

David, C. (2004) *After Poststructuralism: Reading, Stories and Theory*, London and New York: Routledge.

Davis, G. (ed.) (2008) *Praising It New: The Best of the New Criticism*, Athens, OH: Swallow Press/Ohio University Press.

Davis, R.C. (ed.) (1983) *Lacan and Narration: The Psychoanalytic Difference in Narrative Theory*, Baltimore, MD: Johns Hopkins University Press.

Davis, T.F. and K. Womack (2002) *Formalist Criticism and Reader-Response Theory*, Basingstoke and New York: Palgrave.

Deleuze, G. and F. Guattari (1986) *Kafka: Towards a Minor Literature*, Minneapolis: University of Minnesota Press [1975].

—— (1987) *A Thousand Plateaus: Capitalism and Schizophrenia*, trans. B. Massumi, Minneapolis: University of Minnesota Press [1980].

DeMello, M. (2012) *Animals and Society: An Introduction to Human–Animal Studies*, New York: Columbia University Press.

Derrida, J. (1973) *Speech and Phenomena, and Other Essays on Husserl's Theory of Signs*, Evanston, IL: Northwestern University Press.

—— (1976) *Of Grammatology*, trans. G. Chakravorty Spivak, Baltimore, MD: Johns Hopkins University Press [1967].

—— (1978) 'Violence and Metaphysics: An Essay on the Thought of Emmanuel Levinas', in J. Derrida, *Writing and Difference*, trans. A. Bass, London: Routledge and Kegan Paul.

—— (1982) *Margins of Philosophy*, Chicago: University of Chicago Press.

—— (1987) 'Devant la Loi', in Udoff (1987) [1985].

—— (1988) *Limited Inc.*, ed. G. Graff, trans. S. Weber, Evanston, IL: Northwestern University Press [1977].

—— (1996) 'From *Différance*', in Ryan (1996) [1982].

—— (2000) 'Structure, Sign, and Play in the Discourse of the Human Sciences', in Lodge and Wood (2000) [1970].

D'haen, T. (2012) *The Routledge Concise History of World Literature*, London and New York: Routledge.

D'haen, T., D. Damrosch, and D. Kadir (eds) (2012) *The Routledge Companion to World Literature*, London and New York: Routledge.

Dickens, C. (1949) *A Tale of Two Cities*, Oxford: Oxford University Press [1859].

Dickinson, E. (1970) *The Complete Poems of Emily Dickinson*, ed. T.H. Johnson, London: Faber and Faber.

Dollimore, J. (1984) *Radical Tragedy: Religion, Ideology and Power in the Drama of Shakespeare and his Contemporaries*, Hemel Hempstead: Harvester Wheatsheaf.

—— (1991) *Sexual Dissidence: Augustine to Wilde, Freud to Foucault*, Oxford: Oxford University Press.

Dollimore, J. and A. Sinfield (eds) (1985) *Political Shakespeare: Essays in Cultural Materialism*, Manchester: Manchester University Press.

Donnell, A. (2006) *Twentieth-Century Caribbean Literature: Critical Moments in Anglophone Literary History*, London and New York: Routledge.

Drakakis, J. (ed.) (1985) *Alternative Shakespeares*, London: Methuen.

During, S. (2005) *Cultural Studies: A Critical Introduction*, London and New York: Routledge.

—— (2012) 'Empire's Present', *New Literary History* 43, 2: 331–40.

Eagleton, M. (ed.) (2003) *A Concise Companion to Feminist Theory*, Oxford and Malden, MA: Blackwell.

—— (2011) *Feminist Literary Theory: A Reader*, 3rd ed., Oxford and Malden, MA: Blackwell.

Eagleton, T. (1976a) *Criticism and Ideology*, London: Verso.

246 BIBLIOGRAPHY

—— (1976b) *Marxism and Literary Criticism*, London: Methuen.

—— (1991) *Ideology: An Introduction*, London and New York: Verso.

Eagleton, T. and D. Milne (eds) (1995) *Marxist Literary Theory: A Reader*, Oxford and Malden, MA: Blackwell.

Eichenbaum, B. (1965) 'The Theory of the "Formal Method"', in L.T. Lemon and M.J. Reis (trans.), *Russian Formalist Criticism: Four Essays*, Lincoln: University of Nebraska Press [1926].

—— (1998) 'Introduction to the Formal Method', in Rivkin and Ryan (1998) [1926].

Eliot, T.S. (1969) *Selected Essays*, London: Faber and Faber.

—— (1972) 'Tradition and the Individual Talent', in Lodge (1972) [1919].

Elliott, J. and D. Attridge (eds) (2011) *Theory after 'Theory'*, London and New York: Routledge.

Emerson, R.W. (2007) 'The American Scholar', in N. Baym (ed.), *The Norton Anthology: American Literature*, vol. B, 7th ed., New York: Norton [1837].

Erlich, V. (1981) *Russian Formalism: History-Doctrine*, 3rd ed., New Haven, CT: Yale University Press.

Ervin, H.A. (ed.) (1999) *African American Literary Criticism, 1773–2000*, New York: Twayne.

—— (2004) *The Handbook of African American Literature*, Gainesville: University Press of Florida.

Faderman, L. (1981) *Surpassing the Love of Men: Romantic Friendship and Love between Women from the Renaissance to the Present*, New York: Morrow.

Fanon, F. (1963) *The Wretched of the Earth*, trans. C. Farrington, New York: Grove Press [1961].

—— (1997) 'On National Culture', in Moore-Gilbert, Stanton, and Maley (1997) [1955].

Featherstone, S. (2005) *Postcolonial Cultures*, Edinburgh: Edinburgh University Press.

Felman, S. (ed.) (1982) *Literature and Psychoanalysis: The Question of Reading: Otherwise*, Baltimore, MD: Johns Hopkins University Press.

Fink, B. (1996) 'Reading Hamlet with Lacan', in W. Apollon and R. Feinstein (eds), *Lacan, Politics, Aesthetics*, Albany, NY: SUNY Press.

Fish, S. (1980) *Is There a Text in This Class? The Authority of Interpretive Communities*, Cambridge, MA: Harvard University Press.

Fludernik, M. (2009) *An Introduction to Narratology*, London and New York: Routledge.

Forsdick, C. and D. Murphy (eds) (2003) *Francophone Postcolonial Studies: A Critical Introduction*, London: Arnold.

Foucault, M. (1972) *The Archaeology of Knowledge*, London: Tavistock [1969].

—— (1977) *Discipline and Punish*, London: Allen Lane [1975].

—— (1978) *The History of Sexuality*, vol. 1: *An Introduction*, trans. R. Hurley, New York: Pantheon Books [1976].

—— (1980) *Power/Knowledge: Selected Interviews and Other Writings, 1972–1977*, ed. C. Gordon, London: Harvester Wheatsheaf.

—— (1985) *The History of Sexuality*, vol. 2: *The Use of Pleasure*, trans. R. Hurley, New York: Random House.

—— (2000) 'What Is an Author?', in Lodge and Wood (2000) [1969].

Freund, E. (1987) *The Return of the Reader: Reader-Response Criticism*, London and New York: Methuen.

Frow, J. (1986) *Marxism and Literary History*, New Haven, CT: Yale University Press.

Fry, P.H. (2012) *Theory of Literature*, New Haven, CT: Yale University Press.

Furniss, T. and M. Bath (2007) 'Postcolonial Poetry', in *Reading Poetry: An Introduction*, Harlow: Pearson.

Fuss, D. (ed.) (1991) *Inside/Out: Lesbian Theories, Gay Theories*, London and New York: Routledge.

Gaard, G. and P.D. Murphy (eds) (1998) *Ecofeminist Literary Criticism: Theory, Interpretation, Pedagogy*, Urbana and Chicago: University of Illinois Press.

Gallagher, C. (1989) 'Marxism and the New Historicism', in Veeser (1989).

Gallagher, C. and S. Greenblatt (2000) *Practicing New Historicism*, Chicago: University of Chicago Press.

Gane, N. (2006) 'When We Have Never Been Human, What Is to Be Done? Interview with Donna Haraway', *Theory, Culture, & Society* 23, 7–8: 135–58.

Garber, M. (1992) *Vested Interests: Cross Dressing and Cultural Anxiety*, New York and London: Routledge.

Garrard, G. (2004) *Ecocriticism*, London and New York: Routledge.

—— (2012a) *Ecocriticism*, 2nd ed., New York and London: Routledge.

—— (ed.) (2012b) *Teaching Ecocriticism and Green Cultural Studies*, Basingstoke and New York: Palgrave Macmillan.

Garvin, P. (ed.) (1964) *A Prague School Reader on Esthetics, Literary Structure and Style*, Washington, DC: Georgetown University Press.

Gates, H.L. Jr (1987) *Figures in Black: Words, Signs and the 'Racial' Self*, Oxford: Oxford University Press.

—— (1988) *The Signifying Monkey: A Theory of African-American Literary Criticism*, Oxford: Oxford University Press.

—— (ed.) (1990) *Reading Black, Reading Feminist*, New York: NAL.

—— (1992) 'African American Criticism', in Greenblatt and Gunn (1992).

—— (1998) 'The Blackness of Blackness: A Critique on the Sign and the Signifyin' Monkey', in Rivkin and Ryan (1998) [1989].

Genette, G. (1980) *Narrative Discourse*, Oxford: Blackwell [1972].

Gerstner, D.A. (ed.) (2006) *Routledge International Encyclopedia of Queer Culture*, London and New York: Routledge.

Giblett, R. (1996) *Postmodern Wetlands: Culture, History, Ecology*, Edinburgh: Edinburgh University Press.

Gilbert, S.M. and S. Gubar (eds) (1979) *The Madwoman in the Attic: The Woman Writer and the Nineteenth-Century Literary Imagination*, New Haven, CT: Yale University Press.

—— (2007) *Feminist Literary Theory and Criticism: A Norton Reader*, New York: Norton.

Glendinning, S. (2011) *Derrida: A Very Short Introduction*, Oxford: Oxford University Press.

Glotfelty, C. and H. Fromm (eds) (1996) *The Ecocriticism Reader: Landmarks in Literary Ecology*, Athens, GA: University of Georgia Press.

Goldberg, D.T. and A. Quayson (eds) (2002) *Relocating Postcolonialism*, Oxford: Blackwell.

Gordon, C. (ed.) (1980) *Power/Knowledge: Selected Interviews and Other Writings, 1972–1977*, London: Harvester Wheatsheaf.

Graff, G. (1987) *Professing Literature: An Institutional History*, Chicago and London: University of Chicago Press.

Graham, M. (ed.) (2004) *The Cambridge Companion to the African American Novel*, New York: Cambridge University Press.

Gramsci, A. (1998) '"Hegemony" (from "The Formation of Intellectuals")', in Rivkin and Ryan (1998) [1971].

Greenblatt, S. (1980) *Renaissance Self-Fashioning: From More to Shakespeare*, Chicago and London: University of Chicago Press.

—— (1981) 'Invisible Bullets: Renaissance Authority and its Subversion', *Glyph* 8: 40–61.

—— (1989) 'Towards a Poetics of Culture', in Veeser (1989).

—— (1990) 'Resonance and Wonder', in Collier and Geyer-Ryan (1990).

—— (1991) *Marvellous Possessions: The Wonder of the New World*, Oxford: Oxford University Press.

—— (2004) *The Greenblatt Reader*, ed. M. Payne, Malden, MA and Oxford: Blackwell.

Greenblatt, S. and G. Gunn (eds) (1992) *Redrawing the Boundaries: The Transformation of English and American Studies*, New York: MLA.

Gregg, M. and G.J. Seigworth (eds) (2010) *The Affect Theory Reader*, Durham, NC: Duke University Press.

Gregson, I. (2004) *Postmodern Literature*, London: Hodder Arnold.

Greimas, A.J. (1983) *Structural Semantics*, Lincoln: Nebraska University Press [1966].

Griffiths, G. (2000) *African Literatures in English, East and West*, Harlow: Longman.

Gross, A. and A. Vallely (eds) (2012) *Animals and the Human Imagination: A Companion to Animal Studies*, New York: Columbia University Press.

Habib, M.A.R. (2008) *Modern Literary Criticism and Theory: A History*, Oxford and Malden, MA: Blackwell.

Halberstam, J. (1998) 'F2M: The Making of Female Masculinity', in Rivkin and Ryan (1998) [1994].

Hall, D.E. (2003) *Queer Theories*, Basingstoke and New York: Palgrave Macmillan.

Hall, D.E. and A. Jagose (eds) (2012) *The Routledge Queer Studies Reader*, London and New York: Routledge.

Halley, J. and A. Parker (eds) (2011) *After Sex: On Writing since Queer Theory*, Durham, NC: Duke University Press.

Hallward, P. (2003) 'Jacques Rancière, Politics and Aesthetics: An Interview', *Angelaki* 8, 2: 191–211.

—— (2006) *Out of This World: Deleuze and the Philosophy of Creation*, London: Verso.

Hamilton, P. (2003) *Historicism*, London and New York: Routledge.

Haraway, D. (1988) 'Situated Knowledges: The Science Question in Feminism and the Privilege of Partial Perspective', *Feminist Studies* 14, 3: 575–99.

—— (1990) 'A Manifesto for Cyborgs: Science, Technology, and Socialist Feminism in the 1980s', in L. Nicholson (ed.), *Feminism/Postmodernism*, New York and London: Routledge [1985].

—— (1997) *Modest_Witness@Second_Millennium.FemaleMan©_Meets_OncoMouse*, London and New York: Routledge.

—— (2008) *When Species Meet*, Minneapolis: University of Minnesota Press.

Harrison, N. (2003) *Postcolonial Criticism: History, Theory and the Work of Fiction*, Cambridge: Polity.

Hartley, L.P. (1953) *The Go-Between*, London: Hamish Hamilton.

Haslett, M. (1999) *Marxist Literary and Cultural Theory*, Basingstoke and London: Macmillan; New York: St Martin's Press.

Hawkes, T. (2003) *Structuralism and Semiotics*, 2nd ed., London: Methuen.

Hawthorn, J. (1998) *A Concise Glossary of Contemporary Literary Terms*, 3rd ed., London: Arnold; New York: Oxford University Press.

Hayles, N.K. (1997) 'The Posthuman Body: Inscription and Incorporation in *Galatea 2.2* and *Snow Crash*', *Configurations* 5, 2: 241–66.

—— (1999) *How We Became Posthuman: Virtual Bodies in Cybernetics, Literature, and Informatics*, Chicago: University of Chicago Press.

—— (2000) 'Flickering Connectivities in Shelley Jackson's *Patchwork Girl*: The Importance of Media-Specific Analysis', *Postmodern Culture*, 10, 2 [e-journal].

—— (2005) *My Mother Was a Computer: Digital Subjects and Literary Texts*, Chicago: University of Chicago Press.

—— (2006) 'Unfinished Work: From Cyborg to Cognisphere', *Theory, Culture & Society* 23, 7–8: 159–66.

—— (2008) *Electronic Literature: New Horizons for the Literary*, Notre Dame, IN: Notre Dame University Press.

—— (2012) *How We Think: Digital Media and Contemporary Technogenesis*, Chicago: University of Chicago Press.

Hegeman, S. (2012) *The Cultural Return*, Berkeley and Los Angeles: University of California Press.

Herbrechter, S. (2013) *Posthumanism: A Critical Analysis*, London: Bloomsbury.

Herman, D. (ed.) (2007) *The Cambridge Companion to Narrative*, Cambridge: Cambridge University Press.

Hoban, R. (1982) *Riddley Walker*, London: Picador [1980].

Hoggart, R. (1958) *The Uses of Literacy: Aspects of Working-Class Life with Special Reference to Publications and Entertainments*, Harmondsworth: Penguin [1957].

Holden, P. and R.J. Ruppel (eds) (2003) *Imperial Desire: Dissident Sexualities and Colonial Literature*, Minneapolis: University of Minnesota Press.

Holland, N.N. (1975) *5 Readers Reading*, New Haven, CT: Yale University Press.

—— (1991) *Holland's Guide to Psychoanalytic Psychology and Literature-and-Psychology*, New York: Oxford University Press.

Homer, S. (2005) *Jacques Lacan*, London and New York: Routledge.

hooks, b. (1982) *Ain't I a Woman? Black Women and Feminism*, London: Pluto [1981].

—— (1992) *Black Looks: Race and Representation*, Boston, MA: South End Press.

—— (1997) 'Revolutionary Black Women: Making Ourselves Subject', in Moore-Gilbert, Stanton, and Maley (1997) [1992].

Huggan, G. (2004) '"Greening" Postcolonialism: Ecocritical Perspectives', *Modern Fiction Studies* 50, 3: 701–33.

Huggan, G. and H. Tiffin (2010) *Postcolonial Ecocriticism: Literature, Animals, Environment*, London and New York: Routledge.

Humm, M. (1995) *Practising Feminist Criticism: An Introduction*, London and New York: Prentice Hall/Harvester Wheatsheaf.

Hutcheon, L. (1988) *A Poetics of Postmodernism: History, Theory, Fiction*, New York and London: Routledge.

—— (1989) *The Politics of Postmodernism*, New York and London: Routledge.

Innes, C.L. (2007) *The Cambridge Introduction to Postcolonial Literatures in English*, Cambridge: Cambridge University Press.

Iser, W. (1980) *The Act of Reading: A Theory of Aesthetic Response*, Baltimore, MD: Johns Hopkins University Press.

Jagose, A. (1996) *Queer Theory: An Introduction*, New York: New York University Press.

Jakobson, R. (1987) 'What Is Poetry?', in K. Pomorska and R. Rudy (eds), *Language and Literature*, Cambridge, MA: Belknap Press [1934].

—— (2000) 'Closing Statement: Linguistics and Poetics', in Lodge and Wood (2000) [1960].

Jameson, F. (1981) *The Political Unconsciousness: Narrative as a Socially Symbolic Act*, Ithaca, NY: Cornell University Press.

—— (1984) 'Postmodernism, or the Cultural Logic of Late Capitalism', *New Left Review* 146: 54–92.

Jancovich, M. (1993) *The Cultural Politics of the New Criticism*, Cambridge: Cambridge University Press.

Jefferson, A. and D. Robey (eds) (1986) *Modern Literary Theory: A Comparative Introduction*, 2nd ed., London: Batsford.

Johnson, B. (1980) *The Critical Difference*, Baltimore, MD: Johns Hopkins University Press.

Johnson, E.P. and M.G. Henderson (eds) (2005) *Black Queer Studies: A Critical Anthology*, Durham, NC: Duke University Press.

Kane, R. (2005) *A Contemporary Introduction to Free Will*, New York: Oxford University Press.

Kerridge, R. and N. Sammells (eds) (1998) *Writing the Environment*, London: Zed Books.

Knight, S. (1980) *Form and Ideology in Detective Fiction*, London: Macmillan.

Kristeva, J. (1984) *Revolution in Poetic Language*, New York: Columbia University Press [1974].

Lacan, J. (1977) 'Desire and the Interpretation of Desire in *Hamlet*', *Yale French Studies* 55–56: 11–52 [reprinted in Felman (1982)].

—— (2001) *Écrits: A Selection*, London and New York: Routledge.

Lawrence, D.H. (1960) *Women in Love*, Harmondsworth: Penguin [1922].

—— (1972a) 'Morality and the Novel', in Lodge (1972) [1925].

—— (1972b) 'The Spirit of Place', in Lodge (1972) [1924].

—— (1972c) 'Why the Novel Matters', in Lodge (1972) [1936].

Lazarus, N. (ed.) (2004) *The Cambridge Companion to Postcolonial Literary Studies*, Cambridge: Cambridge University Press.

—— (2011) *The Postcolonial Unconscious*, Cambridge: Cambridge University Press.

Leavis, F.R. (1932) *New Bearings in English Poetry*, London: Chatto and Windus.

—— (1936) *Revaluation: Tradition and Development in English Poetry*, London: Chatto and Windus.

—— (1962) *The Great Tradition*, Harmondsworth: Penguin [1948].

—— (1967) *English Literature in Our Time and the University*, London: Chatto and Windus.

—— (1975) *The Living Principle: 'English' as Discipline of Thought*, London: Chatto and Windus.

Lee, V. (ed.) (2006) *The Prentice Hall Anthology of African American Women's Literature*, Upper Saddle River, NJ: Pearson/Prentice Hall.

Lemon, L.T. and M.J. Reis (trans.) (2012) *Russian Formalist Criticism: Four Essays*, 2nd ed., Lincoln: University of Nebraska Press [1965].

Lévi-Strauss, C. (1982) *The Way of Masks*, Seattle: University of Washington Press.

Lilly, M. (1993) *Gay Men's Literature in the Twentieth Century*, New York: New York University Press.

Lodge, D. (ed.) (1972) *20th Century Literary Criticism*, London and New York: Longman.

—— (1975) *Changing Places: A Tale of Two Campuses*, London: Secker and Warburg.

—— (1984) *Small World*, London: Secker and Warburg.

—— (ed.) (1988) *Modern Criticism and Theory: A Reader*, London and New York: Longman.

—— (1988) *Nice Work*, London: Secker and Warburg.

Lodge, D. and N. Wood (eds) (2000) *Modern Criticism and Theory: A Reader*, 2nd ed., Harlow: Longman; New York: Pearson.

Loomba, A. (2005) *Colonialism/Postcolonialism*, 2nd ed., London and New York: Routledge.

Loomba, A., S. Kaul, M. Bunzl, A. Burton, and J. Esty (eds) (2005) *Postcolonial Studies and Beyond*, Durham, NC: Duke University Press.

Lorde, A. (1984) *Sister Outsider: Essays and Speeches*, Freedom, CA: Crossing Press.

—— (1998) 'Age, Race, Class, and Sex: Women Redefining Difference', in Rivkin and Ryan (1998) [1984].

Lukács, G. (1970) 'Art and Objective Truth', in A. Kahn (ed.), *Writer, Critic and Other Essays*, London: Merlin.

—— (1972) 'The Ideology of Modernism', in Lodge (1972) [1957].

Lyotard, J.-F. (1984) *The Postmodern Condition: A Report on Knowledge*, trans. G. Bennington and B. Massumi, Minneapolis: University of Minnesota Press [1979].

McCallum, E.L. and M. Tuhkanen (eds) (2011) *Queer Times, Queer Becomings*, Albany, NY: SUNY Press.

Macey, D. (1993) *The Lives of Michel Foucault*, London: Vintage.

McHale, B. (1987) *Postmodernist Fiction*, London and New York: Methuen.

Macherey, P. (1978) *A Theory of Literary Production*, London: Routledge [1966].

Machor, J.L. and P. Goldstein (eds) (2001) *Reception Study: From Literary Theory to Cultural Studies*, London and New York: Routledge.

McHugh, S. (2011) *Animal Stories: Narrating across Species Lines*, Minneapolis: Minnesota University Press.

McLeod, J. (ed.) (2007) *The Routledge Companion to Postcolonial Studies*, London and New York: Routledge.

Malpas, S. (2005) *The Postmodern*, London and New York: Routledge.

Marx, K. (1970) *A Contribution to the Critique of Political Economy*, Moscow: Progress Publishers [1859].

Matejka, L. and K. Pomorska (eds) (2002) *Readings in Russian Poetics: Formalist and Structuralist Views*, Champaign, IL, Dublin and London: Dalkey Archive Press [1978].

Miall, D.S. (2006) *Literary Reading: Empirical and Theoretical Studies*, New York: Peter Lang.

Miller, J.H. (1976) 'Stevens' Rock and Criticism as Cure, II', *Georgia Review* 30, 2: 330–48.

—— (2000) 'The Critic as Host,' in Lodge and Wood (2000) [1977].

Millett, K. (1970) *Sexual Politics*, Garden City, NY: Doubleday.

Mills, S., L. Pearce, S. Spaull, and E. Millard (1989) *Feminist Readings, Feminists Reading*, Hemel Hempstead: Harvester Wheatsheaf.

Milne, D. (2001) *Reading Marxist Literary Theory*, Oxford and Malden, MA: Blackwell.

Milner, A.J. (2002) *Re-imagining Cultural Studies: The Promise of Cultural Materialism*, London: Sage.

Montrose, L. (1983) '"Shaping Fantasies": Figurations of Gender and Power in Elizabethan Culture', *Representations* 1, 2: 61–94.

—— (1989) 'The Poetics and Politics of Culture', in Veeser (1989).

—— (1992) 'New Historicisms', in Greenblatt and Gunn (1992).

—— (1994) '"Eliza, Queene of Shepeardes", and the Pastoral of Power', in Veeser (1994) [1980].

Moore-Gilbert, B. (1997) *Postcolonial Theory: Contexts, Practices, Politics*, London: Verso.

Moore-Gilbert, B., G. Stanton, and W. Maley (eds) (1997) *Postcolonial Criticism*, London and New York: Longman.

Morland, I. and A. Willox (eds) (2005) *Queer Theory*, Basingstoke and New York: Palgrave Macmillan.

Morris, P. (ed.) (2009) *The Bakhtin Reader: Selected Writings of Bakhtin, Medvedev, Voloshinov*, London and New York: Bloomsbury.

Morrison, T. (1982) *Playing in the Dark: Whiteness and the Literary Imagination*, Cambridge, MA: Harvard University Press.

Muller, J.P. and W.J. Richardson (eds) (1988) *The Purloined Poe*, Baltimore, MD: Johns Hopkins University Press.

Mullin, M. (2008) 'Book Review: *When Species Meet* by Donna Haraway', *Theory, Culture, & Society* 25, 7–8: 373–76.

Munt, S.R. (1994) *Murder by the Book? Feminism and the Crime Novel*, London and New York: Routledge.

Napier, W. (ed.) (2000) *African American Literary Theory: A Reader*, New York and London: New York University Press.

Newbolt Report (1921) *Report to the Board of Education on the Teaching of English in England*, London: HMSO.

Newby, E. (1974) *A Short Walk in the Hindu Kush*, London: Picador [1958].

Norris, C. (2002) *Deconstruction: Theory and Practice*, 3rd ed., London and New York: Routledge.

—— (2007) *Fiction, Philosophy and Literary Theory: Will the Real Saul Kripke Please Stand Up?*, London and New York: Continuum.

Oliver, K. (ed.) (2000) *The French Feminism Reader*, Lanham, MD: Rowman and Littlefield.

Parry, B. (2002) 'Directions and Dead Ends in Postcolonial Studies', in Goldberg and Quayson (2002).

—— (2004) *Postcolonial Studies: A Materialist Critique*, London and New York: Routledge.

—— (2012) 'What Is Left in Postcolonial Studies?', *New Literary History* 43, 2: 341–58.

Parvini, N. (2012) *Shakespeare and Contemporary Theory: New Historicism and Cultural Materialism*, London and New York: Bloomsbury.

Peterson, C. (2011) 'The Posthumanism to Come', *Angelaki* 16, 2: 127–42.

Pieters, J. (2001) *Moments of Negotiation: The New Historicism of Stephen Greenblatt*, Amsterdam: Amsterdam University Press.

Plain, G. and S. Sellers (eds) (2007) *A History of Feminist Literary Criticism*, Cambridge: Cambridge University Press.

Povinelli, E.A. (2011) 'The Persistence of Hope: Critical Theory and Enduring in Late Liberalism', in Elliott and Attridge (2011).

Pratt, M.L. (1992) *Imperial Eyes: Studies in Travel Writing and Transculturation*, New York and London: Routledge.

Propp, V. (1968) *The Morphology of the Folk Tale*, 2nd ed., Austin and London: University of Texas Press.

Quayson, A. (2000) *Postcolonialism: Theory, Practice or Process?*, Cambridge: Polity.

—— (ed.) (2012a) *The Cambridge History of Postcolonial Literature*, Cambridge: Cambridge University Press.

—— (2012b) 'The Sighs of History: Postcolonial Debris and the Question of (Literary) History', *New Literary History* 43, 2: 359–70.

Rabaté, J.-M. (ed.) (2003) *The Cambridge Companion to Lacan*, Cambridge: Cambridge University Press.

Rabinow, D. (ed.) (1984) *The Foucault Reader*, New York: Random House.

Rajamannar, S. (2012) *Reading the Animal in the Literature of the British Raj*, New York: Palgrave Macmillan.

Rajeev, S.P. (2006) *Postcolonial Poetry in English*, New York: Oxford University Press.

Rancière, J. (2009) *Aesthetics and Its Discontents*, Cambridge: Polity [2004].

Ransom, J.C. (1938) *The World's Body*, New York: Scribner.

—— (1941) *The New Criticism*, Norfolk, CT: New Directions.

—— (1972) 'Criticism, Inc.', in Lodge (1972) [1937].

Renfrew, A. (2013) *Mikhail Bakhtin*, London and New York: Routledge.

Richards, I.A. (1926) *Science and Poetry*, London: Kegan Paul, Trench, Trubner.

—— (1929) *Practical Criticism*, London: Kegan Paul, Trench, Trubner.

—— (1972a) 'Communication and the Artist', in Lodge (1972) [1924].

—— (1972b) 'The Four Kinds of Meaning', in Lodge (1972) [1929].

Rimmon-Kenan, S. (1983) *Narrative Fiction: Contemporary Poetics*, London: Methuen.

Rivkin, J. and M. Ryan (eds) (1998) *Literary Theory: An Anthology*, Malden, MA, and Oxford: Blackwell.

—— (2004) *Literary Theory: An Anthology*, 2nd ed., Malden, MA, and Oxford: Blackwell.

Robbins, R. (2000) *Literary Feminisms*, Basingstoke and London: Macmillan; New York: St Martin's Press.

Rooney, Ellen (ed.) (2006) *The Cambridge Companion to Feminist Literary Theory*, Cambridge: Cambridge University Press.

Rosendahl Thomsen, M. (2008) *Mapping World Literature: International Canonization and Transnational Literatures*, London: Continuum.

—— (2013) *The New Human in Literature: Posthuman Visions of Changes in Body, Mind and Society After 1900*, London: Bloomsbury.

Royle, N. (ed.) (2000) *Deconstruction: A User's Guide*, Basingstoke and New York: Palgrave.

Rule, J. (1975) *Lesbian Images*, Trumansberg, NY: Crossings Press.

Ryan, K. (ed.) (1996) *New Historicism and Cultural Materialism: A Reader*, London: Arnold; New York: Oxford University Press.

Said, E. (1991) *Orientalism*, Harmondsworth: Penguin [1978].

Salih, S. (2002) *Judith Butler*, London and New York: Routledge.

Saussure, F. de (1959) *Course in General Linguistics*, New York: McGraw-Hill [1915].

Scholes, R. (1974) *Structuralism in Literature: An Introduction*, New Haven, CT: Yale University Press.

Searle, J. (2005) 'Literary Theory and Its Discontents', in D. Patai and W.H. Corral (eds), *Theory's Empire: An Anthology of Dissent*, New York: Columbia University Press [1994].

Sebeok, T. (ed.) (1960) *Style in Language*, Cambridge, MA: Technology Press/ MIT; New York: John Wiley.

Sedgwick, E. Kosofsky (1985) *Between Men: English Literature and Male Homosocial Desire*, New York: Columbia University Press.

—— (1990) *Epistemology of the Closet*, Berkeley and Los Angeles: University of California Press.

—— (1994) *Tendencies*, New York and London: Routledge.

—— (ed.) (1997) *Novel Gazing: Queer Readings in Fiction*, Durham, NC: Duke University Press.

Selden, R. (ed.) (1995) *The Cambridge History of Literary Criticism*, vol. 8: *From Formalism to Poststructuralism*, Cambridge: Cambridge University Press.

Shklovsky, V. (1998) 'Art as Technique', in Rivkin and Ryan (1998) [1917].

Showalter, E. (ed.) (1985a) *The New Feminist Criticism*, New York: Pantheon.

—— (1985b) 'Towards a Feminist Poetics', in Showalter (1985a) [1979].

—— (2005) *Faculty Towers: The Academic Novel and Its Discontents*, Philadelphia: University of Pennsylvania Press.

Sinfield, A. (1986) *Alfred Tennyson*, Oxford: Blackwell.

—— (1992) *Faultlines: Cultural Materialism and the Politics of Dissident Reading*, Oxford: Oxford University Press.

—— (1994) *The Wilde Century: Effeminacy, Oscar Wilde and the Queer Moment*, London: Cassell.

—— (2005) *Cultural Politics – Queer Reading*, 2nd ed., London and New York: Routledge [1994].

—— (2006) *Shakespeare, Authority, Sexuality: Unfinished Business in Cultural Materialism*, London and New York: Routledge.

Skura, M. (1992) 'Psychoanalytic Criticism', in Greenblatt and Gunn (1992).

Smith, B. (1985) 'Towards a Black Feminist Criticism', in Showalter (1985a) [1977].

Spivak, G. Chakravorty (1995a) 'Can the Subaltern Speak? Speculations on Widow Sacrifice', in Ashcroft *et al.* (1995) [1988].

—— (1995b) 'Three Women's Texts and a Critique of Imperialism', in Ashcroft *et al.* (1995) [1985].

—— (1999) *A Critique of Postcolonial Reason: Toward a History of the Vanishing Present*, Cambridge, MA: Harvard University Press.

—— (2000) 'Discussion: An Afterword on the New Subaltern', in P. Chatterjee and P. Jeganathan (eds), *Community, Gender and Violence*, London: Hurst.

—— (2004) 'Righting Wrongs', *South Atlantic Quarterly* 103, 2–3: 523–81.

Stam, R. and E. Shohat (2012) 'Whence and Whither Postcolonial Theory?', *New Literary History* 43, 2: 371–90.

Steiner, P. (1984) *Russian Formalism: A Metapoetics*, Ithaca, NY: Cornell University Press.

Stepto, R. (1991) *From Behind the Veil*, 2nd ed., Urbana: University of Illinois Press [1979].

Striedter, J. (1989) *Literary Structure, Evolution, and Value: Russian Formalism and Czech Structuralism Reconsidered*, Cambridge, MA: Harvard University Press.

Sturrock, J. (2003) *Structuralism*, 2nd ed., with a new introduction by J.-M. Rabaté, Oxford and Malden, MA: Blackwell.

Sullivan, N. (2003) *A Critical Introduction to Queer Theory*, Edinburgh: Edinburgh University Press.

Thoreau, H.D. (2007) *Walden*, in N. Baym (ed.), *The Norton Anthology: American Literature*, vol. B, 7th ed., New York: Norton [1854].

Todorov, T. (1969) *Grammaire du Décaméron*, The Hague and Paris: Mouton.

—— (1975) *The Fantastic: A Structural Approach to a Literary Genre*, Ithaca, NY: Cornell University Press [1970].

—— (1977) *The Poetics of Prose*, Oxford: Oxford University Press [1971].

Tompkins, J.P. (ed.) (1980) *Reader-Response Criticism: From Formalism to Post-Structuralism*, Baltimore, MD: Johns Hopkins University Press.

Udoff, A. (ed.) (1987) *Kafka and the Contemporary Critical Performance: Centenary Readings*, Bloomington: Indiana University Press.

Vakoch, A. (2012) *Feminist Ecocriticsm: Environment, Women, and Literature*, Lanham, MD: Lexington Books.

Veeser, H.A. (ed.) (1989) *The New Historicism*, London and New York: Routledge.

—— (ed.) (1994) *The New Historicism Reader*, London and New York: Routledge.

Viswanathan, G. (1989) *Masks of Conquest: Literary Study and British Rule in India*, New York: Columbia University Press.

Waldan, P. (2013) *Animal Studies: An Introduction*, Oxford: Oxford University Press.

Wall, C. (ed.) (1989) *Changing Our Own Words*, New Brunswick, NJ: Rutgers University Press.

Warhol-Down, R. and D. Price Herndl (eds) (2009) *Feminisms Redux: An Anthology of Literary Theory and Criticism*, 3rd ed., New Brunswick, NJ: Rutgers University Press.

Washington, M.H. (ed.) (1989) *Invented Lives: Narratives of Black Women (1860–1960)*, London: Virago [1987].

Weil, K. (2012) *Thinking Animals: Why Animal Studies Now?*, New York: Columbia University Press.

Westling, L. H. (1996) *The Green Breast of the New World: Landscape, Gender, and American Fiction*, Athens, GA: University of Georgia Press.

Whitman, W. (2007) 'Song of Myself' in N. Baym (ed.), *The Norton Anthology: American Literature*, vol. B, 7th ed., New York: Norton [1855].

Williams, J. (2005) *Understanding Poststructuralism*, Chesham: Acumen.

Williams, J. and H. Steffen (2012) *The Critical Pulse: Thirty-Six Credos by Contemporary Critics*, New York: Columbia University Press.

Williams, L.R. (1995) *Critical Desire: Psychoanalysis and the Literary Subject*, London: Arnold.

Williams, R. (1961) *Culture and Society, 1780–1950*, Harmondsworth: Penguin [1958].

—— (1977) *Marxism and Literature*, Oxford: Oxford University Press.

—— (1996) 'Base and Superstructure in Marxist Cultural Theory', in Ryan (1996) [1980].

Williams Page, Y. (ed.) (2011) *Icons of African-American Literature: The Black Literary World*, Santa Barbara, CA: Greenwood.

Willis, S. (1987) *Specifying: Black Women Writing the American Experience*, Madison: University of Wisconsin Press.

Wimsatt, W.K. (1965) *Hateful Contraries: Studies in Literature and Criticism*, Lexington: University of Kentucky Press.

Wisker, G. (2006) *Key Concepts in Postcolonial Literature*, Basingstoke and London: Palgrave Macmillan.

Wolfe, C. (2003) *Animal Rites: American Culture, the Discourse of Species, and Posthumanist Theory*, Chicago: University of Chicago Press.

—— (2010) *What Is Posthumanism?*, Minneapolis: University of Minnesota Press.

—— (2011) 'Response to Christopher Peterson, "The Posthumanism to Come"', *Angelaki* 16, 2: 189–94.

Woods, G. (1998) *A History of Gay Literature: The Male Tradition*, New Haven, CT: Yale University Press.

Woods, T. (2009) *Beginning Postmodernism*, 2nd ed., Manchester: Manchester University Press.

Wright, E. (1998) *Psychoanalytic Criticism: A Reappraisal*, 2nd ed., Cambridge: Polity.

Wright, W. (1975) *Sixguns and Society: A Structural Study of the Western*, Berkeley: University of California Press.

Young, R. (2001) *Postcolonialism: An Historical Introduction*, Oxford and Malden, MA: Blackwell.

—— (2012) 'Postcolonial Remains', *New Literary History* 43, 1: 19–42.

Zimmerman, B. (1985) 'What Has Never Been: An Overview of Lesbian Feminist Criticism', in Showalter (1985a).

—— (1992) 'Lesbians Like This and That: Some Notes on Lesbian Criticism for the Nineties', in S. Munt (ed.), *New Lesbian Criticism: Literary and Cultural Readings*, Hemel Hempstead: Harvester Wheatsheaf.

Žižek, S. (2007) *How to Read Lacan*, New York: Norton.

INDEX

Contemporary Literature in *The Basics*

Contemporary Literature: The Basics

Suman Gupta, The Open University

'Contemporary Literature' is among the most popular areas of literary study but it can be a difficult one to define. This book equips readers with the necessary tools to take an analytical and systematic approach to contemporary texts. The author provides answers to some of the critical questions in the field:

- What makes a literary text contemporary?
- Is it possible to have a canon of contemporary literature?
- How does a reader's location affect their understanding?
- How do print, electronic, and audio-visual media impact upon contemporary literature?
- Which key concepts and themes are most prevalent?

Containing diverse illustrative examples and discussing the topics which define our current sense of the contemporary, this is an ideal starting point for anyone seeking to engage critically with contemporary literature.

October 2011 – 190 pages
Pb: 978-0-415-66870-5| Hb: 978-0-415-66871-2

For more information and to order a copy visit
http://www.routledge.com/books/details/9780415668705/

Available from all good bookshops

Poetry in *The Basics*

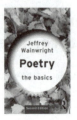

Poetry: The Basics:

Jeffrey Wainwright, poet, translator, and critic;
Manchester Metropolitan University

Now in its second edition, *Poetry: The Basics* demystifies the
traditions and forms of the world of poetry for all those who find
it daunting or bewildering. Covering a wide range of poetic voices
from Chaucer to children's rhymes, song lyrics and the words of
contemporary poets, this book will help readers to appreciate
poetry by examining:

- technical aspects such as rhythm and measures
- different tones of voice in poetry
- the relationship between 'everyday' and 'poetic'
  language
- how different types of poetry are structured
- how the form and 'space' of a poem contribute to its
  meaning
- some of the ways contemporary poets set to work.

A must-read for all those wishing to get to grips with reading and
writing poetry, this book is a lively and inspiring introduction to its
many styles and purposes right up to the present-day.

February 2011 – 268 pages
Pb: 978-0-415-56616-2| Hb: 978-0-415-56615-5

For more information and to order a copy visit
http://www.routledge.com/books/details/9780415566162/

Available from all good bookshops

Pros and Cons, A Debaters Handbook, 19th Edition

The English-Speaking Union [ESU].

Pros and Cons: A Debaters Handbook offers a unique and invaluable guide to the arguments both for and against over 140 current controversies and global issues. Since it was first published in 1896 the handbook has been regularly updated and this nineteenth edition includes new entries on topics such as the right to possess nuclear weapons, the bailing out of failing industries, the protection of indigenous languages and the torture of suspected terrorists.

Equal coverage is given to both sides of each debate in a dual column format which allows for easy comparison. Each entry also includes a list of related topics and suggestions for possible motions.

The introductory essay describes debating technique, covering the rules, structure and type of debate, and offering tips on how to become a successful speaker. The book is then divided into eight thematic sections, where specific subjects are covered individually.

September 2013 – 292 pages
Pb: 978-0-415-82780-5| Hb: 978-0-415-82779-9

For more information and to order a copy visit
http://www.routledge.com/books/details/9780415827805/

Available from all good bookshops

Shakespeare in *The Basics*

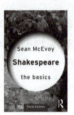

Shakespeare: The Basics

Sean McEvoy, Royal Holloway, University of London

Now in its third edition *Shakespeare: The Basics* is an insightful and informative introduction to the work of William Shakespeare. Exploring all aspects of Shakespeare's plays including the language, cultural contexts, and modern interpretations, this text looks at how a range of plays from across the genres have been understood. Updates in this edition include:

- Ecocritical, queer, presentist and gendered discussions of Shakespeare's work
- Studies of new performances including Tennant and Tate's *Much Ado About Nothing*
- Critical discussions of race and politics in *Othello* and *King Lear*
- Case studies of modern film versions of Shakespeare's works
- A chronology of Shakespeare's work and contemporary events

With fully updated further reading throughout and a wide range of case studies and examples, this text is essential reading for all those studying Shakespeare's work.

May 2012 – 280 pages
Pb: 978-0-415-68280-0 | Hb: 978-0-415-68279-4

Available from all good bookshops

Media Studies in *The Basics*

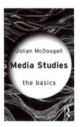

Media Studies: The Basics

Julian McDougall, Bournemouth University, UK.

There have been seismic shifts in what constitutes (the) media in recent years with technological advances ushering in whole new categories of producers, consumers and modes of delivery. This has been reflected in the way media is studied with new theories, concepts and practices coming to the fore. Media Studies: The Basics is the ideal guide to this changing landscape and addresses core questions including:

• Who, or what, is the media?
• What are the key terms and concepts used in analysing media?
• Where have been the impacts of the globalization of media?
• How, and by whom, is media made in the 21st century?

Featuring contemporary case studies from around the world, a glossary and suggestions for further reading, this is the ideal introduction to media studies today.

May 2012 – 214 pages
Pb: 978-0-415-68125-4| Hb: 978-0-415-68126-1

For more information and to order a copy visit
http://www.routledge.com/books/details/9780415681254/

Available from all good bookshops

Film Studies in *The Basics*

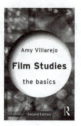

Film Studies: The Basics

Amy Villarejo, Cornell University, USA

Film Studies: The Basics is a compelling guide to the study of cinema in all its forms. This second edition has been thoroughly revised and updated to take account of recent scholarship, the latest developments in the industry and the explosive impact of new technologies. Core topics covered include:

- The history, technology and art of cinema
- Theories of stardom, genre and film-making
- The movie industry from Hollywood to Bollywood
- Who does what on a film set

Complete with film stills, end-of-chapter summaries and a substantial glossary, *Film Studies: The Basics* is the ideal introduction to those new to the study of cinema.

July 2013 – 280 pages
Pb: 978-0-415-58496-8| Hb: 978-0-415-58495-1

For more information and to order a copy visit
http://www.routledge.com/books/details/9780415584968/

Available from all good bookshops